The Brethren of the Common Life

The Brethren of the Common Life

By

DR. ALBERT HYMA

Professor of History, University of Michigan

AUTHOR OF
Renaissance to Reformation, etc.

Wipf & Stock
PUBLISHERS
Eugene, Oregon

Wipf and Stock Publishers
199 West 8th Avenue, Suite 3
Eugene, Oregon 97401

The Brethren of the Common Life
By Hyma, Albert
Copyright©1950 Wm. B. Eerdmans Publishing Co.
ISBN: 1-59244-682-5
Publication date 5/6/2004
Previously published by Wm. B. Eerdmans Publishing Co., 1950

To

CORNELIA STEKETEE HULST

*In recognition of the indispensable
assistance rendered in the
composition of
this book*

Preface

THIRTY years ago the present writer composed a history of a powerful religious movement known as the Devotio Moderna. At that time the historians of Europe and America evinced little interest in this phase of late medieval culture. As a result it was difficult to locate the original sources and to evaluate the contributions of those men and women who participated in the work begun by Gerard Groote and his associates. The founders of the Devotio Moderna had so long been treated with indifference that the greatest of Dutch historians ignored to a large extent their institutions and literary productions. In Great Britain and Germany the general public also was ignorant of the atmosphere in which such influential writers as Thomas à Kempis and Erasmus labored.

But during the past fifteen years a large number of scholars have turned their attention to the Devotio Moderna, with the result that thousands of manuscripts have been carefully examined and their contents made known. The outstanding mystics, reformers, and humanists who were connected with the movement are now much better understood by us than they once were. For this reason a second history can now make its appearance which presents a clearer delineation than was possible before. The leading figures together with their books and their constitutions have become more familiar to us all, and the author can speak with greater confidence than he did in the days of pioneering.

Albert Hyma

CONTENTS

Introduction

SOMEWHERE among the wooded hills of Westphalia the little river known as Oude (or Old) Yssel takes its source. Descending through forest, heath, and meadow on a northwestward course, it soon crosses the borders of Holland. Here both it and its neighbor the Rhine come up against the plateau Veluwe, or "Barren Meadow." Confronted by this plateau, the Oude Yssel turns northward, and for the rest of its course is called simply Yssel; while the Rhine turns mostly westward, but discharges about a ninth of the water with which it enters Holland into the former Zuiderzee by way of the Yssel. Today the old "South Sea" has a new name: Yssel Lake.

Once on a northward course the Yssel changes greatly in character. Slowly it winds past thriving cities—no longer an obscure little river, but a dignified stream whose quiet waters have nearly finished a long journey. The valley through which it now flows is very attractive, and is made doubly attractive by the striking contrast between the verdant meadows along the gentle waters and the dusty heaths of the Veluwe. Down in the valley are fertile banks with green pastures and smiling grain fields; on the plateau are stunted pines and barren sanddunes. Below, the busy hand of man has planted willows and elms, has transformed the monotonous green into the radiant colors of flowers and shrubbery, and has built a multitude of homes; on the solitary heaths of the Veluwe few fragrant garden spots are found, few riversides, and few prosperous homes.

Four or five centuries ago, the contrast between the valley of the Yssel and its nearer environment was even stronger than now. For at that time the Veluwe, to the westward, was far more weird and forsaken. In spring and autumn, when the Rhine, Yssel, and Grebbe[1] overflowed their banks, it would appear like a huge sand heap, devoid of human and animal life. On stormy days the wind would shriek among the tops of the

9

lonely pines and the sand would swirl through the air. This spectacle was in itself sufficient to frighten away most invaders. East of the Yssel the landscape was almost equally desolate. Three different zones could be distinguished there, parallel with the river. First came the fertile strip of land bordering the stream; then the sand hills with their extensive forests of oaks and pines, but not wholly without cultivation, particularly along the little brooks which had their source in the higher land far-ther to the east. The third zone was nothing but a waste of heaths, forests and moors, showing but very few signs of human habitation.[2]

In this valley were situated the cities of Deventer, Zutphen, and Kampen, with Zwolle close by. Deventer was near the center. Bordered on both sides by lonely expanses of heath and fen, Deventer was only to a relatively small degree subjected to the influence of international commerce. True, it was a pros-perous town, but not a mighty port like Bruges or Antwerp; nor was it exposed so much to foreign influences as were the cities of Utrecht, Leiden, Amsterdam, and Dordrecht. Did the green pastures and the silent waters encircling the town perhaps foster in religious men of Deventer that spirit of mysticism which attracted a Thomas á Kempis and impelled him to leave his home at distant Kempen for the Yssel country?

Great mystics have always loved to seek communion with God on the banks of quiet rivers, in forests and deserts. It was of such a country that David wrote: "The Lord is my shepherd; I shall not want. He maketh me to lie down in green pastures; he leadeth me beside the still waters. He restoreth my soul".

However this may be, the valley of the Yssel became the center of a great religious movement – the "Devotio Moderna," or "New Devotion," which developed the institution of the Breth-ren of the Common Life. It was in this valley that the *Imita-tion of Christ,* next to the Bible the most widely read book in Europe, was composed. Here the *Spiritual Ascensions* was written by Gerard Zerbolt of Zutphen, as well as the *Rosary of Spiritual Exercises* by John Mombaer or Mauburn, which two works later had a profound influence on Ignatius Loyola. Not only did Loyola use Zerbolt's work as the pattern for his *Spirit-*

ual Exercises, but Luther gave it the highest praise, as will appear. In this valley also Gerlach Peters composed his *Soliloquy,* which became the mystical text-book of the Port Royalists or Jansenists in France. Here John Cele lived, the first important teacher to introduce the study of the Bible into the elementary schools. And here Gansfort and Erasmus acquired the ideals of reformation which they in turn passed on to Luther, Zwingli, and Calvin.

The "New Devotion" succeeded another religious movement, which had found its most perfect expression in the works of Bernard of Clairvaux, and Francis of Assisi; and in the cathedrals of Amiens, Rouen, Reims, Paris, Brussels, and Cologne. This movement had led to far-reaching monastic reforms; it had touched the hearts of the masses, inspiring them to rise to higher ideals than the worship of self, and the amassing of material riches, honor, and fame among mortals. Learning had been a living force. France had been the chief center of this older movement; its monks had brought monastic reforms to the Low Countries and Germany; and its literature had served as a model; beautiful Gothic houses of worship had been erected, seldom if ever surpassed in grandeur and ennobling simplicity.

But the thirteenth century had been followed by the fourteenth, a century notable for its spirit of strife and discontent. National and dynastic wars had brought misery to Western Europe, and no country had suffered more than France. With the loss of economic strength came the gradual eclipse of France as a dominating force in the realms of learning, literature, and art[3]. And England was scarcely in a better position than its neighbor across the Channel[4]. The same can be said of the Holy Roman Empire, where many evil forces were gradually undermining the prosperity of the people.[5] And what of the Church? Was it not growing from bad to worse as time went on, the more the clergy neglected their duties? Everywhere a decline in moral standards was noticeable, and everywhere a reform was badly needed.

What Europe of the fourteenth century apparently lacked was some great Apostle, a man able to organize a lasting movement for reform; a man who could preach, write, and draw thousands of others behind him, who in their turn would preach, write, and found schools where the rising generation might learn the ideals of the great leader himself. It was the fortune of the Yssel valley to produce such a man; for Gerard Groote, the founder of the Brotherhood of the Common Life, not only preached and wrote, but induced thousands of others to follow his example. He was the spiritual ancestor of Thomas à Kempis, Wessel Gansfort, Hegius, and Erasmus; the inaugurator of the "New Devotion," or Christian Renaissance. Through his influence the schools of Deventer and Zwolle were to become the seats of a revival of learning that was soon to spread all over Western Europe and be carried into the New World.

How did it happen that Groote and the movement he inaugurated became devoted to the reform of the schools as well as of the Church? Why did the "New Devotion," which, as has been said, was a religious movement, extend its influence to the realm of education, and why should one call it the "Christian Renaissance"? The word Renaissance means literally *rebirth,* and the term Christian Renaissance, therefore, should refer to a great rebirth of Christianity. At the same time it should denote some movement which, like the Italian Renaissance, produced a revival of learning. This was exactly the scope of the "New Devotion." Thus far it has been commonly believed that the revival of learning North of the Alps was a product of the Italian Renaissance. We shall consider whether this actually was the case; whether the reform of the schools at Deventer and Zwolle, and of those reformed after their pattern grew out of the Italian Renaissance; and whether Groote and Cele in 1374 were inspired by the Italians, or originated their own ideas.

Perhaps the physical geography of the Yssel valley had something to do with the twofold reform instituted by Groote and his followers. The cities in the Yssel country, though surrounded by immense heaths and moors, and situated somewhat apart from the busiest thoroughfares in the West, were nevertheless commercial centers and shared in the prosperity of Bruges, Ghent, and Antwerp. They formed a part of the Low Countries, where from the days of Charlemagne until the end of the fifteenth century the currents of Western thought met and intermingled[6]. Through this middle region French monastic reforms, epics, and chivalry passed into Germany; and whatever ideas came from Germany to France traveled mostly by way of the Low Countries[7].

It was here that intellectual as well as religious and commercial currents met and mingled; and from here they issued forth. The Flemish towns were the first in Transalpine Europe to supplant the monasteries as chief seats of learning and art[8]. Under the rule of the dukes of Burgundy, Bruges and Ghent became the wealthiest cities North of the Alps, not excepting Paris and London. In the middle of the fifteenth century the court at Bruges outshone even the court at Paris[9]. Then followed the rise of Antwerp and Brussels, which brought more wealth, more leisure, and consequently more learning to the Low Countries. Never before had the world seen such a port as Antwerp, since in this city for more than half of the sixteenth century nearly all the great routes of commerce converged — something which has never happened before nor since in any other port.[10] The Low Countries, therefore, shared with Italy the honor of being the most opulent districts in Europe at the very time that the "New Devotion," or Christian Renaissance made its influence felt throughout the West.

Just as France bought wares of Italy in the Low Countries, so did Paris receive many fruits of the Italian Renaissance by way of the Low Countries. The same can to a large extent be said of Germany, Switzerland, England, and Scandinavia. How this "New Devotion," or Christian Renaissance, between 1380 and 1520, absorbed the wisdom of the ancients, the essence of Christ's teachings, the mystic religion of the Fathers and the saints of medieval Europe, as well as the learning of the Italian humanists; how it assimilated all these ingredients and presented them in a new dress to the old world and the new, will be shown in the following pages.

CHAPTER I

Gerard Groote

UNTIL the third decade of the twentieth century Gerard Groote did not appear as a prominent figure in the history of the Netherlands. Outstanding historians like Professor Robert Fruin and Professor P. J. Blok paid very little attention to him and the movement he inaugurated. In the courses devoted to Dutch history few pupils ever heard much about his preaching or his books, not to mention the Brotherhood of the Common Life. But in recent years it has become fashionable among Dutch scholars of note to reserve for him a modest place beside the great admirals, governor-generals, scientists, and painters who hitherto nearly monopolized all space in the hall of fame. The man who dared to defy the scribes and pharisees of his time and suffered a mental crucifixion for his boldness has finally come into his own. We may henceforth speak of him as the founder of two powerful institutions which rank with others of far greater fame but of much less influence in the modern world.

1. Groote's Life (1340-1384)

Gerard Groote was born at Deventer in the year 1340. His father, Werner Groote, was a prominent member of the municipal government, being a *schepen*, or alderman. He had married Heilwich van der Basselen, who according to our only original source still extant gave birth to the boy in the month of October. Werner Groote belonged to a prominent merchant guild which engaged in the purchase and sale of cloth. The city of Deventer was a member of the celebrated Hanseatic League; during the fourteenth century it flourished mightily, together with the great cities of northern Germany, such as Hamburg, Bremen, and Lübeck. The Groote family occupied a pretentious home

15

in the Bagijnestraat, or Street of the Beguines. Here little
Gerard grew up to be a handsome boy, and later a highly intellectual youth.[1]

Unfortunately the father did not long survive the arrival of
the dreaded Black Death in the city of Deventer; he passed
away about the year 1350, while his wife died on July 24, 1350.
Those years of pestilence must have made a terrible impression
upon Gerard's mind. He had no brother or sister except one of
illegitimate birth called Bernard, who succeeded Werner Groote
in the merchant guild. But Gerard found a worthy guardian
in Johannes Groote, or Ockenbroeck, who seems to have married
a sister of Werner Groote. This uncle lived on the street called
Brink, which in the region of the Yssel Valley usually was the
square in the center of the city. This may once have been the
house belonging to Gerard's mother, for in one of the original
sources we read that he was born in this particular house.[2]

Gerard attended for several years the excellent school attached to the venerable church called St. Lebwin, the same school
in which more than a century later the famous Erasmus studied.
We know very little about this period in Gerard's life, but it
appears that he received some education in the ancient German
cities of Aachen and Cologne. In 1355 he matriculated in the
University of Paris, where he stayed three years, obtaining the
degree of Master of Arts in 1358.[3] He also studied magic at that
time, a fact which caused him much regret in later years. At
Prague also he sought to improve his knowledge.[4] But here
he did not remain long. He devoted about eight years at the
University of Paris to the study of law, after having received
his degree just mentioned. In some of the university documents
dating from the years 1363 and 1366 he is mentioned as a student in the faculty of law.[5]

Formerly the historians of the Netherlands completely ignored
the legal studies of Groote in Paris. The chroniclers in the
Yssel Valley had known nothing about those eight fruitful years
spent by Groote in the law school. As a result his importance
in the history of the Dutch Reformation was seldom fully understood. He could never have accomplished the task he set
out to perform if he had not been thoroughly familiar with the

Canon Law and the *Corpus Juris Civilis.* His appearance before the higher clergy in the Bishopric of Utrecht during the summer of 1383, when he himself was but a mere deacon, would seem preposterous if it had not been for his tremendous learning.

How are we to account for the honors bestowed upon him by the government of his native city if we overlook his legal training in France? The municipal council of Deventer dispatched him to the court of Pope Urban V at Avignon, where he negotiated successfully problems concerning tolls and other dues. In 1359 he had returned to Deventer, and there he had distinguished himself as a capable scholar.[6] It is doubtful that he spent much time there in this particular period; for various reasons he preferred Paris above Deventer. He admitted later that he was one of those "wandering students" who could not long be satisfied with one school, or home, or woman. He made love to women "in every green woods and upon every mountain," so he frankly stated in one of his letters.[7] When many years later he composed a learned work on the married life, he was in a position to discuss the subject not merely from a religious but also from a medical standpoint.[8] His escapades kept him away from Deventer, as we suggested, for more than one reason. No wonder that later he was so profoundly impressed by the experiences of St. Augustine, who had also "wasted his substance" and dabbled in heresies and black magic before he turned from the ways "of this world."

About Groote's mission to Avignon the sources present little concrete information. From the beginning of January to the end of August 1365 he was being consulted by the municipal council of Deventer. It offered him a handsome sum of money to defray his expenses, but to the surprise of the aldermen he refused to accept it, and at the end of the year 1365 he traveled at his own expense from Paris to Avignon. On February 7, 1366, he requested that the papal court appoint him pastor of a congregation at Ouderkerk in the Bishopric of Utrecht. He did not by any means, however, neglect the affairs of his native town, for we read in the documents that on August 20, 1366, and on January 14, 1367, Henricus van Rijpen arrived from Avignon with letters from Gerard Groote.[9]

Although his parents had left him a fortune from which he earned about two hundred gold pounds a year, he was not satisfied with this income. As early as 1362 he was promised a prebend in the ancient city of Aachen (Aix-la-Chapelle), which he finally received during the winter of 1368-69, while he was suffering from a serious illness. He spent some time in that city, but soon removed to Cologne, where he lived in great luxury, having obtained a second prebend in the city of Utrecht. All the chronicles devoted to his life mention his wayward life, for the contrast between the period before and after his conversion was most striking. Thomas à Kempis aptly remarked that "he walked in the ways of this world." [10]

One day, however, a mystic stopped Groote on the street and asked him: "Why do you stand here, intent upon empty things? You ought to become another man." The appeal made some impression on him, but not sufficient to alter his mode of life.[11]

A second warning came to him in his native city, where next we meet him. He was living with his uncle as his father had died nineteen years previous. There he fell very ill. Nevertheless, the pastor of his uncle's parish church refused to administer the sacrament of communion to him, for he refused to give up the study of astrology and magic. The illness grew worse until finally Groote thought his end was near. Suddenly he realized how many years he had spent in quest of self-aggrandizement. At Cologne in particular he had wasted his opportunities. Experience had taught him how great was the need of reform in every part and office of the Church. But he had paid no heed to the deplorable state of affairs among the clergy, especially in the higher ranks. Just as a drowning man in one brief moment reviews all the events of his past life, so did Groote on his sickbed at Deventer go over the days of his lost youth. He had much reason to condemn himself. He ordered his books on magic to be burned, and it seemed as if he was henceforth to be a changed man. But no, as soon as the disease left him, his good resolutions vanished also. We may safely conclude, however, that the warnings he had received at Cologne and at Deventer prepared the way for his final conversion, which took place shortly after the illness at Deventer.

In 1374 Groote and an old friend, named Henry of Calcar, met at Utrecht. They had both been students at Paris, where an intimate friendship had knitted their souls with ties of common ideals and aspirations. But Henry had already yielded to the warning voice of conscience, while Gerard still hesitated. After a long talk Groote was convinced of the necessity of amending his life. This third and last appeal had struck home; it resulted in a complete conversion.[12] Finally resolved to amend his ways, he returned to Deventer once more. First he gave up his two prebends;[13] next he ceded the use of his house to a few poor women, keeping only two small rooms for his own use;[14] then he entered upon the task of mastering his lower self. A terrific struggle, indeed! Yet Groote did not fail. The greater the load of his former wrongs seemed to him, the stronger his desire became to root up the last vestiges of his sin, and to replace the conquered vices by virtues.

Thus he battled for five long years, the last two of which he spent in the Carthusian monastery of Monnikhuizen near Arnhem, where his friend Henry of Calcar had been prior.[15] At Monnikhuizen Groote became an ascetic. Spurred on by the example of the other monks, he began to mortify the flesh, hoping thereby to overcome his sinful nature more rapidly and completely. His life at Monnikhuizen has been described by Thomas à Kempis: "Dressing in a long and coarse garment of hair-cloth, totally abstaining from the use of flesh and other lawful things, and passing a considerable portion of his nights in watching and prayer, he forced his feeble body into complete subservience to the spirit."[16] The Carthusian monks were delighted with their enthusiastic disciple. Groote was never able thereafter wholly to escape from their influence, although his writings and his acts after 1379 reveal a changed attitude, which was further developed by his disciples after he had passed away.

There was one other person who exerted a considerable influence upon Groote during the period of his spiritual struggles. This was John Ruysbroeck, prior of Groenendaal, the Augustinian monastery in the forest of Soignies, near Brussels. Spending most of his time out of doors, a friend of birds and flowers, a lover of the contemplative life, he had tried to solve the mysteries of the universe, and had learned much. "Before I saw you," he told Groote, "I knew you were coming." He found a responsive listener in Groote, but the latter was unable to follow Ruysbroek's theories of the kingdom of heaven, the secret of love, the union of the human soul or spirit with God, the various stages of the active and the contemplative life, the hierarchy of angels, and kindred subjects. Groote had not yet made much progress in mysticism as an abstract system of thought. And Ruysbroeck knew that. Therefore he said to Groote: "Some day you will understand."[17]

The first visit by Groote to Groenendaal must have taken place in the year 1375 or 1376. Groote had brought one of his most intimate friends with him, named John Cele, rector of the school at Zwolle,[18] the teacher who was to inaugurate the reformation of the schools in the Netherlands and western Germany. We know much about Groote's friendship with Cele and shall see his influence in Cele's work.

In 1379 Groote's years of preparation were at an end. The Carthusian monks of Monnikhuizen, astonished at his gifts of argumentation and persuasion, told him that so great a light of religious ardor as he possessed should no longer remain beneath the roof of their little monastery, and advised him to go out among the people and preach.[19] This advice Groote gladly followed. But he had too much reverence for the priesthood to don the garb of such an exalted calling,[20] and thought the rank of deacon good enough for him. Consequently he was ordained deacon shortly before the first of January, 1380, by the Bishop of Utrecht.[21]

Beginning with the cities near the Yssel, he preached the gospel of repentance at Deventer, Zwolle, Kampen, Zutphen, Amersfoort, Amsterdam, Haarlem, Leiden, Utrecht, Gouda, Delft, Ghent and many smaller places. He labored in the spirit of John the Baptist, says Thomas à Kempis, laying the axe to the root of the tree. His magnetic personality, burning zeal to win souls, and power of conviction carried their message straight to the heart. The people came for miles to hear him, many of them leaving their work unfinished and their meals untouched. The huge churches in the larger cities did not have enough room to hold the surging crowds. Remembering his own experiences, he warned the people of a future which might bring bitter regret and severe punishment. He addressed the clergy in Latin, the masses in the vernacular.[22]

One day Groote addressed a considerable group of clerical dignitaries at Utrecht, and reproved them severely for their most flagrant sins: immorality, simony, and laziness, mental and physical.[23] He had himself seen the evils that were undermining the Church, for he had been a monk himself, and before that had held two prebends, so was quite familiar with the state of affairs in his day. He had personal acquaintance with a great many priests, and fully realized how widely hypocrisy, immorality, greed, and self-indulgence were rampant among all ranks of the hierarchy. Many were wolves in the form of shepherds, as he knew, and said that he knew!

But Groote was equally concerned about the people, the wandering sheep, who were roaming about without the guiding help of their spirtual guardians, and exhorted them to be directed by their own consciences. For they possessed the reflex image of divinity within their breasts. He preached to them about Christ's commandments, and urged them to imitate the life of Christ, as he, Groote, himself was trying to do. To love God above all things, and one's neighbors as one-self, those were the two commandments, he said. We should try to eradicate vice and supplant it with newly acquired virtues, for we human beings, having been endowed with a spark of divinity, are not totally depraved. We should purge the impure flesh in which the soul condescends to dwell until our body's death. Our soul should be allowed no longer to remain obscured by the dense mists of sin woven around it by evil thoughts, words, and deeds. Man has fallen low, but he does not have to remain in the dust. Let him realize the tremendous possibilities of future glory or future punishment. He must choose, and is free to choose, though all his acts have been predestined from eternity.

With this appeal to all classes of men and women Groote aimed to teach others what he had already experienced himself. Instinctively the people felt that a new prophet had appeared, a man of extraordinary experience and power. As he went from town to town, he sent one of his disciples ahead to post the announcement of his intended address on the church door.[24] Then the people would come and look, tell their neighbors about the great news, and make the necessary preparations to hear the sermon. The farmer would hear of it, and take his family to town, leaving his crops to take care of themselves; shops were closed, almost everybody came.

Wherever Groote came to preach, a group of men and women, aroused from apathy, changed their lives and continued his work in their locality by personal example and appeal, and by lending religious books to their neighbors.[25] This was the beginning of the great religious movement, named "Devotio Moderna," which will be the subject of our study. In Deventer, Zwolle, Kampen, Zutphen, Doesburg; also in Arnhem, Utrecht, Amsterdam, Haarlem, Leiden, and Delft the fires of devotion were kept burning brightly after Groote had passed on. He himself gathered about him a band of twelve disciples at Deventer.[26] Among this number was a young man of about thirty, named Florentius Radewijns, who had given up his prebend at Utrecht to be in closer touch with Groote.[27] In Deventer he was vicar of the altar of St. Paul in the church of St. Lebwin,[28] and soon it became a custom for Groote's followers to hold meetings in the vicar's house. A few of them came to live with him, while others followed Groote on his journeys, or remained at home. These meetings in the house of Radewijns were the earliest visible beginnings of the society or congregation of the Brethren of the Common Life.

Groote continued his labors as itinerary preacher till the year 1383. His success had been great, but he had made many enemies among the mendicants and the secular clergy, by pointing out the evils among them. They were the more exasperated because with his great learning and his pure, unselfish mode of life he had easily confounded their wits. Their temporary defeat engendered a jealous, spiteful hatred for the man who had so boldly attacked them. They went to the Bishop of Utrecht and made their complaint; they told him that Groote had attacked and denounced them; and that he had tried to lead masses away from the folds of the Church. Now the sheep were leaving their true shepherds, they said, in order to follow after a man who was not even a priest. Should not such a person be commanded to stop preaching entirely? The Bishop listened and assented. No deacon was henceforth to preach in public; Groote was silenced.[29]

But Groote, though he obeyed the edict, decided not to sit idle in the future. He and his friends appealed to the Pope. The latter cautiously waited before he took decisive action. The case before him was remarkable and unusual. A lone deacon had taken upon himself the task of reproving the higher clergy. On August 14, 1383, he had appeared in the city of Utrecht before the diocesan synod, where the Bishop presided and listened with amazement to the vehement accusations leveled against his own colleagues. Groote, previously disturbed by certain forms of heresy that had been openly taught by members of the mendicant orders, and greatly concerned over the wicked deeds of secular priests, appeared as another John the Baptist, and laid bare the most flagrant sins of the higher clergy. But had he said anything contrary to the Gospel of Christ?

Florens van Wevelinchoven, Bishop of Utrecht, was not personally offended. He had observed that Groote was being attacked by three classes of persons: (1) the heretics, whom we shall mention below, (2) the immoral clergy, and (3) the mendicant monks, who complained that he had founded a new religious order without the permission required from the Pope. The good Bishop had no desire to placate the heretics, nor the bad clergy. But he was of the opinion that laymen should not be encouraged in the formation of semi-monastic congregations. Against the character of Gerard Groote he had nothing to say, and yet he did not wish to offend the powerful Dominicans and Franciscans who disliked the Sisters of the Common Life in Deventer. So he had chosen the lesser of two evils, and henceforth all deacons in the bishopric of Utrecht were forbidden to preach.

Pope Urban VI would be pleased to learn that Groote had not refused to accept the papal authority nor the creed of the Roman Catholic Church. Groote had issued a proclamation attesting his orthodox faith and his subjection to the papal chair. His friends had sent messages to the Bishop of Utrecht indicating that Groote had won the support and respect of virtuous clerics and laymen. Although the Bishop had not withdrawn his edict, he would do nothing to harm Groote and his followers beyond the terms of his decree. On October 21, 1383, the learned William Salvarvilla of Liége sent a letter to the Pope in which he suggested that Groote receive personal and apostolic permission to preach again in the Diocese of Utrecht. He and Groote agreed that a priest by the name of Bernard be dispatched to Rome with proper credentials and letters. We possess an interesting letter addressed by Groote to this priest, who was living at Deventer and was told to receive from Radewijns the necessary papers for his trip. At this time Groote was far removed from the scene of strife, having withdrawn to the little town of Woudrichem. The whole winter passed and still no reply came from the Bishop of Utrecht nor Pope Urban VI.[30]

But no matter how long he had to wait for papal sanction, he would not disobey the orders of the good Bishop. Several Dutch authorities used to hold the theory that Groote finally started preaching again, since Thomas à Kempis wrote: "For a time he refrained from preaching, and during the interval he contented himself with private exhortations." But no reliable source states definitely that Groote preached again in public, and those who accused Thomas of having presented erroneous reports were sadly mistaken in their hasty judgment.

One reason why the Pope's reply was so slow in coming is that he had removed from Rome to Naples, as Salvarvilla informed Groote in a letter dated February 3, 1384. When Bernard finally had an audience with him, he found justice. The testimonials he bore with him and the honest tale he told could not fail to impress the pontiff, who gladly extended the hand of Christian fellowship to the great Dutch reformer. Unfortunately Groote was dead before Bernard returned to Deventer with the official grant of permission so eagerly sought by the fiery preacher.[31]

The exile at Woudrichem had long been terminated, and at least six fruitful months of writing, translating, and exhorting had followed in the city of Deventer. The end of his mortal life was near, but this last year at Deventer may perhaps be considered the most important one in the history of the great religious revival which he inaugurated. He now had more time to reflect upon his past, to instruct his followers, and to speak oftener with the teachers and pupils of the cathedral school. Several boys and young men were employed by him to copy books. Whenever he had a chance, he talked to them about some religious subject, trying to win them for the kingdom of God. They were the material most needed, he thought, for the reform of the Church.[32] Religion and learning must go hand in hand. The clergy ought to receive a liberal education before assuming the leadership of the people. Teachers, on the other hand, would do well to include religious instruction among the other subjects taught by them. These boys, said Groote to himself, will some day be leaders among men. Some of them will enter monasteries, others will teach; one or two among them are likely to become merchants or magistrates, while a few others may rise to the priesthood, or even higher. While their characters are still pliable, the ardor of youth in their veins, it is time to fill their minds with noble ambitions. Hence Groote gladly devoted a considerable share of his energy to the religious training of school boys. He was assisted in this undertaking by his followers, both at Deventer, and at Zwolle. Thus the foundations were laid for the great revival of learning which was started and supervised by the Brethren of the Common Life.

In 1383 Groote entered also upon a new task. It was not enough, he said, that the clergy be educated. The people too must read and decide for themselves. Religion should be personal for all men and women. What good does it do, he reasoned, for a layman merely to go to church? Will that cure his spiritual ills? Certainly not. He must do more than listen to his preacher; he must read and think for himself. And in

order to make this possible, he began to translate portions of
the Bible and a great many church hymns into the vernacular,
at the same time providing these translations with glosses and
other explanations.[33]

A pestilence broke out at Deventer in the summer of the year
1384. One of Groote's followers, named Lambert Stuerman,
caught the disease. Groote felt it incumbent upon him to visit
his beloved friend and became infected himself. There was
no hope of recovery; on the 20th of August he passed away.[34]
But his ideals and his plans did not die with him, as will appear.

2. Groote as Theologian and Philosopher

Groote had gleaned part of his knowledge from the Bible,
the writings of Aibert Magnus, Ambrose, Anselm, Antony, Apu-
leius, Aristotle, Augustine, Bede, Bernard of Clairvaux, Boethius,
Bonaventura, Cassianus, Cato, Chrysostom, Cicero, Climacus,
Cyprian, Demosthenes, Dionysius, Eusebius, Fabricius, Francis
of Assisi, Gregory, Gregory of Nianza, Henry of Ghent, Hip-
pocrates, Isidor, Jerome, Juvenal, Lucan, Lyra, Nepos, Per-
menianus Donatista, Peter of Damiani, Plato, Pliny, Seneca,
Socrates, Suetonius, Suso, Theophrastus, Thomas Aquinas, Va-
lerius, Vegetius, Virgil and the Canon Law with its commentaries.

Another field of knowledge was the contact with his friends,
of whom John Ruysbroeck was one. It was he who had initiated
Groote into the mysterious realm of the contemplative life:
"The creature is in Brahma and Brahma is in the creature; they
are ever distinct yet ever united," says the Indian mystic. Were
it translated into Christian language, it is probable that this
thought — which does not involve pantheism — would have
been found acceptable by Ruysbroeck, for the interpenetration
yet eternal distinction of the human and divine spirits is the
central fact of his universe. Man, he thinks, is already related
in a three-fold manner to his Infinite Source, for we have our
being in him, as the Father, we contemplate him as does the
Son, we ceaselessly tend to return to him as does the Spirit.
So the Superessential Life is the simple, the synthetic life, in

which man actualises at last all the resources of his complex being. The active life of response to the Temporal Order, the contemplative life of response to the Transcendent Order, are united, firmly held together, by that eternal fixation of the spirit, the perpetual willed dwelling of the being of man within the Incomprehensible Abyss of the Being of God, *qui est per omnia saecula benedictus.* 'To this divine vision but few men can attain, because of their own unfitness and because of the darkness of that Light whereby we see, and therefore no one shall thoroughly understand this perception by means of any scholarship, or by own acuteness of comprehension. For all words, and all that men may learn and understand in a creaturely fashion, is foreign to this and far below the truth that I mean. ' "[35]

Groote, also, became a mystic. His mysticism, however, differed considerably from that of his aged friend. In spite of his great reverence for Ruysbroeck, he could never persuade himself to adopt those views which the church of Rome considered heretical. From the day of his conversion at Utrecht in 1374 Groote saw very little value in abstract thinking. He never became more than a distant admirer of Ruysbroeck, and similarly refused to subscribe to the views of the scholastic philosophers. He was not a Thomist, though he has been thought one. In his opinion Thomas Aquinas wasted a great deal of time on topics of no practical value whatsoever. There is but one work of Groote left in which he enunciates purely philosophical views. This is the *Sermon,* or *Treatise, on the Birth of Christ,* which in all probability he addressed to a learned body of clerics. In this sermon he most explicitly disapproves of barren types of scholastic philosophy, and does not mention the name of Thomas Aquinas, while in some of his other works he only refers to this philosopher as an authority on theological or moral questions, never as a philosopher whose views he admires.

The theology and philosophy of Gerard Groote was based chiefly upon the New Testament, and the Fathers; in a lesser degree also upon the works of Greek, Roman, and medieval philosophers. If we are to compare his ideas with those of any other philosopher, we might say that his works betray the exceedingly powerful influence of Augustine. And if we are to give a name to Groote's philosophy, we might safely call it Augustinian.

With Adam the whole human race fell, says Groote. There have been wise men like Solomon, humble men like David, strong men like Samson, yet every one of these was but a shadow of what he might have been. Man, created in the image of God, has fallen low, unspeakably low. Once enjoying the pure reflex light of divinity, he now is no longer able to fathom the mysteries of life. His fall was the inevitable result of disobedience to the *"Lex Dei,"* the immutable law of God. Whenever man disobeys that law, he sins, for sin is disobedience. And since the *"Lex Dei"* is the highest of all laws, one should never obey the command of any man, be he the Pope himself, if such a command should oppose God's law; for is not the Pope also subject to the *"Lex Dei"?* Before the Fall, man had this law engraved in his heart, but since that time his intellect has grown dim, and the more he sins, the further he is removed from the *"suprema ratio,"* or supreme source of wisdom. God is the Alpha and the Omega, from whom all things develop, and to whom they all return, either in a natural way or through grace. Sin obscures the intellect, evil enfeebles the will; slowly the light of wisdom vanishes as the obstinate sinner turns farther and farther away from the supreme Law-giver, who offers peace and joy through humble obedience.

But man is not wholly depraved. He still possesses a small spark of divinity within his breast, a radiant gleam of light, which may be fanned into a bright flame. God is a spirit, and all who worship him must obey the voice of their spirits. We should aim to cultivate the inner life, for the kingdom of heaven is within us, as Christ said; here in the innermost depths of our hearts we may find the voice of God. Similarly, the kingdom of evil is also within us, for from the corrupt heart of man come forth all sinful thoughts. He who cannot control his inner life will never succeed in governing his outward acts. Let us therefore endeavor to silence the forces of evil, and listen to the Father's voice. It is God alone who can convert the sinful heart. Happy the man that has decided to make room within his heart for Christ, who is continually knocking at the door, patiently waiting for a response. And if the door is once opened, when Christ enters with his sweet conversation, then the wisdom from heaven will fill that human temple with the peace which passes all understanding. "When I read the psalms," said Groote to his friend, John Brinckerinck, "hidden manna is flowing into my inner self, so that I experience no fatigue in reading, but sweet rapture instead."[36] Groote constantly urged his disciples to seek communion with God the Father, a spiritual communion with a spiritual God. For God is the *summum bonum;* if we have him, we have all goodness; if we lose him, nothing but evil is left unto us. And why? Because that part of us which is divine cannot exist without the life-giving contact with him who alone can sustain life and nourish our inner selves.

Hence the need Groote felt in common with all other mystics to remain in touch with God. As a Christian mystic he sought this contact through Christ. He made it a point to attend mass every day. "Let me first seek the kingdom," he thought, "and then I shall so much the better be able to serve my neighbor." Consequently he would stay till the end of the mass as often as possible to partake of the communion. It was also his habit to withdraw himself several times a day from the busy life of the outer world for prayer, surrendering himself wholly to God, saying: "Here I am Lord; teach me to do thy will, make mine conform to thine." As a mystic Groote maintained that the reading of good books should at all times be supplemented by meditation and prayer, for contact with God Himself he considered the only way of obtaining the highest wisdom. Whenever he was conscious of this contact between himself and God, his "soul would leap with joy." Songs of thanksgiving would escape from his fervent lips, for at such moments "that wonderful peace promised by Christ would settle upon him."[37]

And what is the tie which unites man with his maker? Groote held that it is love, and love only. "Try to love," he said, "for in loving you shall find the kingdom of heaven. If once you have found this kingdom, you will enjoy righteousness, peace, and joy in the Holy Ghost. Without these three gifts all outward show of piety, such as fasting, and mortification of the flesh, will be of no avail." But how is one to show one's love for God? By sitting in one's cell, aloof from the outside world? Not at all, for he who really loves God, loves all of God's creatures. "Although one should avoid too much idle conversation with 'worldly people,' one ought never to shun their presence, but work among them, trying to make them also participants of the joys celestial, far superior as they are to any delights bestowed by our bodily senses." Groote had tasted the supreme felicity love brings to all those who cheerfully lay their dearest treasures upon the altar of self-sacrifice.[38] Thomas à Kempis tells that "when Groote felt the force of love in his heart, his soul would sing with joy, and his spirit, as a flame, was borne upward to God."[39] Groote constantly exhorted his disciples to cast out jealousy for sympathy, spite for charity, rancor for love. "Close your eyes to your neighbor's defects," he would say, "and try to discover his good qualities, which are always worth considering; nay more than that, they are the only side of his character it is well for you to dwell upon. For our soul's health can only be sustained by thoughts of love. And strange to say, the more love we spend, the more we receive, together with much joy in the spirit. We must also fight melancholy, despondency, dejectedness: these are the enemies of our spiritual existence." Groote found it quite easy to love even his enemies, after once having tasted the heavenly bliss which attends every act of whole-hearted forgiveness. "The health of his soul," says Thomas à Kempis, "gave to his food a savor beyond that of any pleasant meat. . . .He sent away his guests joyful in the Lord."[40]

Groote was more than a philosopher, more than a mere mystic. He carried on an active campaign against the dying scholasticism of his day. "Why should we indulge in those endless disputes," he would say, "such as are held at the universities, and that about subjects of no moral value whatsoever?" "Do not therefore attend court," he advised, "and if you are asked to go, send a substitute." When he referred to the works of philosophers, he always singled out those passages which had practical value. Among the philosophers of ancient Greece and Rome he preferred men like Plato, Socrates, and Seneca, who had endeavored to solve certain moral problems for the benefit of their fellow-men. "Words merely serve to convey our thoughts to others," he wrote one day; "they are the servants, not the masters of sense and expression."[41]

The same spirit which impelled Groote to attack the decadent scholasticism of his time induced him also to combat indolence, physical as well as mental. He wanted no women to live in his house at Deventer, for example, who did not want to gain their own livelihood with their own hands. "At present," he wrote in a certain letter, "I am firmly resolved to accept no one who is able to work, but wants to beg for her meals somewhere in the city. All those shall work who are in a condition to do so, and if the time should come when they cannot perform manual labor any longer, then it will be early enough for them to accept alms. This I say, because labor is necessary for the well-being of mankind. In trying to avoid physical exertion, these women fall into the danger of idleness, thereby forgetting the study of their own inner selves, and wander from house to house, inquisitive and restless, prying into other people's affairs, ignoring their own duties."[42] On the ground of indolence Groote also attacked some of the mendicant friars, who in return showed him and his followers after him no small amount of hostility.

What Groote wanted was more Christianity, plain and simple. To follow in the footsteps of Christ, to bear his cross in humble submission, that was Groote's aim. For that reason he gave up his prebends, ceded his house to some devout women, and compassed land and sea to tell others about Christ's message; he tried to return good for evil, to treat the obstinate with patience, the suffering with sympathy, the impudent with forbearance. Thus he labored for four years and a half, loved by the masses, and followed by thousands of grateful disciples. He was not a profound scholar, not a great philosopher. The subtle arguments of the learned doctors at Paris, Cologne, and Prague he regarded as foolishness. He sought nothing but the conversion of sinners, the formation of a harmoniously developed character

on the part of his disciples, and the extension of God's kingdom
on earth. Groote was neither Thomist, nor Scotist; he did not
imitate Ruysbroeck as a lover of solitary nooks in forest or
monastery, but preferred a life of action among men. He wanted to be a Christian, and the movement he set on foot was a
Christian Renaissance.

3. Groote as Reformer

Groote was deeply concerned about the Church. Indeed,
among the reformers of the fourteenth and fifteenth centuries
he occupies a leading position. Few men were so well acquainted with the decline in moral standards among all ranks of the
clergy as he, and very few, if any, so bitterly lamented the impending collapse of the Church. Instead of ignoring the dangers which were threatening the Church from within, he sought
to stay the evil by attacking those who were the cause of the
wide-spread demoralization: monks, priest, and bishops, as well
as common people. He tried to rouse them all from their mental and spiritual lethargy.

In the first place he endeavored to extend the meaning of the
word *religio,* which in his time was not the equivalent of the
English word *religion,* but served to distinguish the monks, or
regular clergy, from other people. He protested against the
wrong interpretation of the word *religio.* "If devout women,"
he wrote, "separate themselves from the world, and try to serve
God in the privacy of their homes, without taking monastic
vows, they are just as religious as the nuns in their convents. To
love God and worship him is religion, not the taking of special
vows. For the cause and purpose of things give them their
names and forms. If it is, therefore, one's aim to live a religious
life, his way of living becomes religious in God's opinion, and
according to the judgment of our consciences." On another
occasion he said· "Truly religious men are not confined by
place, time, or manner of men." "All these," he continued,
"who live aloof from the world to serve God, who despise temporal honors; leading chaste lives, obedient and poor: they are
religious people."[43]

"No one may found a new religious order," continues Groote, "without the Pope's permission, but it is not wrong, I believe, for two or more persons to live together in observance of certain established rules, or the rule of all rules, namely, the blessed Gospel; that is not forbidden, I think. The mere name *religio* signifies but little; it is not the name which determines the nature of a thing. Names are conventional. Therefore, the *Horologium*[44] is right in saying: 'Many so-called religious people go about in cowls and wear other outward garbs of religion, but within they are lions, bears — terrible beasts.' There are many who are not protected by the name *religio,* and yet they may be more religious than those whom the Church calls religious."[45]

In the year 1379 Groote departed from the monastery, and never returned to it. Did he afterwards perhaps cherish so much reverence for the monastic life that he never dared to enter a monastery again?[46] We know that he had great respect for a pious monk who left his friends and relatives for the sole purpose of worshiping God more perfectly. Whenever he made acquaintance with persons who showed a burning desire to come into closer relation to God, and seemed to be eminently fitted for the monastic state, he did not hesitate to praise and recommend monasticism.[47] To others, who had taken monastic vows, he was accustomed to write frequently, reminding them of the reason why they entered the monastery. Since they had decided to serve God in comparative seclusion, they should no longer indulge in gossip, but should close their ears to rumors, quarrels, wars, and festivals; they should live soberly, and perform their daily tasks with alacrity.[48] Many other examples might be adduced to show that Groote approved of monasticism,[49] though his approval was not unqualified. Some people seemed to be particularly well fitted for the monastic life, but not he, nor those among his disciples whose ability to instruct the young, to preach to the masses, to remind the clergy of their shortcomings, or to comfort the poor and the afflicted, impelled them to employ their talents in the service of their neighbors, instead of burying them in the solitude of a lonely cell. Hence we find him writing to one of his followers: "I dare not advise you to enter a monastery, though it is not for me to judge,

being ignorant of God's ways.   My desire is that you remain in
the world, and be not of the world."[50] When John Cele, rector
of the school at Zwolle, wanted to discontinue his work as teacher and become a monk, Groote urged him to remain at Zwolle,
where he was doing such splendid work, not only among the
school boys, but also as a preacher.   Though Groote perfectly
understood and never failed to appreciate the merits of monasticism, he was by no means blind to the laxity of discipline
noticeable in nearly all monasteries.   Monks were not less prone
to sin than other men.   Hence he vigorously attacked the
greatest monastic evils: immorality, simony, and indolence.[51]

Groote's attitude towards the secular clergy and the Church
in general was that of a reformer, not that of a revolutionist.
He did not engage in negative criticism alone, as many of the
humanists did, but supplemented his criticism with constructive
plans.   He was not satisfied with conditions as he had himself
seen them at Deventer, Aachen, Cologne, Paris, Utrecht, and
Avignon, for he loved the Church too much not to be grieved
at its dangerous condition.   However, he did not attack the
doctrines or dogma of the Church.   "Everything I have preached is in complete accordance with the teachings of the Church,"
he wrote; "wherever I have been wrong I shall gladly retract.
I submit myself to the authority (judgment) of the Church."[52]

The Church, in Groote's opinion, was a divine institution;
its teachings were promulgated by servants of God, who had
been inspired by the Holy Ghost.   In the realm of dogma or
doctrine, therefore, the Church was supreme, and its teachings
infallible.   Although he drew a careful distinction between the
Bible and other religious writings, he did not go so far as later
reformers and say: "I submit myself only to the authority of
the Scriptures," for he was firmly convinced that since Christ
had promised to remain with His church until the end, it would
be preposterous for him to lay claim to a better knowledge of
the Bible than the Church Fathers and the medieval saints
possessed.[53]

Groote never dreamed of calling the Church supreme in the
realm of morals, however, for he said: "There are some men
today who exalt the judgments of the Church, because to them

they are better known than the commandments of God, or the
laws of nature, since they are ignorant of these laws, due to the
darkness of their hearts; they are disposed, as were the Scribes
and Pharisees, to transgress the law for the sake of human traditions, or the regulations of the Elders, for the instructions of
the Church are more familiar to them than the laws of nature,
or the commandments of God."[54] Far from wishing to break
the Church, he deplored the schism within the Church and exclaimed: "I wish that both popes with all their cardinals would
sing a *'Gloria in excelsis'* in heaven, and that a true Eliakim
would bring peace and harmony upon earth. This schism cannot be healed without some terrible blow to the Church, which
has long been in a position of decrepitude, ready to fall to
pieces, and now the head itself is in a sad condition."[55]

The most exalted office a man could fill on earth, in Groote's
eyes, was the cure of souls, and even the Pope was a greater man
as priest than as head of the Church.[56] Consequently the worst
form of simony was that of accepting or dispensing such a bene-
fice for money. The cure of souls should be a thing quite
spiritual, quite divine. And it should be a bishop's duty to
appoint for these spiritual tasks only men who had been endowed with a clear mind, whose hearts were pure, and whose
aims were unselfish. If a bishop could not find trustworthy
shepherds for his sheep, he had better resign his office, in spite
of all the regulations found in the Canon Law and all the laws
enacted by the Church.[57]

Groote's views on the sacraments are closely allied with his
opinion regarding the duties of the clergy. "If the Pope should
command you," he says to the lower clergy, "or a bishop, or any
other superior, under whatever form of penalty, even that of
excommunication, suspension, deposition, or privation, to administer the Holy Supper, and you have not repented of certain
mortal sins, no human law of obedience can compel you to do
it; on the other hand, you should refuse to administer the sacrament in question, heedless of all temporal loss or calumny.[58]
For the laws and regulations of the Church are on the same level
with those enacted by all human agencies."[59] "The sacraments," continues Groote, "have power independent of the

Reformed view

priest who administers them, and his sins have no effect on the nature of the sacrament; all one's pollutions are taken away by one's faith in Christ, nor can any sinner pollute the divine sacraments."[60]

As for the sacrament of penance, no priest, says Groote, has the right to forgive any sins of any person who has not confessed all his evil deeds and decided never, if possible, to repeat them again. For if the sinner intends no repentance, absolution is idle; in such cases the priest must repeal his pronouncement of forgiveness. The sole condition required in this transaction is the sinner's repentance. All the priest can do is to act when the sinner is sincere in his confession and has resolved to amend his evil ways.[61] Great caution is required of him, for suppose he forgives sins which God as yet cannot forgive, what benefit will the sinner receive? The priest presents the sinner to the Church as absolved from his load of sin, whereas the Church Triumphant or the Immaculate Church, that is, the inner circle of true believers terrestial as well as celestial, refuses to accept him. He is introduced at the outer gate, but is repelled by those within the enclosure.[62] The priest's chief aim should be to convert sinners, for the conversion of sinners is a greater work than the creation of the world. "I believe," said Groote, "that prayer is more beneficial than mechanical rules and transactions; admonition is better than absolution, for after all it is God alone who can convert sinners.[63] Suppose somebody takes his neighbor's property, and is unrepentant, then all his confessions are of no avail, and every one who absolves him is simply a servant of the devil."

It should be noted that Groote had no desire to break away from the Church. He even tried to silence four "heretics." In one of his letters we find him addressing a certain "Brother John," who had preached against him at Zutphen, Zwolle, and Kampen. "Your words were full of idle boasting and blasphemy," he tells him; "thus far I have suffered you to continue, but now I can stand it no longer. You shall retract, else I shall take you before the Roman Curia. Beware, if you still persevere in your obstinate course, after these friendly warnings."[64] John probably heeded Groote's warning, but the other three men Groote attacked publicly. One of them was Bartholomew, an Augustinian friar from Dordrecht, a friend and to a great extent a follower of a curious sect, known as the "Free Spirits,"[65] who preached the following doctrines: "God is neither life, nor light, nor nature. The divine essence is my essence, and my essence is divine essence. Just as man cannot exist without God, God is unable to live without man's aid. Divinity is dependent on man. Man is perfect God. Man from eternity is God in God. Man is never born, but has existed from eternity. The aim of every man should be to lose himself in the Nothingness of the Godhead; then he will be like Christ, both God and man. Every man, therefore, is saved through the immanence of the Holy Ghost, not through Christ's sacrifice. There is only one sin: to remain under the law of good works, rewards, and punishment; consequently there is but one virtue: to free oneself from these. And again, there is no evil in such imaginary sins as lust, pride, theft, hatred."[66] Groote wanted to silence preachers who taught such doctrines. "Bartholomew enters inns," he wrote, "and gets many friends there, for he finds fault with no one. Nothing is so dangerous as to preach about God and perfection, and not to point out the way which leads to perfection. Penitence is hardly necessary in his opinion; tell him that if he is to preach any longer, he must show the people the way to heaven through Christ by following in His footsteps, not by ignoring the imperfection of man, and the existence of sin. I mean to listen to him in secret with a notary public, catch him at his game, and make it impossible for him to continue his present work as servant of the devil."[67] After some delay he finally succeeded in having Bartholomew silenced by the Bishop of Utrecht.[68]

Now the question naturally arises, Was Gerard Groote the "hammer of heretics" that one rhymed source called him?[69] Were those critics correct who in recent years accused him of inquisitorial investigations and persecutions?[70] What these writers overlooked was Groote's zeal to preserve the purity and authority of the Church, paying little attention to mere heresies but reproving wicked deeds and words. In this respect he most truly imitated Jesus of Nazareth rather than the medieval inquisition.[71]

His significance as a reformer in the fourteenth century has seldom been properly analyzed. Not until the year 1942 did a comprehensive biography of Groote make its appearance, and before 1938 only scattered works of no great scope were devoted to his life and writings. But in 1940 and 1941 extensive publications attested the rising interest in his life and teachings. In the Netherlands a society was founded which is now actively engaged in preparing an edition of his *Opera Omnia*. This is the *Geert Groote Vereeniging,* which recently published a Dutch translation of the biography of Groote by Thomas à Kempis. It was published as No. 155 of the publications issued by this society, and in the near future we may look for some remarkable developments. At the same time some useful work is being done in the United States. One notable book is the admirable dissertation by Professor William Spoelhof, which deals with the development of religious toleration by Groote and his followers.

What made Groote so important in the history of western Europe was his successful attempt to revive the primitive Christian Church. Contrary to the opinion of hostile critics, he paid very little attention to the many heretical beliefs current in his day. But he did consider seriously the evil lives of heretics. When a learned friend named Salvarvilla wondered why he did not care to help heal the Great Schism in the Western Church, he told this scholar that outward schisms were caused by lack of inner power and love. We must first heal the schism in our hearts, so he reasoned. His main theme always was the acquisition of spiritual power rather than the building of concrete structures. What could he accomplish in Rome or Avignon if ordinary members of the Church were being lost because of sinful living?[72]

There is a hidden power in the famous book entitled the *Imitation of Christ* which has made it the most widely read work ever composed in Europe. It flowed from the pens of Groote's disciples as easily and as logically as did the books of the New Testament in the Near East. A man of tremendous spiritual power gathered around him twelve chosen disciples, of whom one became a traitor. He founded two institutions which reminded thoughtful men and women of the first church in Jerusalem. The scribes and pharisees of his day he unmercifully flayed and was promptly silenced by them, as had happened in a similar case at the Holy City. After his death his sayings were jotted down and his program was executed. From the Yssel Valley in all directions his influence spread, largely unseen but most powerful just the same. George Elliot knew something about this phenomenon when in the famous novel, *The Mill on the Floss,* she portrayed the tremendous change that came over the young woman in the story who found in her attic a copy of the *Imitation.* Thousands of such cases could have been recorded from actual facts.

Groote established a Christian Renaissance, not an inquisition. He wanted to instill personal religion rather than mere doctrines. In that respect he resembled Erasmus, who at times was a faithful child of the Devotio Moderna. What did he care if a certain man or woman erred in matters of doctrine as long as one tried to imitate the life of Christ? Seeing how corrupt a large number of clergymen were, he hoped to rally all laymen to his side, which was also a characteristic of Christ in Palestine. The Netherlands was much like the Holy Land. A small country, devoid of great natural resources, lay on the western shore of a huge continent. The route of trade traversed it as did the Oriental arteries of commerce in the days of the Apostles. "From all nations under the sun" the merchants and tourists came to the Low Countries. The travelers brought with them many new ideas, and upon their return they took to their respective communities a message of hope and cheer for a wicked world. Before long some of the most venerable monasteries in France, Germany, and the southern Netherlands bowed before the spiritual scepter of Windesheim, which began its humble existence two years after Groote's death, but soon saw its reformers carry the new gospel to hundreds of older institutions. In this manner did Groote operate long after his death. Those who still insist in looking upon him as an inquisitor must examine him anew. Then they will understand why he spent so much energy in reforming both clergy and laity.

Groote made his position quite clear in his well-known *Sermon Against the Immoral Clergy*, delivered in the year 1383 before the higher clergy in the Bishopric of Utrecht. He established five points which in recent years have attracted much attention among Dutch scholars. One of them discovered in an ancient manuscript a summary of the sermon and a good explanation of the five points. They are: (1) that an unworthy priest does not detract from the value of the sacrament administered by him, (2) that a priest who openly lives in immorality must be avoided by the faithful members of the congregation, (3) that according to Thomas Aquinas it would be very sinful to partake of the sacrament administered by such an immoral priest, (4) that those prelates who permit a sinful priest to function in his parish are guilty of a grave misdemeanor, and (5) that every woman who by living with a priest should cause scandal to the Church must leave him forthwith.[73]

These views of Groote were not remarkable; they merely indicate that he wanted sincerely to reform the Church along orthodox lines. In some respects, however, he preached views that were justly deemed heretical or revolutionary. He was indifferent to the visible structure, as manifested in buildings and the hierarchy. Christ was the real head, and the Pope counted for very little. For this attitude he has been adversely criticized by Roman Catholic scholars in the Netherlands.[74] Furthermore, he was of the opinion that any Pope may fall into error and heresy, and he made much of natural law, claiming that a Pope receives his office both through human and through divine law, whereas modern Catholicism recognizes only the divine law.

Of great interest to the historian is Groote's extraordinary position toward heretics, which as a rule has been sadly misinterpreted by Dutch scholars of note. According to him a heretic may retain saving faith, notwithstanding the verdict of Thomas Aquinas and other learned authorities. He reasoned that a heretic loses only as much of the faith as is involved in his particular heresy, while nearly all other scholars entertained a most pessimistic view regarding skeptics. What impressed him particularly was the failure on the part of the higher clergy to live up to the high standards set by Christ. Why should they spend so much time and energy in preaching about useful topics. In the University of Paris, for example, the jurists and theologians taught doctrines that were truly false and misleading. Suppose those doctrines were not called heresies, were they perhaps not worse than heresies? Groote actually came to the conclusion that the whole world would soon be destroyed, because the clergy had abandoned its high calling. A great Church Council might still save the Church, but the chances were not bright.[75]

Groote's concern about the evil clergy reminds us of the statements made by Jesus of Nazareth, whom he wanted to imitate with heart and soul. Some of his most important criticisms have recently been discovered in ancient manuscripts. One letter had been known only in abbreviated form, and we may well surmise that in the three great collections of his correspondence found respectively in The Hague, Liége, and Magdeburg, the scribes eliminated the terrific attacks upon the clergy. In 1940 a Dutch translation of the letter was published, indicating the revived interest recently displayed in the Netherlands. Groote quoted freely from St. Bernard, Jerome, Augustine, and Gregory the Great. He talked about "blind leaders of the blind," and about "wolves in sheep's clothing."[76] In this manner he created a tremendous demand for reformation which could not fail to affect many of his countrymen. That he also attracted the attention of those who would not reform is readily understood. Illuminating is the learned discourse of one scholar whose treatise was published for the first time in 1941, together with Groote's reply. The former intimated that Groote was much too severe.[77]

From the day of Groote's conversion he never was a friend of lazy friars, for he hated indolence. "It is well for a true Christian," he would say, "to cede his possessions to the poor. This will compel him to work for his daily bread. Poverty without begging is a boon to the pilgrim, for he should be freed from all temporal encumbrances.[78] Man is only a steward here on earth, wherefore it is his duty to confine his expenditures to a small minimum. Why should one be jealous of one's neighbor who is leading a life of luxury?" Groote himself had spent all his possessions for the extension of God's kingdom upon earth. So little, in fact, he had reserved that sometimes he had to ask one of his friends for a small loan. In his poverty he aimed to imitate Christ. "O Lord of all riches," he exclaimed, "why didst thou elect such humble garments? Why didst thou choose to sit on an ass which was found tied to a gate near a public road, upon which even the humblest man was free to ride, and worse, on a colt upon whose back no man had ever sat, as it had thus far been used for the meanest sorts of employment? Rejoice, ye poor ones, for this seeming poverty is but a guise, since he, though poor in earthly goods, was master of all, magnificent, royal, divine! Follow in his footsteps, ascend the road which leads from ignominy to glory, from toil and strife to peace and rest, to heights sublime."[79]

All obstacles should be removed which might in any way obstruct his path, wherefore he deemed it best for men such as he not to marry or to be at all familiar with women. He shunned them himself: to the women in his house he seldom spoke except through a closed and curtained window.[80] Basing his views upon certain passages found in the New Testament and in the writings of St. Augustine,[81] he exhorted the lower clergy who wished to serve God above all things not to marry:[82] "Marriage is a hindrance to him who intends to develop his spirtual nature, for it brings sorrows of its own, as well as joys, cares, and much worldly thought. There are many men who have had to give up their career as scholar or philosopher, as the inevitable result of their friendships with women."[83]

To those for whom he thought marriage fitting, he also offered serious counsel. His disciples should choose devout wives — chaste, virtuous, and true — and one must not assume that he can draw an ungodly woman to God.[84] The marriage tie is sacred, for marriage is a symbol of the eventual union between Christ and his church. Therefore it is a man's duty to love his wife as much as the Church is loved by Christ; he has no right to frequent inns and loaf about town at night. Christ does indeed love his Church, and readily forgives the sins of his beloved, as husbands and wives should remember, cover each other's defects, avoid quarrels and ill-feeling. For perfect love hides all the faults of its object.[85]

It would not be right to call Groote a pessimist. He thought that it was always best to dwell more upon the hope of eternal glory rather than upon the pains of hell.[86] As for the theory of good works, he wrote: "Christ would rather see a wife obedient to her husband and quietly performing her daily tasks than any ascetic doing penitence, and not obedient, or kind-hearted."[87] "Asceticism," he stated on another occasion, "is often very harmful, for the devil will frequently use it as a tool, telling the person in question that it is a very helpful method for the religious student, and yet all this watching, praying, and fasting will often cause mental diseases, anger, or pride. Man is prone to think that he can do good on his own initiative, thus taking too much pride in his own work, which if really good, is not his work, but that of God. Hence there are many people who pray much and inflict physical hardships upon themselves, while within they are unrighteous and avaricious."[88]

Groote himself did not lead a gloomy life, for he felt he had lived in that peace which passeth all understanding, and all temporal delights. The happiness enjoyed by him when conscious of this blessed peace was plainly visible upon his features. The reading of the Scriptures gave him great joy. When his friend Cele was depressed and worried about his shortcomings and his weakness amidst the many temptations he had to encounter, Groote wrote him an encouraging letter: "Be happy in the Lord, for nothing is so helpful in temptation as mental happiness and confidence in God." "It is our duty," he says, "to make ourselves worthy habitations, where Christ will be pleased to dwell. The Holy Ghost will readily assist us in acquiring virtue, for virtues are indeed gifts of the Holy Ghost. Far above the sacraments, above miracles and prophecies stand virtue and love. All virtues are to be employed as tools wherewith we can increase love; through love they unite us with God the Father, and the Holy Ghost. Just as many twigs sprout from

one common root, so are many virtues shaped by one force —
namely, love. Our enemy Satan knows very well that all external
works and all spiritual exercises without love and faith are
valueless. He persuades many to perform good works, telling
them that thereby they will obtain salvation. Thus by devoting
all their attention to these 'good works,' they neglect their inner
selves, where salvation and the kingdom of heaven may be
found."[89]

The greatest of all virtues was humility. "The more we realize
our own imperfections," says Groote, "the nearer we approach
perfection." "Before all things," he continues, "and in all things
study specially to become humble inwardly. For it is far better
to do but little good out of obedience to God's will than to do
a great deal more on one's own account, since the lesser becomes
the greater before God. 'Good will' means to acquiesce in God's
will, for everything that occurs is an act of God's will. God
speaks to us through his acts. Blessed is he who obeys God's
voice and bears in mind that everything which befalls him is
predestined by God, even the wrongs done by others. False accusations and slander he ought to bear in peace, for God knows
best. Let him say to his Creator: 'Lord, all that is mine and my
own self I surrender to thee; I renounce my will for thy sake.
This is the greatest thing I have been able to do in this
world.' "[90]

4. Groote as Educator

Groote also was deeply interested in education. He never
became a teacher himself, nor did he expect much of mere formal study as an aim in itself. Such subjects as geometry, arith-
metic, rhetoric, logic, grammar, poetry and astronomy, he
thought, were of very little use to him. "Whatsoever doth not
make thee a better Christian," he once said, "is harmful." He
asserted that for him it was really a waste of time to get a degree in medicine, for such a degree would bring no practical
results. The same was true of a degree in civil and canon law.[91]
Yet he was by no means opposed to learning as his writings
plainly show.

Groote loved books. He never had enough of them, and eagerly acquired each new addition to his library. Sometimes five copyists were kept busy writing manuscripts for him. His friends bought books or lent them to him. So much he thought of his library that he arranged for a committee of three men to be in charge of his books after his death. These three are called "guardians of Groote's books" in the documents of that time. Groote not only read books whenever he had a chance, he simply devoured them, says one of his biographers. There were times when he would wonder whether it really was right for him to love those books so passionately, but when he reproached himself for this "thirst of his after mere book-learning," he very soon would dismiss his misgivings.

He devoted himself to encourage learning in school boys, often inviting them to his house, where he had them copy books for him and talked with them about their work at school, their aims and ideals. As they opened their hearts to him, he formed plans to help the boys who had no home and practically no friends at Deventer. If they needed good food and clothing he provided it, and he arranged for them to lodge with kind matrons who treated them as their own children. Furthermore, he reasoned that the boys needed capable teachers, men of sound learning, and of character, men who would try to win their love, and refrain from any kind of punishment until their friendly admonition had failed utterly.[92] They should be university men, if possible. Hence we find Groote busy at work in the Yssel valley, trying to secure comfortable quarters for the homeless, and capable teachers for all. At Deventer, Zwolle, and Kampen he cultivated the friendship of both teachers and their employers.[93] The most intimate friend he seems ever to have had was John Cele, the teacher at Zwolle from 1374 or 1375 to 1417. "These two men were one heart and one soul," says Thomas à Kempis.[94] Partly through Groote's influence Cele obtained his position as rector of the city school at Zwolle. At first he had not been inclined to teach, but Groote showed him the crying need of education for all classes of men and women, particularly for the clergy. "How are these men to instruct the masses," he would often remark, "if they have no knowledge to give, their brains being empty and void of all sound learning"? Cele's business was to teach. When after some time he decided to enter a monastery, where life would be much easier for him, Groote did not rest till he had persuaded him to continue teaching. He urged him to go to Prague, to study at the university, while at the same time he found a substitute for him at Zwolle. The reforms introduced into the schools of Zwolle and Deventer were therefore the direct outcome of Groote's educational activities. Their history will be treated further in the following chapter.

We have followed Groote's activities as student, scholar, reformer, and educator. His career as the accomplished son of a wealthy magistrate, his experiences as a holder of two prebends, the conversion which came to him in 1374, these and other factors we have endeavored to place in their proper light. He made a great impression on the men and women of his time, as the following eulogies show.

William de Sarvarvilla, cantor of the University of Paris, wrote in a letter addressed to Pope Urban VI, which induced the latter to grant Groote a license to preach, shortly before he died: "Truly he was 'The Great,' for in his knowledge of all the liberal sciences, both natural and moral, of civil law, canon law, and of theology, he was second to no one in the world, and all these branches of learning were united in him. He was a man of such saintliness and gave so good an example of the mortification of the flesh, his contempt for the world, his brotherly love for all, his zeal for the salvation of souls, his effectual preaching, his reprobation and hatred of wickedness, his withstanding of heretics, his enforcement of the canon law against those that broke the vow of chastity, his conversion to the spiritual life of divers men and women who had formerly lived according to the world, and his loyalty to our Lord Urban VI — in all those things I say he gave so good an example, that many thousands of men testify to the belief that is in them that he was not less great in these virtues than he was in the aforesaid sciences."[95] William Vornken, prior of Windesheim, calls Groote the "Fountain of the Devotio Moderna," and adds: "The fathers of the former congregation say, Through what act of grace or miracle came it to pass that as master Gerard Groote was preaching and sowing the seed everywhere, there were added to him so suddenly and unexepectedly men of such kind and so great, for these were of one mind with him, and every one of them in each city and place burned with the zeal with which he also burned to exhort and convert a people that was stiff-necked. O happy day on which that great Gerard was born amongst us, for he was the fount and source whence flowed the waters of salvation to our land, so that what before his time had been parched became a pool, and the thirsty land, springs of water."[96] Thomas à Kempis claims that Groote "illuminated the whole country with his life, words, ways, and doctrine."[97]

In 1424 John Vos of Heudsen, prior of Windesheim, and leader of the Devotio Moderna, said on his death-bed to the monks of his monastery and the Brethren of the Common Life from Deventer, Zwolle, and Hulsbergen (near Hattem, also in the Yssel country): "Groote was the first father of this our reformation, the source and origin of the Devotio Moderna; he was an apostle in this country who kindled fires of religious fervor in the cold hearts of men, and drew them to God."[98] John Busch, who had been sent from the Yssel valley to Erfurt, Magdeburg, Hildesheim, and other cities of central Germany, where he helped to reform many a monastery, also called Groote "the fountain-head of the Devotio Moderna."[99] This same opinion was expressed by Ruysbroeck's biographer at Groenendaal.[100] Then we have the series of biographies written in Dutch, which describe the lives of Groote and his followers at Deventer. In the chapter devoted to Groote it is set down: "All religious fervor in this country for one hundred miles around was caused by master Gerard."[101] And when the news of Groote's death reached the convent of Weesp near Amsterdam, a devout sister wrote the following notice in her manuscript: "Gerard Groote, with his holy life and example, has enlightened the whole bishopric of Utrecht."[102]

It is obvious that the men and women of the late fourteenth and early fifteenth centuries who were of the Devotio Moderna considered Gerard Groote their spiritual father. He was in fact the founder of the Brotherhood of the Common Life and the Windesheim Congregation, which instituted the only lasting reforms of the whole fifteenth century, corrected the Vulgate, translated parts of the Bible, sent thousands upon thousands of religious books throughout Western Europe, reformed schools and textbooks, comforted the sick, consoled the afflicted, fed the poor, lodged the homeless, and composed that well-nigh perfect fruit of Christian mysticism: *De Imitatione Christi*, or *Imitation of Christ*.

To conclude, Gerard Groote, as founder of the **Devotio Moderna**, became to some extent the spiritual father of all the men educated by the Brethren of the Common Life and by their pupils, such as Thomas à Kempis, Gansfort, Erasmus, Dringenberg, Hegius, Murmellius, Agricola, Beatus Rhenanus, Wimpheling, Luther, Zwingli, Bucer, Calvin, and Loyola, as we shall see in the following chapters.

CHAPTER II

The Rise of the Devotio Moderna

AMONG Groote's followers at Deventer and elsewhere three groups or classes may be distinguished. They all had decided to change their lives, but many among them preferred to remain at home, where they could live just as religious a life, they said, as in a monastery or as members of a definitely organized society or brotherhood. To this class belonged the pious women who lodged so many poor school boys at Deventer, Zwolle, and several other places. But soon we lose sight of these unorganized little bands. Many of them became affiliated later with the Brethren and Sisters of the Common Life, who constituted the second class of Groote's disciples; or they joined the third class, namely the Augustinian Canons and Canonesses Regular of the Windesheim Congregation. It is to the last two groups, accordingly, that the following pages are devoted.

1. Groote is the Founder of the Brotherhood of the Common Life

On the 21st of September, 1374, Groote ceded the use of his house to some poor women. Five years later he drew up a constitution for the little society,[1] in which he clearly set forth the reason why he had asked these women to live in his house. Not to found a new monastic order, he wrote, had they come to live here, or a beguinage, but simply to find a place where they might worship God in peace. Only those could secure admittance who were not bound by monastic vows; nor were they expected to take such vows on entering the house. They should all be free to leave if they chose, though they could not re-enter, after once having taken their departure. All the inmates of the house would remain members of the local parish church, just as

49

all other laymen. Their clothes should in no respect be different from those of the other women in the city, for they were neither nuns nor beguines. One might even be a member of the society without living in the *"Meester-Geertshuis,"* or Master Gerard's house, at all. At first they had one matron, later two. The matrons were to act as treasurers of the house, and would have authority to make all the members perform manual labor. Their orders were expected to be promptly obeyed. In case of ill-behavior the matrons would consult with two other sisters as to the form of punishment for breach of discipline. The offender would in most cases lose her share in the common savings. But if more serious offences were committed, such as theft, stubbornness, or too great a familiarity with men, the guilty person would have to be expelled. After Groote's death the city council of Deventer would be asked to deal with such cases.[2] During the first few years, when the new society counted but a limited number of members, the two matrons took care of all the business transactions, such as buying supplies, matters of discipline, and supervision of the sisters' daily tasks. Later a division of labor was created. A provisor was chosen, and in 1383 Groote appointed John van den Gronde as the first rector. A procurator was appointed in 1435 and the various tasks of the sisters were also supervised after Groote's death by members specifically directed by the superiors.

The constitution of the "House of Master Gerard" further stated that the members were to live soberly, wear simple clothes, avoid familiar intercourse with men, and restrict their visits to a limit of eight days and a distance of not more than ten miles. No one would be expected to cede her property, on entering the house; the sisters would all work in common and share the expenses together, while the income would be equally divided. Every member of the house who was able to work would be expected to contribute her share of manual labor, for Groote did not want the sisters to beg under any circumstances. Each member, however, was to perform those tasks for which she was specially fitted by nature. Soon the sisters became great adepts in agricultural pursuits; they had a flourishing dairy business, and many of them earned neat little sums through their skill in sewing, knitting, weaving, spinning, and similar purely feminine employments.

In composing this constitution for the Sisters of the Common Life, Groote prepared the way for a mightier organization, known later as the Brethren of the Common Life. Shortly after he left the Carthusian monastery of Monnikhuizen near Arnhem, he had succeeded in recruiting a number of devout followers. In 1380 a man joined them who was destined to become the leader of the Devotio Moderna. This man was called Florentius Radewijns. Born at Leerdam in the year 1350, he had gone to Prague in 1374, and received a master's degree in 1378.[4] Thereupon he had gone home to Gorinchem,[5] where he lived with his parents till the news of Groote's fame as preacher reached him[6]. This must have happened in the year 1380, for Groote had not yet left the Yssel valley. So much impressed was he by Groote's imposing personality that he decided to imitate him in all things. One of the first things he did was to give up his prebend at Utrecht, in order to be nearer to Groote. At Deventer he became vicar of the altar of St. Paul in St. Lebwin's Church.[7]

It was in Radewijns' vicarage that Groote's twelve disciples used to meet, though not all of them actually lived in this house. When did these disciples begin to live the common life? One writer thinks in 1372; that is, two years before Groote's conversion. Another one sets down a later date: 1381 or 1382. Still another one places the date several years after Groote's death; while another authority on the Brethren of the Common Life claims that the brothers did not even have a rector until thirty or forty years after the organization was firmly established.[8]

The sources, however, show plainly that Groote, shortly after his return from the monastery of Monnikhuizen near Arnhem, began to preach in the cities along the Yssel. Among his numerous followers there were twelve who clung quite faithfully to the master, except one of them, called a backslider, and traitor.[9] Groote advised some of them to live together in one house, where they could exhort each other, work and pray together — in short,

serve God with greater chance of success.[10]   We also read that
Groote had several boys and young men copy books for him.
The boys were often invited to his house.   He purposely paid
them a little each time so that they would have to come quite
often and have a talk with him.   It was not these boys whom
Groote urged to live together in one house.   And not only
Groote invited school boys to his house, but also some of his
followers at Zwolle and Deventer, most of whom were soon to
become known as Brethren of the Common Life.   Hence the
founders of the new organization were not those school boys
who were asked to Groote's house from time to time.   The fact
is, there were also girls among the young people entertained by
Groote's friends.   Moreover, the sources do not at all tell us that
these boys and girls who were given financial or other assistance
by Groote and his followers founded the congregation or brotherhood, called Brethren of the Common Life.[11]   It is only some
modern critics who make that assertion, and wrongly so.

Among the twelve disciples at Deventer there were several
copyists, who made their living by copying books, and some of
them, we saw, were living in Radewijns' vicarage.   Now these
copyists wanted to join their funds.   Accordingly, Radewijns
came to Groote one day and said to him: "Master, what harm
should there be in our uniting our weekly earnings, and living
the common life"?   "Unite your funds"?   Groote exclaimed in
surprise.   "Impossible, for the mendicant monks would surely
attack us for trying to found a new monastic order".[12]   But as
Radewijns would not give up his plan so readily, Groote finally
answered that in case they would in the near future lead the
common life, he would gladly be their leader and instructor.[13]

Should one call Florentius Radewijns then the founder of
the Brethren of the Common Life?   For did not he suggest to
Groote the idea of uniting the funds?   It should be remembered,
however, that Groote had composed the constitution for the
Sisters of the Common Life before Radewijns had ever heard of
him.   And it was Groote himself who had stipulated that the
sisters should combine their wages and share the common ex-

penses. For this reason the mendicants had already attacked him.

He had even found it necessary to defend them in a sermon at Deventer, together with the beguines, who also united their earnings.[14] When the men in Radewijns' house wanted to lead a life similar to that of the Sisters of the Common Life, he naturally hesitated, and pointed out to them the great danger of attack from his enemies, the mendicant monks, who were living a life of indolence and hated Groote for his love of poverty and manual labor. But his hesitation did not last long, for he knew well that the Canon Law would protect them. He mapped out their future mode of life, drew up a schedule for their daily tasks and their religious exercises, and would undoubtedly have made further arrangements, if the hand of death had not suddenly intervened, as it did on the twentieth of August, 1384. Groote was indeed the founder of the new brotherhood, though his plans were only materialized after his death.[15]

2. Groote is the Founder of Windesheim

On the afternoon of the twentieth of August, 1384, a pathetic scene was enacted at Deventer. In one of the houses on the Bagynestraat a group of men were standing around Groote's bed. Their beloved master was dying. They saw his life ebbing fast and trembled. And he himself was conscious of their dismay. There was a long silence. But at last he opened his eyes and spoke: "My friends," he said, "do not fear, and let not your hearts be troubled. You will not have to give up your present mode of life. In order that you may protect your temporal possessions I advise you to build a monastery, where those among you best fit for the monastic life may find shelter and perform their work in peace, while at the same time it will protect the others who prefer to remain in the world." "But which order shall we join"? they asked. "The Augustinian," he answered, "for their rules are not so harsh as those of the Carthusians and Cistercians."[16]

Groote also gave a last message to the Sisters of the Common Life. He had regretted the fact that only middle-aged women were willing to join the little society. But better times would come, he thought. "When I shall have departed hence," was his final remark, "I shall send some little flowers from above, benignant spirits, which will swell your numbers."[17]

Thus we are told by John Busch and Thomas à Kempis, the two most reliable historians of the Windesheim circle. Their narratives do in no respect contradict each other, as some writers have thought, who failed to read Thomas à Kempis carefully.[18] On the contrary, they are supported by other trustworthy sources. It was not John Busch, for seven years the pupil and assistant of John Cele at Zwolle, who indulged in flights of the imagination, but those modern scholars who insist on overthrowing the best sources we have. Groote, it appears, had openly attacked Bartholomew of Dordrecht, a mendicant monk, and the clergy at Utrecht besides. They were furious. Moreover, Groote, as founder of the Sisters of the Common Life, had instituted a semi-monastic organization which was looked upon by mendicant monks as a hostile rival of their order. He was also translating parts of the Bible into the vernacular, preached against indolence, abhorred all forms of begging, and bitterly denounced those monks and priests who failed to perform their duty. Last but not least, he had a group of disciples who were holding regular meetings in the vicarage of Radewijns. One half of these disciples were actually living with the vicar. They copied books for Groote and for others, and were surely going to live the common life. Perhaps they had already given up their private property. At any rate, they were founding a monastic order, it seemed, without taking the customary vows, or asking the pope for his sanction.

Whenever these copyists were seen on the streets, they were addressed as Beghards and Lollards, hooted at, and commended to burn in hell, or some other suitable place of torture. The common people, and those among the lower classes who frequented inns or lounged about the streets all day, were instigated by some monks to slander Groote's disciples. These monks composed songs in which Groote was mocked and ridiculed.[19]

Then there were many laymen as well as clergymen who had attended Groote's sermons, and had felt some compunction about their evil ways, but finally had decided to ignore Groote's appeals. They gradually moved away farther and farther from the path so persistently pointed out to them by Groote. Finally the clergy resented his attacks. For it seemed to some as if he had singled them out for reproval. Groote had advised them to give a large share of their possessions to the poor, to visit the sick and afflicted, to take care of the homeless, and to shun all forms of indolence, intemperance, and immorality. The man was insane, they said to each other. And look at those copyists: always writing books on religion, and never ready to visit us in the tavern and the dance-hall. Do you think we would lead such miserable lives as those wretched copyists are doing? Thus they argued, glad to find support among other members of the clergy, both secular and regular.

Groote was aware of these things. He had already told Radewijns to act with caution. As the people grew bolder each day, and the mendicants increased their attacks, the situation began to look serious. The brethren, not being protected by monastic vows, were uneasy and held daily consultations in Radewijns' vicarage. Finally they came to the conclusion that a monastery should be built where a part of them could live and by their example lead and protect the others. They were to join the Augustinian Canons Regular.[20]

But Groote's end was near, as we have seen. Though he must be considered the founder both of the Brethren of the Common Life and the Windesheim Congregation, he left his work unfinished. Would he also leave his disciples without a leader? Great was their affliction in having to lose so kind and so learned a master. But as he looked up for the last time at his faithful followers, now only eleven in number, his eyes rested upon the one he loved best. "I will not leave you defenseless," he said, "I appoint Florentius as your new leader. He will instruct you, and help you, as I have tried to do." And then he departed.

3. Florentius Radewijns

So highly in fact did Groote respect his faithful friend that he had urged him to become a priest. As for himself, we know, he thought he was too great a sinner to join the ranks of the priesthood. But Radewijns was endowed with special gifts of devotion. No one was kinder than he to the poor, the sick, and the afflicted. He often went to visit the suffering. Many a meal he was wont to send to certain famishing families in the slums of Deventer. A list was kept by him of all the poor people in the city. The feeble-bodied and all others who through no fault of their own were in need of material assistance, he supplied with food and clothing, and the poorer class of school boys with pens, ink, and paper. One lenten season there was great scarcity of food and of work, so that an unusually large number of poor people came to Radewijns for help; whereupon he, finding himself unable to give assistance to so many at once, persuaded his friends and followers to add one hour a day to their work for the period of one week. The extra money thus saved he handed over to the "Overseer of the Poor" at Deventer. During the month of May he was accustomed to gather herbs for the sick. He would invite all those people to his house who were afflicted with ulcers, sores, and other skin diseases. They were then given a bath in warm water, perfumed with aromatic herbs. A clean bed was also prepared for each patient, where they were told to rest themselves, after first having received a cup of wine.[21]

Radewijns did not even shrink from lepers, and to the maimed and deformed he was particularly kind. "I once knew a leper," says Thomas à Kempis, "who used to abide outside the walls of the city. Florentius would often sit beside him and talk to him." "I have seen," he continues, "one blind of an eye, and one lame of one foot, who were both converted by him." At times he was consulted by so many people that he had no time even to go to church.[22] And who was there who could comfort the people as did Radewijns? Involuntarily their hearts were filled with new hope and happiness at one touch of his hand, or a single glance from those starry eyes which bespoke tender sympathy. The moment one approached him, one's troubles and anxieties would suddenly subside. What was there in this singularly attractive person to shed about him as it were a halo of almost celestial felicity? Was he so great an orator? Did he perhaps cast the hypnotic spell of fiery eloquence upon the fascinated crowds?

Among all the men Thomas à Kempis had met before he wrote the *Imitation,* Radewijns, he thought, was the one who had taught him most about the Cross of Christ. We should learn of him, Christ had said, by imitating him.[23] And how could we imitate him best? By taking his yoke upon us, the yoke of humility, and charity. One should try to sympathize with the poor and afflicted, visit the sick, comfort orphans and widows, and be ready to perform the most humble tasks at home. We should never seek our own good, Radewijns used to say, but rather consider only our neighbor's welfare. Thus one might become a Christian, in his opinion. And Radewijns was wont to practise what he preached. He was always ready to take an active share in his neighbor's sorrows. Naturally, his feeling of pity was instinctively felt by all who came near him. Thomas à Kempis himself had often experienced a thrill of rapture simply in being near his teacher and master. A few words from Radewijns' lips would comfort all. "This," says Thomas à Kempis, "I have often tried and experienced myself."[24] Is it any wonder that Thomas à Kempis, who had spent several years in Radewijns' presence, often used to look upon his stay at Deventer with a feeling of reverence and intense gratitude? Florentius Radewijns was a man who lived the ideals of the *Imitation of Christ.* Whether he formulated those ideals we shall consider later.

But Radewijns was also a famous preacher. From far and near the people used to come to his house, where he or one of his followers addressed them in their own language.[25] These sermons were held in the open air, and particularly on holidays the crowds that assembled in the garden of the vicarage were quite large. Gradually it became a custom among the people to write down parts of Radewijns' discourses, for they were so easy to understand and so practical. He spoke to them in their own dialect, unadorned with pompous foreign quotations. Had not Christ done the same in his day? Had he preached in a foreign language? Why should Radewijns then employ Latin or fine speeches in reminding the people of Christ's message to his followers? Plain speech, simple words he used. And these were kept alive in the shops, the mills, and the farm-houses.

Though fully aware of his duties as a member of society, Radewijns loved the contemplative life. "I often used to look at him in the choir," says Thomas à Kempis, "and whenever I saw him, I was careful not to chatter, so impressed I was by his great religious fervor. When he was walking on the street, he seldom would notice the greetings of his friends, being engrossed in meditation. Scarcely five or six words would he speak at our supper-table. But when he was alone, then his mind became illuminated with so pure a light of divine radiance that whether he was reading the Old Testament or the New Testament, always some mystic interpretation of every passage came to him."[26]

As a faithful follower of Christ, Radewijns loved the simple life, wearing plain garments even after he had been ordained priest, avoiding dainty food, and reading only such books as might aid him in improving his character. His followers he exhorted to do the same. Novices and other inexperienced people should avoid the study of subtle questions, he used to say. But in one respect he failed to grasp the true meaning of Christ's teachings. "He did not consider with due care the weakness of his body," Thomas à Kempis wisely remarks. As a result of his excessive fasting, he ruined his digestive organs, losing all taste for different foods, mistaking wine for oil or beer. Often his friend Everard Eza of Almelo, one of Gerard Groote's most influential disciples, would warn him of his folly, and cure him for the time being.[27] Fortunately Everard induced him to take more rest and to work more often in the open air. He had to admit, however, that if it had not been for Radewijns' prayers and the grace of God, he must have died long before his time.

In spite of his weak body Radewijns had an imposing personality. His presence in the choir was sufficient to banish all jesting. Thomas à Kempis himself did not stir when he was near. Says Thomas: "Even though he were not looking at me, yet I did not dare to talk in the choir, so I feared and respected his presence. Once he came up to me, to sing with me out of my book. I stood as if rooted to the ground and did not dare to move."[28] There were people who fearlessly insulted Groote's disciples after his death, but not those living in Radewijns' house; and although a few condemned the habits of Brethren of the Common Life at Deventer, they nevertheless all agreed in praising Radewijns.

His knowledge of human nature was remarkable. Each one of his followers he treated in such manner as to stimulate his heart and mind. When reproach was needed he would freely employ it, but if one could be won through gentleness, praise, or jest, he was glad to employ those means also. He was not weak in his kindness, or proud in his coolness. Great talents he had none, nor was there any particular virtue or vice observable in his character. The man's whole personality had undergone a harmonious development. Thoughtful and prudent, painstaking, calm, persevering, free from violent passions, and devoid of special talents, he was always composed, a perfect master of his lower self, harsh to his own nature, but filled with love and sympathy for his neighbor. Such was the man appointed by Groote as the leader of the Devotio Moderna, according to his biographers.

The works he wrote himself enable us to give a few more particulars. Radewijns was neither a scholar nor a great author in our sense of the word. Many paragraphs in his writings appear to have been copied from the Fathers and the works of medieval mystics. One of his writings, called *Omnes inquit artes*, is merely a collection of excerpts; and the only real composition from his hand, known as the *Tractatulus de Spiritualibus Exercitiis*, or *Treatise on Spiritual Exercises*, contains many a sentence copied verbally from Bonaventura, Cassianus, and other writers. But they do show us what sort of a thinker Radewijns was; they reflect his theological and philosophical views.

Kingdom of God
purity of heart

Our aim and final destination, Radewijns writes, is the kingdom of God. The road which leads to that goal is purity of
heart. All our labors, our watching, fasting, meditation, prayer,
and reading of the Scriptures are only means employed by us to
eradicate vice, ere we ascend toward the plane of perfect love.
And as we advance on our road we shall be able to resuscitate
the slumbering memories of the spirit — memories of a glorious
past and of a still more glorious future. In keeping steadily
before our eyes the destination at the end of our road, we shall
continue to exercise our spiritual nature, lest our first ardor
should cool. These spiritual exercises will finally enable our
weary souls to enter the harbors of rest and peace, after a long
voyage across the seas of time. We, as pilgrims, wandering aim-
lessly in the desert of time, should seek the joys of heaven upon
earth, which can be done most effectively by checking the desires
of our mortal bodies, for the way of the spirit is life, and the
way of the flesh is death.[29]

As the pilgrim advances upon the highway of this mortal life,
faint memories come to him of a lost heritage. Sometimes, when
he pauses in his way to look about him, he catches feeble
glimpses of his happy past before the fall of man. At such moments it is the voice of the spirit which urges him to turn his
steps homeward once more, by purifying his heart from the stains
made by sin. For the purer his heart, the clearer his memory
will become; he will then regain that marvelous secret of immortal life: love. The two chief ends of all religious or spiritual
exercises, therefore, are the purging of our heart from sin, and
the cultivation of love.[30] Perfect love is never acquired by any
one, except he first has cleansed his heart from vice and supplanted evil by virtue. Consequently the more successful we
are in purging our hearts, the greater our love will become. Our
final aim, therefore, is love; everything else is but a means to
reach that end. Through the Fall our mind or reason has become
blind to the truth, our will perverted, our memories unstable.
Man is a depraved being, but through Christ's sacrifice he is
not hopelessly lost, nay he may gain a better fate than those
spirits which are not allowed to enter mortal bodies.[31] But he

must act, although his soul has already been saved through faith. For Christ's sacrifice, implemented by our personal faith, does not purify our heart nor reform our mind.

All virtue, says Radewijns, is contained in love. He compares man with a musical instrument; man in his present state is out of tune with the Infinite. When one is converted, one's improper and imperfect affections or emotions are changed into pure love; one will then love God for God's own sake. All our reading, meditations, and prayers should be concentrated chiefy upon the abolition of sin, thus making room for love. Love, we must remember, is worth more than the negative attitude of fighting vice; it is the end, the crown of human existence. Nothing but love can lead us to the heavenly country. Love for God in the first place, then love for our neighbor. We must strive to promote mutual friendships, practise modesty, suppress hatred, jealousy, and spite, and be careful in admonishing others. Obedience is the greatest virtue: it perfects our humility. It is in fact very sinful to seek one's own welfare rather than that of one's neighbor.

Radewijns urges his readers to exercise themselves in the acquisition of brotherly love, to read the Bible, to pray often, to confess their sins, to perform their daily tasks with alacrity, and to cultivate a healthful discipline of mind and morals. Manual labor should be performed by all, but not all forms of manual labor were fitted in his opinion to favor the practise of spiritual exercises; those which resembled the spiritual exercises in kind were preferable, such as copying religious writings. No one should study to acquire knowledge for its own sake, for there is no true learning except that which teaches us to acquire love through the conquest of evil.[33] The whole Bible was written for one end only; if one succeeds, and remains steadfast, one will not need to read the Bible any longer.[34] There surely can be no use in studying difficult passages in the Bible, according to Radewijns. He thought no human brain could grasp the meaning of those passages, unless one were aided by the Spirit.

Somewhere within our inner selves a mysterious force resides, called conscience. It should be our daily care to stimulate this force into action. Usually it suffers from neglect, grows feebler and feebler till its voice is but faintly distinguished. Know thyself, Socrates had said, and Radewijns repeated this message. Examine your inner nature, he wrote, and arouse your conscience from its long slumber. Pray, watch, and work, lest the force of habit overwhelm you. One should meditate frequently on the ultimate approach of death, the sufferings of Christ, and the final judgment. He also gives directions for fighting various vices, which he copied largely from the works of Cassianus and David of Augsburg.[35] We should also seek the blessings of solitude and silence, for when human voices are absent, God will come to talk with us. Especially should we seek a few moments of this conversation with God shortly before retiring at night.

Virtue, says Radewijns, can only be acquired through grace. We of our own selves can never overcome evil, so low have we fallen. Even our good works are not wholly good, but mixed with imperfections of various kinds. If we humiliate ourselves, however, as Christ once did, this grace will come to us in abundant measure. And how can we best cultivate this virtue of humility? By frankly admitting how depraved we have become since the fall of man, how prone to evil, how powerless in fighting vice; by patiently bearing with accusations, insults, and calumnies heaped upon us by slanderous tongues, and by giving all the credit to God, if perchance we should succeed in overcoming vice. Thus we shall find love, the greatest of all blessings. Love will bring peace, and much inward joy, though not unalloyed with grief about our continued shortcomings. When once this love has come to us, we shall seek to draw more souls to Christ, which we can do most successfully on holy days, when people have more leisure and are in a better position to listen to our appeals.[36]

After the purgative way comes the illuminative way. Man will then begin to understand God's tenderness to him, and will fathom the mystery of the fall of man and of his redemption through Christ. Christ's sacrifice on the cross is in fact the greatest event in the history of the human race.[37] No one can realize this more perfectly than he who has felt the load of sin gradually being lifted from his weary back and shoulders. With tears of joy he will look upon that central cross at Golgotha, where all at once the whole guilt of humanity was paid for, where the redemption of all souls was bought at a terrific price. Christ our savior and example, the chief factor in every man's life, should therefore have the chief and best place in every man's life.[38] Thus wrote he who for sixteen years was the leader of the Devotio Moderna.

4. The Brethren of the Common Life at Deventer

In the year of Groote's death the religious revival inaugurated by him gained a foothold in those places where he himself had preached, or where his followers had begun to continue his work, namely at Deventer, Zwolle, Doesburg, Zutphen, Kampen, Almelo, Utrecht, Amsterdam, Haarlem, Leiden, etc. But among all these cities and villages only those situated nearest to the Yssel valley succeeded in retaining the master's best thoughts. Naturally there were Deventer and Zwolle which at once assumed a leading position in the history of the Devotio Moderna, and kept the fires of religious zeal burning, when all the others gradually lost their first ardor.

During Groote's lifetime the question of the common life had been brought up for discussion. Groote had assured his followers that he would gladly become their leader and protector, in case they should decide to follow the mode of life practised by the women in his own house at Deventer. Some of them were to build a monastery, he had said, while the others would remain at Deventer. The monastery was not built at once, however. Two years elapsed before the brethren felt the need of seeking protection there. For they had not yet begun to lead the common life, wherefore the mendicant monks left them comparatively at ease, seeing that their society did not resemble a monastic organization. The brethren used to meet in a very informal way. Some of them were living with Radewijns in the vicarage, but not a few merely came to visit at stated times. Not long after Groote's death an important event took place. Radewijns had been accustomed to keep charge of the money earned by the men living in his house. When he noticed their indifference to merely temporal advantages, such as wealth, fame, and honor, he decided to unite their wages, and make of them one common fund. From that day they were Brethren of the Common Life. The exact date of this is not clear; it naturally must have happened between Groote's death and the foundation of the new monastery. For they built that monastery because they had offended their rivals, the mendicant monks, by founding a semi-monastic oranization, having united their funds and shared their expenses in common. It had now become a vital necessity for them to build the monastery, where some could live and all would find protection.[39]   Since Groote died on August 20, 1384, and the monastery was founded in 1386, we may assume that the common life was begun before 1387, and probably during the fall of 1384 or the year 1385, inasmuch as Groote had drawn up definite rules in August or July, 1384.

There were at this time ten men living in the vicarage with Radewijns at Deventer.[40]   An important character was John of Huxaria or Höxter. The brethren were so impressed by this man's religious fervor that for a time they were uncertain whether they should elect him as their rector or Radewijns, the acknowledged leader of the Devotio Moderna; finally they chose Radewijns.[41]   According to the obituary of the Brethren of the Common Life at Deventer,[42] John of Höxter died on the 7th of January, 1387. Consequently the brethren must have chosen their choice before this date.

The next event of importance took place in the year 1391, when the "House of Florentius" was founded, the first real house of the Brethren of the Common Life, and named after the first rector, Florentius Radewijns. Till 1391 the brethren had been living in the vicarage with Radewijns. As their number increased from year to year, they finally decided to move to more comfortable quarters. There was a devout lady, called Zwedera of Runen, the wife of a nobleman, who had heard of their plight.

She offered them a house and lot, situated in the Pontsteeg, in exchange for two small buildings in the Enghe Straat. This house in the Pontsteeg was torn down and replaced by a fine new building, the "House of Florentius." Most of the brethren now moved from the vicarage to the "House of Florentius," taking their books and furniture with them.[43]

Still another house was founded during the life of Radewijns: the "*Nova Domus,*" "*Domus Pauperum,*" or the new house for poor clerks. It was built in 1398, and intended for the poorer class of pupils attending the school.[44] For the Brethren of the Common Life faithfully continued Groote's policy in helping poor boys and girls to get an education. Radewijns and his followers often invited them to their house, providing them with material and spiritual sustenance. "Behold," Radewijns wrote in 1398, "we take these youths into our house, inexperienced as they are, changeable, having as yet no definite aims or exerting much will power, but they are tractable and pliable. Oh what would happen, if one, or two, or three of us would persuade these boys to work, and teach them discipline, and humility"? Many devout burghers at Deventer would take an interest in the younger boys, due to Radewijns' influence. One Lambert van Galen always had eight of them in his house, and a certain Bye van Dunen also took care of eight boys. These boys were all consigned to the people by the brethren in the "House of Florentius." For only after 1400 did the Brethren of the Common Life take in boys who had not yet finished their work at the cathedral school.[46]

Upon the whole we may say that the brethren during the rectorate of Florentius Radewijns conscientiously tried to imitate the lives of Apostles as set forth in the New Testament. It was the simple life they led, a life of work and devotional exercises. Says Badius Ascensius, the celebrated humanist and printer, who had received his early education from the Brethren of the Common Life at Ghent:

"All were to approach as near as possible the life of the Apostles and of the primitive church of Christ, so that in the whole congregation there should be one heart, and that no one should consider or call anything his own. No one should seek outside the house the cure of souls, ecclesiastical benefices, or worldly occupations for the sake of gain; but clerics who should be found worthy would be promoted to cures that were not too lucrative. All should dwell together in chastity and poverty, and should be clad in that manner of dress which Gerard Groote had approved. No one should beg from door to door; and in order that they might not be driven to this by want, all should avoid idleness, and according to their abilities should transcribe books, or instruct children. They were to take care that they themselves and all whom they should teach, should venerate and worship God with the deepest piety. They should love their neighbor with due charity, and should assist the poor with alms, according to their means. All should observe brotherly love. To their superior or spiritual Father in all lawful and just concerns they should yield unquestioning obedience, considering that their highest merit consisted in charity and submission. All earnings accruing from their labor in common or in private they should, according to the apostolic rule, lay at the feet of the Superior, and if perchance they left the Brotherhood, they should carry nothing with them."[47]

When Thomas à Kempis lived in the house of Radewijns (1398-1399) there were about twenty inmates, three of whom were laymen.[48] And in a document of the year 1396 we read that there should be at least four priests and eight clerics, that is, twelve members belonging to the clergy; the number of laymen was not specified.[49] Gradually their number increased for their fame soon spread even into distant countries. Many priests, says one biographer attracted by the rumor of Radewijns' virtues and those of his followers, came to Deventer and submitted themselves to Radewijns' rule, laying open to him their hearts. Particularly from Westphalia they came in great numbers. It was not long before the mendicant monks and their friends heard of the growing repute of the Brethren of the Common Life. Groote's fear had not been ill-founded. In spite of the new monastery they had built, the men at Deventer who now remained behind, were not sufficiently protected, having taken no monastic vows. One of their friends and protectors, named John ter Poorten, a prominent member of the city council, was publicly attacked as "Pope of the Lollards."[50]

Not satisfied with instigating the people and inventing sundry unofficial attacks, the Dominicans began to look for other ways of harming the brethren. They carefully studied the Canon Law and its commentaries, thereby hoping to prove that the Brethren of the Common Life had no right of existence. To live the common life without taking monastic vows was a crime, they said. No one had a right to found a new religious order without the pope's consent. And here were those upstarts at Deventer who had never asked for the pope's consent. They had a rector whom they had decided to obey, yet they took no vows of obedience. They earned their daily bread with their own hands, had definite rules and regulations, read sacred writings in the vernacular, and even held addresses to the people in their own language. All this they did without waiting for any one's permission. Surely, so strange and newfangled an institution was an offense to the Church!

The attacks grew fiercer, as time went on, for the jealousy of the mendicant and other monks increased in correspondence with the rising power of the new brotherhood. The Augustinian Canons Regular of Windesheim heard of these attacks. In 1395 they drew up a document in which they defended their friends at Deventer. The Brethren of the Common Life were virtuous men, they wrote. They taught no heresy of any kind, represented no secret societies or lodges, did not preach outside of the churches, had assumed no rules, no new monastic garments, had taken no new vows, and their whole mode of life had been approved by Gregory XI.[51]

This document was not sufficient, however, to stop the enemy's assaults. What was worse, in 1398 another enemy appeared in the form of a terrible pestilence. William of Vianen first caught the disease. Ten brothers were infected and died. They were nursed by John Ketel, their pious cook, but he also passed away in 1398. Then the remaining brethren, led by Radewijns, decided to leave the city and go to Amersfoort across the Veluwe, leaving a few members behind to take care of their property at Deventer. At Amersfoort the brethren continued their work with new energy. They had taken several school boys with them, for whom they found suitable quarters among Groote's disciples at Amersfoort, where the first brethren-house west of the Yssel had been founded in 1395. Here the men from Deventer copied books, and preached to the people in the vernacular, especially on holidays, "instructing them by example and doctrine." But it was not a happy time for them. They were now staying far away from the home they had built with their own hands and means. The attacks of their enemies continued, and the pestilence was sweeping one after another to the grave in Deventer. True, they were living with friends who were hospitable and kind, but still these friends were comparative strangers to them.

A spirit of sadness pervades the letters written by the fugitives at Amersfoort to the men at Deventer. "Let us go and die with them," says Gerard Zerbolt of Zutphen, one of the brethren who had gone to Amersfoort, "or else let them come and die with us, though we are able to die here and you to live there. What will life be worth to me, after they have passed away?" And when they were told that one of their beloved friends at home had followed the others to the grave in their absence, they were almost overwhelmed with grief. Their next three letters also breathe anguish. The brethren appeared to have lost all interest in life, so down-cast they were. But in their last letter the dawn of a new hope breaks. They are expecting to return to Deventer soon! "Just as the members of one body all suffer together and console each other," they now write, "so do they also exult in each other's good fortune. The expectation of our return home is a great source of joy to us. Florentius is going to Amsterdam soon and when he returns, we hope to go back home to you."

And what of their other enemies, the mendicant monks? Suddenly their attacks were rendered forceless by a scholar, who came to their aid at the right moment. This new defender of the brethren was Gerard Zerbolt of Zutphen, a man of considerable learning and sharp insight into all questions pertaining to law and tradition. A much greater scholar than Radewijns himself, he was more successful in affairs. With a sort of prophetic vision he perceived the dangers encircling the new brotherhood on all sides, when the brothers themselves were scarcely aware of impending trouble. They had written a great deal about the sorrows of separation, but the dangers from without they could not perceive.

The crisis came in 1398. Radewijns had been at Utrecht and at Amsterdam. The brethren at Deventer and Amersfoort were sure of his success in obtaining privileges from Frederick van Blankenheim, Bishop of Utrecht. But Radewijns had to write home from Amersfoort: "The business of the Lord has made no progress; wherever we turn we meet with obstacles." That was all he could say. He now was homesick. He had resolved to leave Amersfoort for Deventer in secret. His first attempt was a failure, but finally he succeeded in fleeing. Strange though it seems, Radewijns, the first rector of the Brethren of the Common Life, forsook his followers in the thick of the fight. He had been unequal to his task. How fortunate therefore that now his work could be continued by his more vigorous disciple. The name of this disciple we seldom read in the documents of that time, and the chronicles devote only a few pages to the story of his life. He loved to sit in his lonely cell, unknown to the world about him. But by uniting the best thoughts of Radewijns with the scholarly labors of Groote, he became the representative of both types of devotion or mysticism: the simple and the worldly-wise, the practical and the theoretical, the active and the passive.

5. Gerard Zerbolt of Zutphen

Gerard Zerbolt was born at Zutphen in the year 1367.[52] After attending school in his native city he went to a university, probably that of Prague, where he studied hard from early dawn till late at night. But he does not seem to have stayed there very long, for in 1384 we find him at Deventer. Radewijns persuaded him to become a member of the brotherhood at Deventer.[53] A born student, he passed nearly all his time in his room at the

"House of Florentius," reading "sacred writings," that is, the Bible, the Fathers, the Canon Law, and similar works.[54]   He used to be so occupied with his work that he would forget the whole world about him, perfectly oblivious to any changes in the weather for example.   Even at the dinner-table he was wont to continue his meditations.   As soon as the meal was over, however, and the Bible was brought forward, he was all attention.[55] This book-worm, the other brothers reasoned, should be appointed librarian of their house.   And Zerbolt, once in possession of Groote's books, together with his learned discourses which might be manipulated as a key to the books themselves, soon became the foremost scholar among the Brethren of the Common Life.   Thomas à Kempis was a member of the house at that time.   Says Thomas: "Many clerics used to come to him for advice, asking him to solve difficult problems for them. Radewijns often called for him when business transactions had to be undertaken for the house, and particularly when questions of law came up for discussion.   Whenever Zerbolt was confronted with problems too difficult for him to solve, he would write them down and keep them in mind till he would meet some learned doctor.   The scholars and great writers praised him highly for his learning."[56]   Thus Zerbolt gradually prepared himself for the struggle in which he was to bear the brunt. The struggle lasted from 1384 to 1419, but it was decided in favor of the brethren, when Zerbolt collected his arguments in their defense — which he used in soliciting the protection of important church officials — and arranged them in the shape of a treatise, called *On the Common Life*.[57]

It was prohibited to found a new monastic order, Zerbolt admitted, but to live in private houses and share one's expenses with others was quite permissible, as it had been customary in the past; it had been recommended by the saints of old, and approved by the pope.   Those chapters in the Canon Law, Zerbolt continued, which were directed against the founders of new monastic orders, were in no way opposed to the common life as such.   What did the words "religious" and "religion" imply, he asked, and who might be said to be founding new monastic orders in contravention of the Canon Law? Surely, the way in which the Brethren of the Common Life conducted themselves was irreproachable. There were six ways of possessing temporal goods, some of which were far from commendable, but to live outside of monasteries and still to have no property of one's own, was highly praiseworthy. In the first place, it would be in complete accordance with Christ's wish as found in the Gospel of St. Matthew ch. XXVIII (ch. XIX, verse 21): "If thou wilt be perfect, go and sell that thou hast." Secondly, man's natural mind or reason impels him to live a simple life, that is, the common life, though man has sinned against his natural mind or reason, wherefore the common life appears more difficult now. Again many saints and doctors recommend the cession of one's private property for the benefit of the whole society or family, such as Egidius, Thomas Aquinas, and Bede. Where love reigns supreme no one will want to have possessions of his own, and friendship is promoted by the common life, as has so well been said by Seneca. Furthermore, in the primitive, the Apostolic Church, all goods had been in common, and was not the early church the best one? We are taught by nature to lead the common life, for man is indeed a social animal, as Aristotle just remarked. Hence the Stoics used to say that man was born to assist other men, which saying is supported by Genesis II. This is what Plato also asserted in the myth of Timaeus. Paul preached the same doctrine in the twelfth chapter of his Epistle to the Romans, and Ambrose in the first book of the *De Officiis*, Ch. CXXVIII, while there are several chapters found in the Canon Law which exhort all clerics to lead the common life. Augustine also recommended the common life on several occasions.

But now it happens, says Zerbolt, that in our day we are told that the common life is only to be lived by monks and that all the references in the "sacred writings" which approve the common life apply solely to the monastic state. For this reason one very rarely meets with men or women living the common life except in monasteries, though it was not that way in the days of the primitive church and long thereafter. For the same reason it may perhaps seem justifiable to all those monks who have lost all traces of religious fervor, and are filled with iniquity, gradually to do away with the common life altogether. Similarly many evangelical precepts are no longer obeyed although they are most beneficial to all those who still follow them.

Here Zerbolt exposes the secret of the great decline in morals among the clergy, secular as well as regular. At first it was customary for all to follow Christ and obey every one of His commandments in so far as humanly possible. As the first ardor cooled, only the spiritual leaders were expected to do what in preceding centuries had been performed by all. And in Zerbolt's time many members of the clergy had relinquished all hopes and desires of becoming imitators of Christ and his apostles. Zerbolt knew quite well where they failed. Even when the most experienced members of his house at Deventer built a monastery which was generally regarded as a model of piety, Zerbolt remained in the "House of Florentius," as Radewijns, his teacher did. One could practise religion just as well in private homes, he thought and for many years it was his highest ambition to prove this to the outside world.

Zerbolt had by no means exhausted his evidence in favor of the Brethren of the Common Life. Augustine advises us, he continued, in cases of doubt to refer to the older laws, writings, or customs of the Church. We should not hesitate to search among the works of the Ancients. What do we find regarding the theory of the common life? Not only was it practised by the apostolic church but even long before the coming of Christ. The common life was begun in Paradise. And if man had not fallen, this mode of living would still be universal among men. After the state of innocence man was placed under the law of nature, or the natural laws. Even in this state the common life was continued among religious men, and it flourished where love and friendship were cultivated. Many philosophers, although they lived without the guidance of the Scriptures, were taught by the "Law of nature" and the "natural light" that the common life would promote friendship and love. Consequently they also lived the common life. Of the Pythagoreans we read that all the disciples of Pythagoras laid all their money in their midst and among them was great friendship. For Pythagoras had taught them to make one out of many. That was true friendship, he said. On the question of the common life the philosophers of old almost completely agreed with the theologians, hence there was no need of giving other quotations from philosophical writings.

Again, the common life flourished under the régime of the Mosaic law, particularly among the wisest and most virtuous men. There were namely three sects among the Jews, the Pharisees, Sadducees, and Essenes, and of these three the Essenes were the noblest, for according to Josephus they lived in many respects the apostolic life and had all goods in common. This mode of life was reinstated therefore by Christ, observed by the Apostles and their disciples, and continued afterwards. But in the state of glory, when God will be all in all, and the joys of us all the joys of each, and the joys of each the joys of all, then this common life is to be perfected and universally applied. For where all things shall be in common, there will be no discord, but perfect love and unity. And the more sincerely we practise this common life and this love for God and our neighbor, the more rapidly we shall approach this state of glory.

In the last part of the third chapter Zerbolt shows that the dwelling together of pious men in private homes does not necessarily institute an officially recognized "collegium," for these men hold no offices in the Church, and if some of them do, it is certainly not on account of their office that they were admitted as members of their society. The fourth chapter of the *Treatise on the Common Life* deals with the subject of secret societies. Three kinds of such societies are prohibited, Zerbolt writes, namely the assemblies of conspirators, of heretics, and of the seditious. But the Brethren of the Common Life are a quite different sort; they are pious, loyal, orderly. The fifth chapter is devoted to the question of preaching in private houses. This is forbidden, Zerbolt admits, but the members of a group may address and exhort one another, correct each other's faults, and even deliver speeches to the whole group in the house, as long as no one speaks to the common people, which may only be done by the prelates. The same subject is continued in the next chapter, where it is explained that the Brotherhood of the Common Life is quite distinct from all secret societies.

The seventh chapter is perhaps the most interesting one of the whole treatise. It has been printed twice in the original since 1889, and once in the Dutch translation.[58] As early as the year 1400 it had been translated by a monk in Brabant,[59] and not long after this date it spread across all of Germany, being copied in great numbers.[60] In the table of contents this chapter is entitled: "It is Permitted to Read and have Dutch (Germanic) books; what Dutch (Germanic) Books are Dangerous for Lay-men and what are Prohibited." We have seen that Groote shortly before his death translated parts of the Bible and a great many church hymns. If he had lived several years longer, he would undoubtedly have translated a great deal more into Dutch ver-nacular. Now Zerbolt regarded it his duty to continue in part the work left unfinished by Groote. Each disciple performed his fitting share. Cele took over Groote's interest in educational reforms; John Brinckerinck became a leader among the Sisters of the Common Life; Radewijns was the appointed guide of the whole body of Groote's disciples — the great physician of the mentally and spiritually diseased, the friend of the poor, the sorrowful, and the homeless; but Zerbolt inherited the master's love for books, and for learning; it was he who had to defend the new brotherhood with weapons too heavy and cumbersome for Radewijn's use; it was he who became the only distinguished scholar in the house at Deventer, and its most influential au-thor till the days of Hegius, Murmellius, and Erasmus.

To read the "sacred writings," as long as they contain no heresy or errors, particularly, if they are easy to understand, and in so far as they do not disagree with the canonical writings in style or subject matter, is permissible and praiseworthy, claims Zerbolt. This can be proved in the following manner. If lay-men are not allowed to read such books, it will be necessary to state why, that is, because they are laymen and unlearned, and for such it is not fit to read or study religious writings; or, although it is not prohibited for laymen to read them, nevertheless they shall not be permitted to read them in their native tongue. But it would be wrong to make such an assertion. For in the first place, laymen are not forbidden to read such works on account of being laymen, as is plainly inferred from several decisions found in the Canon Law. Augustine even reprehends laymen for being unwilling to read religious writings. Chrysostom does the same. Jerome exhorts even women to study the Scriptures, as is done also by Gregory. There are many laymen today, Zerbolt remarks, who spend a great deal of their time in reading wholly impractical and useless stories and fables about knights errant, the war of Troy, and similar subjects. Would it not be far better for them to study the Scriptures instead? And what does the Bible have to say about this matter? The New Testament commands us more frequently to study God's precepts than does the Old Testament, but in the latter many commandments are given to read and study the Scriptures, as for example in Deuteronomy, Ch. VI and Ch. XI and in many other places. In Deuteronomy, Ch. XI, we read: "Therefore shall ye lay up these my words in your heart and in your soul, and bind them for a sign upon your hand, that they may be as frontlets between your eyes. And ye shall teach them your children, speaking of them when thou sittest in thine house, and when thou walkest by the way, when thou liest down, and when thou risest up. And thou shalt write them upon the door post of thine house, and upon thy gates." That such commandments were not addressed to the clergy only is very plain indeed. From these and many other proofs which might be given, it clearly appears that laymen are not prohibited from reading religious writings, simply because they are laymen.

Now we still have to prove that it is not forbidden to read religious writings in the vernacular. Much evidence can be brought forward to establish this point also. In the first place, we may say that the greater part of the Old Testament was written for the Hebrews in Hebrew, which was the vernacular for them. Similarly, the New Testament was drawn up in the Greek vernacular with the exception of the Gospel of Matthew,

and Paul's Epistle to the Hebrews, which were directed to Hebrews, hence written in their vernacular. Some say that Paul
wrote his Epistle to the Romans in Latin. At any rate, the whole
or nearly the whole of the Bible was written in another language
than Latin.

In the second place, we find that many a missionary translated
parts of the Bible into the language of the people he tried to
convert. Dorotheus writes that Bartholomew, when he came to
India, translated the Gospel of St. Mark into the language used
there. This he surely would not have done, had he thought it
wrong for any one to read the Bible in the vernacular. The
sole reason why the Bible is now read in Latin, is on account of
this language being so widely used. The Hebrews read the Old
Testament in Hebrew, the Greeks had Greek Bibles, the Chal-
deans had the Scriptures in their own language. In the days of
old the Syrians and the Arabs read the Bible in the vernacular.
Ulfilas translated it into Gothic. The Bible has been translated
for the Egyptians, the Slavs, the Armenians, and if one were to
search further he might find a translation of parts of the Bible
in every language under the sun! For when the Holy Ghost
descended upon the Apostles on that great day of Pentecost,
many devout men were present and each heard the Apostles
speak in his native tongue, for a sign that the gospel of Christ
was to be preached in every language on the globe. Yes, in all
languages except the Dutch or Teutonic? Would not that be
a curious, a ridiculous thing? Impossible. Why should not
they, the Brethren of the Common Life, who counted many laymen among their members, be allowed to read the Bible in
the vernacular? Every one endowed with an infinitesimal spark
of intelligence would at once admit that they were permitted
to study the Bible in Dutch. Not only permissible it was, but
meritorious and quite praiseworthy.

But it would not be wise to read all books indiscriminately;
laymen are not allowed to read heretical works for example.
They should study those writings which plainly and openly discuss simple doctrines, as was indicated by Paul in his first Epistle
to the Corinthians, the third chapter, and in the fourth chapter

of the Epistle to the Hebrews. Augustine gives us similar instructions, and Chrysostom also. There are certain parts of the Bible which are more or less obscure, as the Revelation by St. John. Such books ought to be explained and properly interpreted for laymen to comprehend their hidden meaning. What benefit could one derive from the study of books one could never hope to understand? Hugo of St. Victor and Augustine have taken great pains to explain this matter. One should also avoid those books which use profane and abusive language in dealing with the most sacred subjects. There are such Teutonic works in existence, like certain sermons by Eckhardt. And finally, laymen should read no religious works in the vernacular that deviate from the doctrines promulgated by the acknowledged leaders in the Church.

Chapter VIII of the *Treatise on the Common Life* is devoted to the subject of obedience. The Brethren of the Common Life had taken no vows, for they did not intend to form a monastic organization. Consequently they could not bestow so great authority upon their superior or rector as was the case with the regular clergy. Not a single member of their house was obliged or compelled to obey the instructions of the rector. They did not promise to obey any office-holder in such manner. No matter how humble and how ignorant one might be, nobody, however virtuous, talented or noble, could threaten him with punishment, since no one expected him to render homage to any superior in that way. For they had decided to obey Christ only, and to imitate the Apostles. If one were to find the kingdom of heaven, Christ had said, he should become like unto a little child. The greatest men in God's kingdom were those who not only obeyed their superiors, but also their equals, and even their inferiors. In the apostolic church all members had been considered each other's superiors and equals — all as members of one body.

These and similar questions Zerbolt discussed in Chapter Eight of his treatise. All men were expected to render obedience to their superiors, he began, laymen as well as the clergy. For this reason the Church has condemned that sect which claims that man may attain to such perfection in this life that he no longer has to obey any law or commandment issued either by temporal or ecclesiastical powers. But in houses like the one in which Zerbolt was living one found oneself transported into a wholly different atmosphere. Here all men were considered equal.

Yet no society can exist without law and order. It is as with a family, where the father is like a king in his kingdom. The children and the domestics all obey the master of the house, and he takes care of the whole family. Yet there is a great difference also between the house of the brethren and a family. In a family we find inferiors obeying a superior. In the brethren-house one finds equals correcting and admonishing each other as equals, not as a father treats his children. Is such kind of obedience permissible? It is, according to Peter, Augustine, Bernard, and Thomas Aquinas. The fact is, there could not be harmony or peace in such a house without this sort of obedience. It is permissible then for the Brethren of the Common Life to have a rector to take care of the house, and to obey each other's wishes, in order to promote peace and harmony.

Is it also permissible for them to confess their sins to each other? Some declare they should not do this, but these people are wrong, says Zerbolt in Chapter Nine. One may confess one's sins to laymen. In case of necessity one may even confess one's mortal sins to laymen. And as for venial sins, one is permitted to confess them at any time. For in the sixth chapter of James we read: "Confess your faults one to another." And although the learned doctors and theologians are not agreed on this subject, nevertheless we are permitted to confess our sins to laymen. But it seems best to confess to priests whenever possible. To-day the custom of confessing sins to one another is scarcely ever practised. Perhaps because we have so many priests, or because many doctors are opposed to the practice.

It certainly is permissible, Zerbolt continues, to confess daily shortcomings to each other. For such a humble confession almost in itself brings one forgiveness of the sins committed. In the second place, this kind of confession will teach us more clearly the nature of sin, the difference between vice and virtue, and the various remedies for each vice. It is easily understood that for this kind of confessions we do not so much need a person who has the keys of authority, as one with experience in spiritual affairs, who can teach us to fight temptations and the devil's attacks. When somebody reproved Arsenius for confessing his sins to an unlearned farmer who knew a great deal about spiritual exercises, he answered: "I have learned Latin and Greek, but the alphabet of this farmer I have thus far failed to decipher." Thirdly, if one is accustomed sincerely to reveal his shortcomings, he finally becomes ashamed of having to admit the repeated yielding to the same temptation, and firmly resolves to defeat the enemy who sent that temptation. Confession also frees us more quickly from the snares of the tempter.

This non-sacramental confession, Zerbolt argues, was once very common among virtuous men and highly praised, but now it is not common and some consider it wrong. Here we have the secret of the institution founded by Groote: a protest against the formalism of the Church in the fourteenth century. One by one the commandments of Christ had been disregarded as too difficult to follow. Even the clergy generally were disregarding them, and what was infinitely worse, the men who wanted to return to the customs of the apostolic church were attacked by the very leaders in Christendom. The Brethren of the Common Life were called heretics — they were attacked for trying to obey, where their enemies refused to obey. They were not to live the common life, nor to have a rector, nor to read religious books in the vernacular. To confess their sins to each other was said to be prohibited, though James had plainly commanded all Christians to practise it frequently.

What else was wrong about the new brotherhood? Groote had prepared a schedule for the men who had decided to live the common life, according to which they were to regulate their daily tasks. The brethren had chosen a rector soon after Groote's death, and now they had a procurator besides, while some or all of the members practised a certain course of spiritual exercises. Although it is impossible to tell exactly what sort of a constitution they had in Zerbolt's day, inasmuch as the original written constitution was drawn up after 1413,[62] certain it is that they were following definite rules. That was wrong, their enemies said. Hence the tenth chapter of the treatise is intended by Zerbolt to defend this feature of the brotherhood's organization. The same subject is continued in the eleventh or last chapter. To perform manual labor at stated times, and to read books, to fast, pray, and meditate regularly is permitted, says Zerbolt, not only to monks but to all virtuous men. For even the simplest laborers eat, work, rest, and sleep at stated times. Therefore the Brethren of the Common Life too are allowed to have their rules or regulations. And here the treatise ends.

Zerbolt's theological views are most clearly set forth in his *Spiritual Ascensions,* the work which exercised such a profound influence on Catholic Europe of the fifteenth and sixteenth centuries, particularly on Ignace Loyola. Based on and partly copied after the *Treatise on Spiritual Exercises* by Radewijns, Zerbolt's book on the spiritual ascensions repeats the views set forth by Radewijns, which views are supplemented by certain chapters found in the *Reformation of the Faculties of the Soul,* — also written by Zerbolt. They form a course of spiritual exercises, which were practised by thousands, worked over by Mauburn (or Mombaer), and finally incorporated, though changed to some extent, by Loyola in his *Spiritual Exercises,* as we shall have occasion to observe in another chapter.

Man fell from his privileged state of innocence in paradise. This was the first fall; the second fall of man is due to his sins on earth. If one wishes to find the kingdom of heaven, says Zerbolt, one must steadily keep in view whence he originally came — what he was before the fall, in order that he may know how to regain his lost estate, for it is useless to strive after perfection, if one knows not what such perfection implies. Man must in all his spiritual exercises remember his final end: purity of heart and love. To purify the heart is to extinguish evil desire, which we may also call the reformation of the soul or the mind. For Oh man, thy mind, which is more exalted than all mortal creatures, becomes defiled in subjecting itself through improper affection to temporal objects. Explore your sinful nature, strive to realize the extent of your fall, and carefully examine your evil deeds each day. For there is also a third fall, which for example happened to the prodigal son, when he went among the swine. In this condition man continually commits mortal sins.

Since we can distinguish three falls or descents, there must also be three ascents, each divided into several steps or stages. As *Ascent* man ascends the steps, he gradually reforms his intellect, his will, and his memory, for these are the three faculties of the soul. During the first ascent he leaves the ways of the godless, as the prodigal left the swine. He begins to confess his sins and to show repentance. During the second ascent his repentance is sufficient to bring forgiveness, but that is not enough. Three things are needed before he reaches the third ascent, namely: fear of the Lord, hope, and love. Zerbolt begins with fear, for often he had read this text: "The fear of the Lord is the beginning of wisdom." In the first place, this holy fear plainly exposes the evil fruits of sin. One also should reflect often on the approach of death, the last judgment, and the pains in hell. The second step of the second ascent is hope, the hope of future joy. Then follows the third step, where the active life begins. Here one learns to love, after having purified the heart. And here one commences the real exercises.

Zerbolt asks, How are we to purge ourselves from sin, and acquire perfect love? Only through Christ, who is our model and example. For Christ said that no one could come to the Father but through Him. It should be our aim to become his companions, his followers. Secondly, we should love and adore Christ both as God and man, and thirdly, through the example of Christ's humanity, we could rise to great heights of spiritual perfection, while, in looking upon his divinity as our mirror, we ourselves might obtain knowledge of and love for things divine. Just as Radewijns had devoted a considerable part of his *Omnes inquit artes* to the life of Christ, and as Thomas à Kempis, who was now collecting the material for the *Imitation of Christ,* was soon to follow Radewijns, so Zerbolt also reserved thirteen chapters for this same subject.

The third ascent is directed against the evil consequences of the first fall or descent, commonly called original sin. Zerbolt holds that it is our duty to cleanse our hearts in so far as we are able, humanly speaking, from the tares introduced into our blood by Adam's sin with Eve. The first thing to do is to extinguish vice, as Radewijns also had said. Then follow about a dozen other chapters, some of which remind us forcibly of certain passages in the *Treatise on the Common Life,* but they contain nothing new.

Zerbolt wrote his two mystical works shortly before his death, which occurred in 1398. In November, 1398, the Brethren of the Common Life of Deventer had returned from Amersfoort.[64] Radewijns was ill, wherefore Zerbolt was sent to an old friend north of Deventer. On his return he caught an infectious disease and died on the 4th of December.[65] With him the house at Deventer lost its scholar, author, and defense. Radewijns, heartbroken as he was, passed away on the 25th of March, 1400, and the center of the Devotio Moderna shifted northward to Windesheim and Zwolle.

6. Windesheim and Diepenveen

The monastery of Windesheim had been founded in the year 1386, by Groote's followers at Deventer, who wished to materialize his plans. They wanted a permanent place of refuge for those among their number who preferred the monastic life, and a place that might afford a temporary shelter to the brethren left behind at Deventer, in case of need. "For this reason did they decide to build a monastery," says Rudolph Dier, "because they, living the simple, common life, were afraid of further persecutions by rivals, and thus, if some of their members would be actually living in a monastery, the others would be protected by them."[66] The brethren in Radewijns' vicarage had felt no need of such protection until they had introduced the common life. In 1386, however, we find them looking for a site for their new monastery. They found one near Hattem on the Veluwe, about three miles southwest of Zwolle. After having secured permission from the Duke of Gelderland to erect some buildings there, they went to their ecclesiastical lord, the Bishop of Utrecht. Radewijns and six other men were sent to tell the bishop about their plans. "Do not build that monastery in Gelderland," the bishop told them, "but somewhere in my territory east of the Yssel." Now it happened that one of the men, a certain Berthold ten Hove, owned some property there, wherefore the brethren agreed to build on his land, which was situated at Windesheim in the Yssel valley, three miles southeast of Zwolle.[67]

First one man was sent to make the necessary preparations; later five others were added, and one was appointed procurator. They began to work at once. The site was found to be a lonely tract of land with some few willows on it, but no buildings of any kind to house the men. A small elevation was selected for the buildings. This spot, they were told, had never been flooded by the Yssel. Soon gifts came pouring in: Lambert Stuerman, of whom Groote had caught the pest, as they thought, but who had recovered, gave 100 French crowns; some one else gave 200, and a third one 136. Henry of Wilsen, one of six men sent to inspect the grounds, sold all he had, and handed the money over to the brethren at Deventer. Many among his relatives and acquaintances contributed, so that the amount required for the erection of the buildings was soon raised. Encouraged by this the men at Windesheim worked with redoubled energy. In October of the year 1387, the monastery proper, with its church, had been finished.[68] All was now ready for the dedication. The six brethren were to take the vows of chastity, poverty, and obedience. But, although they had been instructed by Groote and Radewijns in the essentials of the Christian religion, they knew practically nothing about the monastic life and its ceremonies. They decided to spend a few days at the Augustinian monastery of Eemsteyn near Dordrecht, where some of Groote's best friends were now practising the rules of the Augustinian Canons Regular with the ardor of new devotion.[69] Here they were kindly accepted and initiated into the rituals of the Augustinian order, which the monks of Eemsteyn had learned from those of Groenendaal, Ruysbroeck's monastery.[69] On the 17th of October the dedication took place. The brethren went through the customary ceremonies, and each of them read from a strip of parchment the vows of obedience, poverty, and chastity. Just those and no others. No vows of obedience to the bishop of Utrecht, no promises of allegiance to any party or power, and no submission to any rules except those they were to formulate themselves. What was the cause of this independent attitude? Perhaps it was, as Acquoy suggests, the inborn love for personal liberty so characteristic of the Frisians and the Saxons.[70]

There stood the little monastery with its thatched roofs among the willows planted beside the still waters. Who would have thought in 1387, that this humble convent would soon be sending its missionaries all over the Low Countries and thence into the farthest outpost of the German lands; that it would bring about the only lasting monastic reform in fifteenth century Europe, and incorporate within its fold some of the most famous monasteries in the West? Though its men were first taught by the monks of Eemsteyn near Dordrecht, Groenendaal near Brussels, and St. Victor at Paris, not long thereafter it surpassed them all in moral force and religious zeal.

This apparently marvelous success may not seem strange, however, to one who has noted how the founders of Windesheim spent their lives. Under the leadership of Henry of Höxter (17 October 1386-17 October 1387) and that of William Keynkamp (October 1387-November 1391) the works of love and faith were plentiful. Particularly during the priorate of John Vos of Heusden (1391-1424) Windesheim was the pride of Groote's followers, and from 1400-1424, it was the center of the "New Devotion." So great was the love among the Brethren of the Common Life at Deventer and their friends at Windesheim in those early years that all their possessions were considered almost as one common fund, placed at the disposal of the one who needed them most:[71] In 1392, Deventer and Windesheim founded the monastery of Mariendaal near Arnhem. John Ketel, the pious cook at Deventer, who possessed 1300 florins, gave the whole sum to the founders, and Radewijns also gave some money.

John Vos of Heusden was in fact the greatest prior Windesheim ever had. Born at Heusden in 1363, he had come to Deventer to receive instruction in the cathedral school of St. Lebwin. Radewijns had introduced him to Groote one day. The first meeting had been decisive. Groote had looked at him with one of those penetrative glances of his, which seemed to pierce one's very soul, and said: "This is the man I have sought; with him I will do something worth while on earth." Till 1388 he had remained with the other brothers in Radewijns' vicarage. But the monastery called him, and in 1391, he was elected prior.

The first thirty years were a time of great moral strength and rapid growth. Of the forty brethren invested before 1424, one half became rectors or priors of monasteries built or reformed under their supervision. For there were other great reformers in those early days besides John Vos of Heusden. There was John à Kempis, a disciple of Groote and later of Radewijns.[72] At Deventer and Windesheim he was a model of piety, and later he became rector and prior of several monasteries in succession. Then there was Arnold of Calcar, sub-prior at Windesheim for 35 years, and Henry Wilde, one of six founders, who was sent to St. Victor at Paris to study the rules of the Augustinian order; Henry Wilsem, once a prominent magistrate at Kampen, and a convert of Groote, Berthold ten Hove, also converted by Groote, John Scuutken, another disciple of Groote, and Albert Wijnberghen.

It should be noted, however, that whatever Windesheim possessed before the year 1400 was a gift from the Brethren of the Common Life and their friends at Deventer. And similarly, when a monastery was built for the Augustinian Canonesses Regular, it was founded by the Sisters of the Common Life of Deventer.

In 1383, the sisters had secured a rector and confessor in the person of John van den Gronde. When Groote was about to die, he had promised to send "little flowers" from heaven. But for several years his promise remained unfulfilled. The rector was getting old, and could devote but a small part of his time to their care, as he often went out preaching, or to hear confessions of the sisters at Zwolle, or the brethren at Mount St. Agnes, three miles north-east of Zwolle. Left without proper guidance, the Sisters of the Common Life at Deventer gradually neglected Groote's instructions; discipline relaxed, and the blessings of manual labor were ignored. When Van den Gronde died, a reform was at once instituted by his capable successor, named John Brinckerinck. This brother was one of the most ardent followers Groote ever had, for he had attended the master on nearly all his trips. He became as close a friend of Groote as John Cele had been. Not being able to find a single monastery in or near the Yssel valley where Christ was imitated, he had joined the Brethren of the Common Life at Deventer. In 1392, he left their house for the "House of Master Gerard," — Groote's ancestral home — this being the year in which Van den Gronde passed away.

Brinckerinck has rightly been called the second founder of the "House of Master Gerard." The moment he entered the building, the sisters felt that their life of ease was ended. They were told to lead the common life again, to work with their own hands and to discontinue begging for alms. "You must either work or leave the house," was his command. But they stayed, for he at once won both their love and respect. It was said that rays of holiness radiated from him. Soon his fame spread beyond the walls of Deventer. From Zeeland, Friesland, Münster, and Cologne all sorts of persons came to the "House of Master Gerard" for counsel and religious instruction. And the sisters, inspired by his saintliness, were full of religious fervor. Soon the old home of Groote was found altogether too small. Four other houses were founded at Deventer during Brinckerinck's life-time. Says one early biographer: "So great a fire of the Holy Ghost was kindled among those saintly sisters in the House of Master Gerard that the whole country around here grew warm with it, and all this as the result of the doctrine and instruction of their father, John Brinckerinck."[73]

Meanwhile some of the clergy were not pleased. Others were filled with holy anger, because the poor women read books in the vernacular, which was considered reprehensible by certain members of the clergy at that time. The sisters should immediately stop this evil practice, they said, and when they saw that their orders were disregarded, they attacked the sisters publicly. At last Brinckerinck found it necessary to defend them in church, where he held a lengthy discourse on the subject of reading books in the vernacular. The arguments used on this occasion he had gleaned from a book he had read in the library of the brethren-house, which probably had been composed by Zerbolt.

There were other reasons why the Sisters of the Common Life were attacked in those early days — the same reasons which caused the Brethren of the Common Life to seek protection in a monastery. Many a time Brinckerinck had to ascend the pulpit in the church of St. Mary at Deventer to defend the sisters. It should not surprise us to learn that they too wanted to found a convent, for the times were so different from what they are today. On the seventeenth of June, 1400, Brinckerinck called the sisters together to draw up the necessary plans. They possessed a piece of land near the Yssel, three miles north of Deventer. Here they decided to build their home. But it was a lonely tract of land they had selected — marshy and unattractive. Ditches had to be dug, stumps rooted up, holes filled with sand; in most places the surface of the soil had to be raised six feet. Undaunted by hardship, fatigue, and discomfiture, the women did the work, assisted by the brethren of the "House of Florentius" and later by hired laborers. Before that year was over, the first buildings, made of wood were finished. In 1401, the sisters bought some more land; in 1406, still more; they built a barn also, and soon they had become prosperous farmers, possessing a fine herd of sheep, cows, pigs, and who knows what else? The monotonous brown of the murky soil had been replaced by soft green grass. And soon the wooden cloister buildings were exchanged for a fine brick convent — the convent of Diepenveen.[74]

7. John Cele and his School

After Zerbolt's death the center of the Devotio Moderna had traveled northward from Deventer to Windesheim and Diepenveen. It was to shift still farther to the north, for in the city of Zwolle a flourishing brethren-house had attracted many devout from Flanders, Brabant, Friesland, Westphalia, and other districts. Soon it opened its doors to a Wessel Ganstort, an Alexander Hegius, and a Rudolph von Langen, and before long it began to send out missionaries to several other cities, such as Groningen, 's-Hertogenbosch, and Doesburg, where daughter-houses were founded. The reform of the school at Zwolle was the beginning of a mighty revival of learning. And although this intellectual revival found its most perfect expression in the labors of Hegius at Deventer, Murmellius at Münster and Dringenberg at Schlettstadt, Zwolle was the place which provided the source material, and gave the movement its impetus.

Among Groote's first and most influential disciples was Henry Foppens of Gouda. Anxious to imitate his master as friend of poor school boys, he bought a house at Zwolle, where he intended to lodge some of them. Also as preacher and leader of the Sisters of the Common Life at Zwolle he became a worthy follower of Groote. Then there was Reynold of Drenen, pastor at Zwolle, and blind John Ummen, a very pious man, who together with two other laymen, named Jacob Wittecoep and Wychmannus Ruerinck, bought a lot next to Foppen's house. On this lot a house was built, where the three laymen in question lived the common life, acting upon Groote's advice. We might therefore call them the first Brethren of the Common Life, for they had kept no private property of their own.[75] On the 5th of July, 1384, the house was sold to Groote, lest the heirs might claim it some day.[76] "These three men," says Jacob Voecht of Utrecht, "were therefore the first Brethren of the Common Life at Zwolle, to which number many others were added later, among whom blind John Ummen was foremost; he became their rector and procurator. Together they moved to Mount St. Agnes, where Groote showed them the site for their new house.[77]

The first brethren-house at Zwolle was not a success, for the men who had founded it moved to a lonely hill, three miles away from the city, where but few people were found to give them employment, and few boys to be cared for. A better fate was reserved for the second institution. On April 4, 1393, Florens van Wevelinkhoven, Bishop of Utrecht, died. His successor, named Frederick van Blankenheim, was a friend of Groote's disciples. The brethren at Zwolle, as soon as they were made aware of the new bishop's friendly attitude, decided once more to found a house, hoping that this time they would not be compelled to seek protection and rest in a solitary place. There was a certain Meynoldus of Windesheim, a disciple of Groote, who had sold his property and had come to Zwolle, where in a humble dwelling he lived with a few poor school boys. Encouraged by the success of the Brethren of the Common Life at Deventer, he wanted to found a house where priests and clerics might live the common life. A suitable site was secured, and a fine building erected, called "House of St. Gregory." This happened in the year 1396.

Who was to be elected rector of the second institution at Zwolle? Meynoldus of Windesheim, the real founder, felt himself unfit for so exalted a task. It was not for him, he said, to become the spiritual guide of the men and boys living with him in his house. One day he came to Florentius Radewijns, rector at Deventer. "Can you lend me one of your clerics"? he asked of Radewijns. "Yes," was the answer, "take this youth with you; his name is Gerard Scadde of Calcar." At the expiration of one year Meynoldus returned to Deventer with Gerard. "The young man should at once be ordained priest," he said to Radewijns "in order that he may become our rector." Radewijns gladly assented. In 1396, then, the Brethren of the Common Life at Zwolle obtained both a new house and a capable rector. They were instructed in the ways and means practised at Deventer; the rules of Deventer, as yet unwritten, became theirs also.[78] And with these rules they acquired religious fervor in great measure, surpassing their friends at Deventer for a time, as will be shown in the following chapter.

Thus far we have but casually mentioned the name of Zwolle's great teacher, John Cele. A native of Zwolle, he received a master's degree at some university — Prague perhaps. Through Groote's friendship he seems to have obtained his position as rector of the city school at Zwolle, in or shortly after the year 1374.   The fact that Groote selected him as his trusted companion on his visit to Ruysbroeck is significant.   Groote often corresponded with him in later years,[79] and also often came to visit him.   In almost every respect Cele tried to imitate his beloved friend.   Not only did he, as Groote had done, refuse to become a priest, declaring that a priest's responsibilities were greater than those of the angels,[80] but he also stayed a short time (1381-1382) at Monnikhuizen, the Carthusian monastery near Arnhem, where Groote also had spent two years.   And, as had been the case with Groote, he found but little satisfaction there. Duty, he thought, had called him back to Zwolle: "His light should no longer be hid beneath a bushel."

Cele brought about the reform of the city school at Zwolle, and succeeded in attracting as many as 1200 boys at a time from districts far removed from the Yssel valley.   He became the founder and originator of what we now call the secondary schools, and it was his school that served as model for those of Dringenberg, Hegius, Murmellius, Melanchton, Sturm, Calvin, the Jesuits, and all their followers.   There were several causes which contributed to his success.   In the first place, after having been taught by Groote to make a careful distinction between the form and the inner essence of things, he pruned away from his curriculum all dead formalism, at least as far as he was able. Of what use was the study of Canon Law, medicine, and astronomy to the average school boy, he used to ask, consciously in imitation of Groote's standpoint.[81]   And as for the study of religion and the harmonious development of one's mental and spiritual self, the Gospels, the Epistles of the New Testament, and other biblical works, together with the Fathers, were a more fruitful source of instruction than the subtle and wholly impractical scholastic disputes engaged in by the learned doctors of Paris and Cologne.   Scholasticism was as good as any other system of philosophy, but there were different kinds of scholasticism: the living and the dead, the practical and the formal, as there were different kinds of religion or faith, such as the theoretical and the personal, such as the religion of Christ versus that of the Pharisees.

John Cele did this thing, which was new. Three times a day (on holidays at least) he read and explained to his pupils selections from the Bible: from the Epistles in the morning, the Gospels in the afternoon, and from some other book in the evening.[82] He exhorted his pupils to write down those parts of his addresses which seemed most useful to them. The life of Christ was continually referred to as the only reliable pattern we could find on earth. To imitate him was Cele's chief aim; it should be theirs also, he said, "Cele himself," says Busch, "as a true imitator of Christ, never taught us anything which he had not previously practised, in order that he might be our example."[83] The pupils were taught to pray both in Latin and in Dutch; Busch gives us both versions of a prayer taught by Cele. He never undertook anything without commending it first to God in prayer, for at all times he felt himself in the presence of God. The one chief cause of his fame, says Schoengen, the archivist at Zwolle, was his maxim: "The kingdom of heaven consisteth not in knowledge and speech, but in work and virtue." Cele was not at all opposed to book-learning. He asserted that God's will or testament was expressed in "sacred writings," and that the Church would long have perished had it not been for the reading of good books. Cele and Zerbolt proved themselves in this respect at least closer to Groote's principles than Radewijns, who stressed the importance of intuition or inspiration more than the scholarly Groote had done. Zerbolt, we remember, had followed Groote's view in realizing the needs of the masses. The farmers and the burghers should read the Bible for themselves, he had argued, and since most of them could not read Latin, they ought to be given an opportunity of reading the Bible in their own tongue. Cele, in following these same views, invited all the inhabitants of Zwolle to attend his discourses, thus giving them a chance to gain a better understanding of the passages he advised them to study.[84]

But there were a great many other books to be studied besides the Bible and the Fathers, in Cele's opinion. Not a single subject was scrapped by him from the curriculum then in vogue. It was wise to examine everything, he thought, but one should learn to select the best, the useful, the practical. There was no harm in the study of geometry, astronomy, logic, and medicine, as long as one used those subjects as a means of reaching a certain end. If one was to become a priest some day, he would not need to know so very much about geometry, for example, nor would the future merchant or farmer have much occasion to study medicine, or astronomy. The Bible should be studied by everybody, for all men were created in God's image; they all should strive to regain a part of their lost heritage. Virtue and love were essentials, character a necessity, if one wished to build up a society where peace and order would reign. One should also develop one's intellect, however. The priest ought to know a great deal about literature and philosophy. The teacher, so long as he avoided as much as possible the merely theoretical, or formal side of things, would be justified in retaining all subjects taught in the schools thus far. Cele, therefore, retained the exercises in scholasticism, grammar, logic, ethics, and philosophy. "But although he took great pains in teaching these subjects with effect," says Busch, "nevertheless he did not thereby diminish his interest — nay, he even increased his zeal in instructing his pupils in the sacred writings, good manners, a saintly and Christian life, and the fear and love of God. For in the morning he would explain an Epistle and in the evening some other part of the Scriptures, addressing the whole school."[85]

Cele was a practical teacher. He saw that no two boys were exactly alike, nor were they equally well supplied with funds. With the Brethren of the Common Life at Zwolle he made arrangements to house them in a suitable manner. Those who could afford it were expected to pay the brothers for their room and board, while Cele asked a certain sum as tuition fee. The poorer class of boys, of whom there were a great number, instead of being compelled to beg for alms, were kindly taken care of by the brethren, and Cele even gave them money for the books, ink, and paper they needed in school.[86] In order to take care of each pupil's individual needs, he divided his school into eight

classes. This arrangement may seem quite simple and natural
to us today. We should remember, however, that this phase of
Cele's reform was an innovation, a pedagogical discovery, we
might say.[87] And this discovery, or invention, led to other discoveries. The "quadrivium" was included in the curriculum,
and last but not least, in the two highest classes special studies
were taught by specialists. As the inevitable result of Cele's
reforms, his pupils generally made more rapid progress at the
universities than most other students.[88]

Another factor which may partly explain Cele's fame was his
way of keeping order in the school-room. The teachers of that
time resorted to various forms of punishment, which in spite of,
or rather as a result of, their harshness failed to bring about
better discipline. Cele rightly reasoned that a teacher's personality was the great factor in the matter of order and discipline. He took a personal interest in every one of his pupils;
as far as he was able, naturally. As to punishment, every form
was too severe, if one had not first exhausted all the ways of
correction taught him by sympathy and love.[89]

If he was right in asserting that the Church would have
perished centuries ago without the use of books, then the clergy
in particular, but all laymen also, should read much. Groote
had held the same, and so had Zerbolt. And since there never
could be too many good books in the world, Cele taught his
students the elements of rhetoric. One feature of his method
was the "rapiarium," or collection of excerpts, which every pupil
of his had to make. From the Gospels and other books of the
New Testament he selected the plainest and most helpful
sayings. These he dictated in a loud voice to the whole school.
"For he wanted his pupils to have the leading events and the
most striking passages found in the Epistles and the Gospels
collected in one copy-book, a theological excerpt-book, in which
the most useful thoughts found in the sacred writings were
gathered in brief extracts. This would enable them more easily
to commit such passages to memory."[90]

The influence exerted by him on the Europe of the fifteenth
century is incalculable. Students, attracted by his fame, flocked

to Zwolle from the bishoprics or principalities of Cologne, Trier, Louvain, Utrecht, Brabant, Flanders, Westphalia, Holland, Saxony, Cleves, Gelderland, and Frisia. Among the thousands of boys who between the years 1374 and 1317, were educated at Zwolle, a considerable number entered monasteries, where they helped to introduce better discipline, and more love for sound learning. "Paris, Cologne, Erfurt, and the Roman Curia testify how many learned men Cele's school sent out," is Busch's complacent remark. The whole population of Zwolle was changed for the better as a result of Cele's educational work. Among the prominent magistrates were found several of his pupils, from which we may infer that many a burgher of Zwolle, if not converted by Groote himself, became through Cele's influence a defender of the principles advocated by the Devotio Moderna. "It is now more than forty years ago," Busch wrote in 1459, "that he migrated hence, and still his name is upon the lips of those who were fortunate enough to be instructed by him."[91]

Although he was very generous in helping his poorer pupils, Cele made a great deal of money with his school. With this money he constructed a fine library in the church of St. Michael at Zwolle. There he placed a large collection of codices on theology, philosophy, and literature, to which all devout citizens were freely admitted. Furthermore, many of Cele's followers imitated his noble example by collecting books and lending them to others.[92] By this also the city of Zwolle became a center of popular learning. The clergy in particular were woefully lacking in sound learning. And if the Church was to be regenerated, if a lasting religious revival, so sadly needed, was to take place, the clergy would have to be instructed first of all, the laymen should be taught to exert themselves, and school teachers must break with the empty formalism and the dying scholasticism which were injuring both the Church and society. This had been Groote's message to the men and women of his day. Radewijns, Zerbolt, Vos of Heusden, Brinckerinck, and Cele each took over a part of Groote's work, repeating his message in their own way. Thus began that mighty religious and intellectual revival, the Devotio Moderna. Soon it succeeded in permeating the lives of the men and women living in the Yssel valley, then it spread in ever-widening circles across the continent. This was made possible by the strong organization built by the Brethren of the Common Life, which will be treated in the following chapter.

CHAPTER III

The Brethren and Sisters of the Common Life

In the preceding chapter we have noted the beginnings of three institutions founded by Groote. First came the home in which the Sisters of the Common Life found a shelter. Next followed the Brethren-house at Zwolle and a similar house at Deventer. Almost simultaneously the monastery at Windesheim was founded. These three institutions lived side by side until the first decades of the sixteenth century, when the storm of the Reformation broke loose upon the peaceful Yssel Valley and engulfed the Devotio Moderna. We shall now examine the history of the Brotherhood of the Common Life, which included or at least gave support to the Sisters of the Common Life.

1. The Brethren at Deventer

From the year in which the "House of Florentius"[1] was built till the death of Radewijns in 1400, the brothers at Deventer led a very quiet and uneventful life. Radewijns was succeeded as rector by Amilius van Buren, an intimate friend of Thomas à Kempis, as will appear in a later chapter.[2] It was his constant aim to preserve mutual love and harmony among the men. Often he would say to them: "There is one thing which we must all adhere to and observe: our status as Brethren of the Common Life; for although the monastic state is preferable in the opinion of the Church, nevertheless he who lives a saintly life outside of a monastery will receive the reward of saintliness."[3]

Amilius carefully guarded the rules of the house, and during his rectorate large numbers of school boys flocked to Deventer, many of whom acquired the habit of visiting the brethren-house,

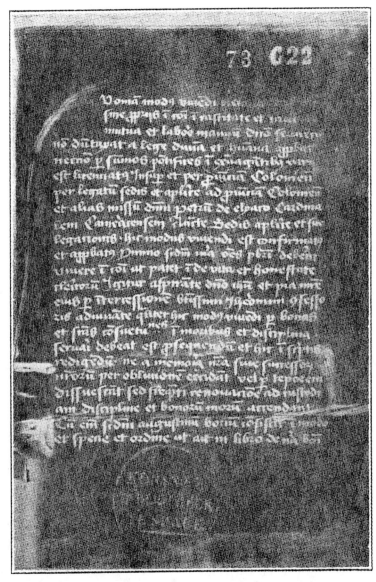

First page of the first constitution of Brethren-house at Deventer, discovered in the Royal Library at The Hague by Albert Hyma and published by him in his first book: *The Christian Renaissance* (Eerdmans, 1924)

where they were regularly instructed in the essentials of the Christian faith.[4]

It naturally followed that the brethren received most of their recruits from these boys. In 1400, the community counted so many members that forty of them were sent to found other houses. One young man went to Münster, where in the same year he induced a small number of followers to lead with him the common life; a few others moved to Delft, also to found a house.[5] The rectorate of Amilius was therefore compared with the reign of Solomon, while Radewijns' rule was thought to correspond to that of David.[6]

But Amilius van Buren did not reign so long as Solomon. During the first week in June, 1404, he felt the end of his life approaching. Calling all the members of the community together, he addressed them in a lengthy speech. "John of Haarlem shall be my successor," he concluded; "obey him, and let no one say to himself that John is still so young, or that you have read much more and know a great deal more than he does. It is our duty to love our fellow-men, and obey them all in order that we may properly humiliate ourselves." On June 10, Van Buren, the second rector of the Brethren of the Common Life at Deventer, passed away.[7]

John of Haarlem ruled the brethren for six years. In 1410, he was succeeded by Godfried Toorn, who was rector for forty years. Although he had to sustain a great deal of hatred and opposition from the enemies of the new brotherhood, his temper always remained serene. The sources also say that he knew how to search the inner recesses of the heart and to delve into the rich mines of theology and jurisprudence. Always looking beneath the surface of form and outward appearances, he was not satisfied with mere style. The brethren were encouraged by him to read as many books as possible, and to select those first which contained the most practical religious and moral teachings. "Father John Vos of Heusden," he used to remark, "was wont to restrain his men from reading Thomas Aquinas and other modern scholastics of his type on obedience and kindred subjects, hoping that they might thus retain their simplicity."[8]

There were two virtues he never ceased to extol: friendship and chastity. "Brethren," he once exclaimed, "we have left all our relatives and acquaintances, our native country and other ties behind; we have come here to dwell together in this house that we might serve the Lord through the common life. If we, therefore, are querulous, impatient, or in any way unkind to each other, we shall become the most miserable among men. You will indeed kill me, if discord should arise among you."[9]

The man who uttered these words was by no means devoid of talent. He had been a teacher at Deventer,[10] and it was during his rectorate that the Brethren of the Common Life drew up their first written constitution. Before 1413, they had failed to secure official recognition from the papal see. True, the monks of Windesheim had defended them in 1395, the alumni of the University of Cologne had approved their mode of life, and Frederick van Blankenheim, bishop of Utrecht, had proved to be their faithful supporter; but the brethren wanted still more. In 1413, Cardinal Pierre d'Ailly came to the Yssel valley as papal legate for the Germanic peoples. He gave the brethren and sisters at Deventer several privileges, amongst them a document in which he officially confirmed the approbations signed by the Cologne jurists in 1398. Whether the cardinal personally requested or suggested that the brethren draw up a written constitution, we do not know. At any rate, it appears from the preamble to their first written constitution that the cardinal's official support had encouraged them to write down these rules which had been in vogue among them, lest their successors should forget their own constitution.[11]

In September, 1450, Godfried Toorn's health began to fail. His successor was elected by the brethren before he died. Six weeks later his death occurred, namely, on the 3rd of November. The new rector was called Egbert ter Beek (1450-1483). During the first year of his rectorate Cusa, the famous cardinal, mathematician, and reformer, came to Deventer. He must have enjoyed himself there, as in this very same city, supported by these very same brethren, he is said to have received part of his early education.[12] Quite naturally he offered them a great many privileges in the form of prebends, and similar things. But the rector flatly refused to accept them, being unwilling to depart from the ways of simplicity and humility taught by the first members of his brotherhood.[13]

Egbert ter Beek distinguished himself for his zeal in upholding the status of the Brethren of the Common Life. Many a day he spent in visiting the daughter-institutions in Flanders, Brabant, Holland, and Westphalia; anxiously watching, lest the encroaching armies of monasticism overwhelm the brotherhood. One day he heard that the rector of the local institution at Doesburg on the Yssel had invited the prior of Windesheim to change his house into a monastery of the Augustinian Canons Regular. He immediately hurried to the scene of operations. Yes, the prior was already there, having begun to invest the brethren. "What on earth are you doing here?" he exclaimed, addressing the brethren. "And what business brings you here"? was his remark to the prior of Windesheim. "Well," answered the prior in question, "have I done any wrong in advancing the brethren to the monastic state, which, as you must admit, is superior to yours"? "I make no objection," was Egbert's reply, "if you merely seek to induce laymen or secular clergy to enter monasteries, but you ought not to usurp our houses. This house has always been ours, and it shall remain ours. It was given to our brethren, in order that they might live the common life, and if any of them should wish to become monks, they would be free to leave the house." Whereupon the bewildered prior, according to our chronicle, quickly left the place.[14]

It was during Ter Beek's rectorate that John Brugman, perhaps the most popular preacher the Low Countries ever produced, was changed from a Saul into a Paul. Even today the people throughout the Netherlands, who as a rule have not the slightest idea who Brugman was, or where he lived, still make him a proverb, often remarking after having listened to an unusually eloquent preacher: "He preaches like a Brugman."[15] Like many a monk of his day, he had for a time been very bitter against the Brethren of the Common Life, who, as conscience but too plainly told him, were living more saintly and Christ-like

lives without the protection of the monastic vows than most so-
called religious people. After his "reformation" he suddenly
changed his attitude, and thenceforth praised the brethren very
highly in his sermons, letters, and treatises.[16]

On the sixteenth day of April, 1483, Egbert ter Beek followed the other four rectors to the grave. A few days later his
body was solemnly carried to the church-yard by the mourning
brethren. Future leaders of the German Renaissance were
among those who attended the funeral, for in that year Alexander Hegius was called to Deventer as rector of the school of St.
Lebwin's and Erasmus was one of the boys who had been given
religious instruction by the brethren for several years past. From
Zwolle the great revival of learning inaugurated by Groote and
Cele had come traveling southward again, selecting Deventer
as its center till the death of Hegius. After 1483, the rectors
of the brethren-house fade away into comparative oblivion.[17]

As for the different buildings used by the brothers at Deventer, a few remarks will suffice. Radewijns' vicarage was later
referred to as the *"Antiqua Domus,"* or the "Ancient House,"
in distinction from the *"Nova Domus,"* or the "New House,"
which was founded about the year 1398, for the school boys of
the cathedral school. The house built in 1391, for the use of
the members themselves, was called *"Domus Domini Florentii,"*
or "Heer Florenshuis," or "House of Master Florentius."
Several plots of ground were added to their property from time
to time, and additional buildings were erected for various pur-
poses. The chief building occupied by the brethren at Deventer during the days of Erasmus was erected in 1441.[18] And
finally, those boys who could find no room in the *"Nova Domus,"* or *"Domus pauperum"* ("New House," or "House for
Poor Boys") were sent to two other houses: the *"Hierony-
mushuis"* ("House of Jerome") and the *"Jufferenhuis,"* or
"Juffer Wibbenhuis" ("House of Lady Wibben").[19]

2. The Brethren at Zwolle

In 1410, the brothers at Zwolle elected Theodore Herxen as
their second rector — the man who for a period of thirty-three

years was to become the acknowledged leader of the Devotio Moderna. Born in 1381, he had received his early education at Deventer. He was one of those devout school boys who were so kindly treated by the brethren of the House of Florentius. As a faithful follower of Gerard Groote, he wanted to train his inner self somewhere in a Carthusian monastery. One day he came to John Vos, prior at Windesheim, and asked him for advice. The prior saw at once how easily this pious youth could be persuaded to enter his monastery. Furthermore, he was rich in earthly possessions, which Windesheim would be able to use to advantage. True, the young man had thus far hesitated to become a monk, inasmuch as his desire to win other souls for Christ had been urging him to remain in the world among people. The monastic state, however, was at that time considered by most religious folk as vastly superior to that of a preacher who had not taken the three vows. Now it happened that in those days the doctrine of self-denial still remained indelibly engraved in the hearts of Groote's disciples. Accordingly, the prior of Windesheim told the young man: "Do not enter this or any other monastery, but go to Gerard Scadde of Calcar, rector of the brethren at Zwolle, and ask him for admission into their house."[19]

On the 23rd of December, 1409, Gerard Scadde of Calcar died. Although Theodore Herxen was only twenty-nine, the brethren, struck by his great religious fervor, and aware of the superiority of his talents as educator, preacher, and scholar, elected him rector in Gerard's place. Herxen was at once a zealous preacher, a skillful teacher, and a versatile writer. How one could most successfully win children and youths for Christ's kingdom he set forth in three of his works, called: *A Book showing how to draw the Little Ones to Christ, A Treatise concerning the Drawing of Youths to Christ,* and *A Book concerning the Praiseworthy Efforts of the Brethren in drawing the Little Ones to Christ.* The Brethren of the Common Life were conscientiously imitating Groote in trying to secure recruits from the boys and girls (though chiefly boys) for God's army on earth. Theodore himself undoubtedly spent many an hour giving these boys religious instruction. Later he wrote down the results of his experiences, in the three above-named treatises.

As preacher and author he won great fame, for he preached to the people in their own language. Two big books were composed by him for laymen, which the brethren used to read from to the people on holidays. Among the many other works he wrote was a book called *Devout Exercises,* which was read a great deal in his time. From far and near people came to him for advice and instruction,[21] and the brethren themselves stood in such awe of him that a mere look of his would send them quailing with fear to their respective rooms. All devout men and women of Zwolle and its environment revered this pious leader of the Devotio Moderna. It was whispered among them that he held daily converse with angels.

His influence must have been great upon some few at least among the many boys who came to him, as their custom was, to confess their sins. The sources tell of a very wayward son of a magistrate at Woudrichem, how his father had sent him to a monastery, whence he had returned home in a short time. Shortly after that he had been sent to Zwolle to attend school. Here he comported himself in a most disgraceful manner. The gravest misdemeanors were but trifles to him. One day he came to Herxen to tell what he had done and ask for absolution. "My dear boy," the rector replied, "no human being can absolve you from your sins, not on account of their great number, but of your state of mind. Not until you have utterly annihilated that evil force within you which prevents you from doing penance, not until you have firmly resolved to commit not one of these offenses any longer, can I absolve you from the guilt which now weighs down upon your soul. Go, and I will pray for you; try to sin no more, and I will struggle with you; and then return unto me once more. Then we shall rejoice together and praise the Lord for his grace, for I must wait till God himself forgives you, ere I can absolve you from sin." The young reprobate went away, vaguely wondering why he, the well-favored son of a prominent magistrate, should be treated thus. But the rector of the brethren did not forget him, for he had been reminded by this youthful sinner of certain parables mentioned in the Gospels, which speak of the great joy in heaven caused by the sincere repentance of truly humble sinners. Finally, through love and sympathy, Herxen gained his end. The boy returned and was absolved.[22]

A man like this was bound to make enemies. Groote had preached the same views about repentance; he too had drawn a careful distinction between the true Church, consisting of a small group of devout believers, and the outer court, where many clergymen were dwelling. Groote, the first leader of the Devotio Moderna, had ruthlessly torn down the idols of indolence, self-indulgence, and mammon worship. His example was now being followed by Theodore Herxen, the fourth and last universally recognized leader of the same movement. And since Groote had been persecuted Herxen could hardly escape the same fate.

There was a certain Liefard, rector of the Sisters of the Common Life in one of their six houses at Zwolle, who had failed to perform his duties as rector and confessor. As Liefard had many rich friends at Zwolle, Herxen was unable to remove him from his office. In the meantime the news of Liefard's scandalous behavior reached the bishop of Utrecht, and the man was imprisoned. Shortly before the imprisonment Liefard's friend, Theodore Henso, pastor at Zwolle, together with cathedral chapter of St. Lebwin at Deventer had begun to compel the Sisters of the Common Life at Zwolle to confess to the chaplains of his parish. This had grieved Herxen very much, for evidently the chaplains in question did not take life so seriously as one might expect of servants of Christ. Herxen went to Cologne, but the archiepiscopal curia of that city was bribed by his enemies at Deventer and Zwolle, wherefore he was now threatened with excommunication. One day the kind, old rector was hissed out of the church by a shouting mob, who, instigated by their spiritual father, cried: "Throw the Beghard into the water." The pastor even prohibited Herxen from hearing confessions of the school boys, although one of his predecessors had given Herxen this privilege, while it had been confirmed by Frederick van Blankenheim bishop of Utrecht.[23]

Herxen was followed by Albert Paep of Calcar (1457-1482). Thinking to divert for a time at least the dangers of attack from the various office-holders in the church of St. Michael he invited the city council and the vicars of the local parish to supper one day. The magistrates were very sociable, but the vicars adopted a haughty attitude toward the humble brethren. "We discovered" says the chronicler," "that we had made no progress, for the vicars did not want to be corrected by us."[24] Although he does not tell us what the brethren wished to discuss with the vicars, we can easily guess their intention. It had long been the custom among the Brethren of the Common Life to confess their own faults to each other, as Zerbolt had pointed out in his *On the Common Life*. Christ had warned his disciples never to speak evil of any one, except to the person who committed the evil in question. That there was a great deal amiss with the Church during the closing years of the fifteenth century must have been apparent to all honest men and women. It had been one of Groote's chief tasks to point out the existing evils, but it was to the clergy themselves in his *Sermon against the Immoral Clergy*. When he addressed the clergy, he spoke of their many faults, and the people's shortcomings were exposed in the people's presence. Such had been Groote's method in trying to reform the Church. His reformation had been continued by the Brethren of the Common Life. But exactly where he had met with the strongest resistance, they also were opposed. Hence Albert Paep, the third rector at Zwolle, had to cancel those suppers with the vicars of the local parish.

Albert Paep was in turn followed by other rectors, whose names need not be mentioned here; and as was the case with the house at Deventer, a few brief remarks about the buildings belonging to the society will suffice. Mention has been made of the chief building, the "House of Gregory," where the brethren themselves lived. Several other buildings were used to house the great crowds of school boys from Frisia, Flanders, Brabant, Westphalia, Trier, Cologne, Liége and Holland. There was the *"Domus divitum scolarium* ("House for Rich Boys") for boys with means; the *"Domus vicina"* ("House next door"), or *"Parva domus"* ("Small House"), also for those whose expenses were paid by their parents or guardians; the *"Domus pro mediocribus"* ("House for the Middle Classes"), where boys were lodged who paid part of their expenses; and the *"Domus pauperum scolarium"* ("House for Poor Students".) As for the property donated to the Brethren of the Common Life at Zwolle, a long list of documents has been published by Dr. Schoengen, which shows that the brethren had other sources of income besides the copying of books.[25]

3. Other Houses of the Brotherhood

The brethren-houses of Deventer and Zwolle until the year 1520, were the two chief centers of the Devotio Moderna outside of the monasteries. By these two all the other houses of the new brotherhood were founded, either directly or indirectly. As early as the year 1395, Radewijns, the first rector of the brethren at Deventer, was asked to found a congregation at Amersfoort. Three clerks were sent by him in the same year.[26] The next place in the Netherlands to ask for a few missionaries of the common life, was the city of Delft, where the magistrates, having heard of the rising fame and the good works of the brethren at Deventer, were anxious to secure a similar society of copyists and teachers. The procurator of the "Nova Domus" together with other members of the house at Deventer were sent to Delft. This seems to have occurred in the year 1403.[27] There also was a house at Hoorn for a few years,[28] which must be looked upon as a daughter-institution of the house at Deventer.

The first house founded by the men of Zwolle was that of Albergen, in eastern Overyssel. Its foundation took place in the year 1406.[29] The next house was founded in 1407, at Hulsbergen near Hattem, a short distance west of the Yssel,[30] and the one after that in 1424, at 's-Hertogenbosch.[31] In 1425, the brethren at Zwolle were compelled to leave their house on account of an interdict.[32]   They moved to Doesburg, where a new community was established in 1426.[33]   The house at Groningen was founded between 1426 and 1432,[34] that of Harderwijk on the Zuiderzee in 1441, also by the brethren of Zwolle, the one at Gouda in 1445 by the brethren at Delft,[35] at Utrecht in 1474, also by the house at Delft,[36] and at Nijmegen in 1469 or 1470, by the brethren of 's-Hertogenbosch.[37]   The Brethren of the Common Life also had a house at Berlikum in Friesland,[38] and at Orten in Brabant but at present we know very little about its history.   The same is true of those other houses which may have existed without leaving us any records of their history.   For as long as the minutes of the annual meetings held by the Brethren of the Common Life of the above-named houses at Zwolle have not been discovered, we shall know very little about the less important houses.

In Germany, the brethren had many houses.   There was a congregation at Münster from the year 1400, founded by Henry of Ahaus, a missionary of the Deventer house.[39]   The same Henry of Ahaus instituted a society at Cologne in the year 1417 or earlier.[40]   There was a congregation at Osterberg near Osnabrück as early as the year 1410, and one at Osnabrück from 1415, at Herford from 1428, at Wesel from 1436, and at Hildesheim since 1440.   The brethren at Cologne founded the houses at Wiesbaden, Butzbach near Mainz, Königstein on the Taunus, and Wolf on the Moselle.   There were important houses at Rostock, Magdeburg, Marburg, Cassel, and Emmerich, and less important ones in Württemberg; also one at Kempen, and at Culm in Poland.[41]   The first comprehensive account of the work done by the Brotherhood of the Common Life in the German lands is that by Professor William Landeen, whose dissertation is entitled, *The Devotio Moderna in Germany*.   He has shown that the famous Professor Gabriel Biel was Rector of the house at Schönbuch.   Another distinguished member was Paracelsus.

In the Southern Low Countries houses of the Brethren of the Common Life were founded at Ghent, Antwerp, Brussels, Grammont, Mechlin, Cambray, Liége, Louvain, and Wynoksberg.[42]

The Sisters of the Common Life also succeeded in founding a large number of houses, particularly in the Yssel valley. At Deventer they had five houses.[48] At Zwolle there were six.[4] There were three houses at Zutphen, two at Doesburg, Kampen and Lochem, two at Utrecht, one at Arnhem, Doetinchem, Gorinchem, and a host of other places.[45] The "House of Master Gerard" at Deventer, the first institution, founded a community at Sonsbeke, Xanten, Essen, and Cologne,[46] and reformed the houses at Neuss, Calcar and Emmerich. The houses of the brethren at Zwolle had charge of nineteen sister-houses.[47]

Not all of the houses founded by the brethren or sisters of Deventer and Zwolle were equally prosperous, however. We have seen how the first institution of the brothers at Zwolle was a failure, inasmuch as the men had left the city for a community where only a few people were found to give them employment and still fewer school boys. Nearly all the brethren at Amersfoort joined the Fransicans in 1399.[48] Between 1399 and 1405, the house regained part of its former strength, but in 1405 the majority of its members entered the monastery of St. Andriescamp, and in 1415 became Augustinian Canons Regular of the Windesheim Congregation.[49] Two years afterwards, however, they left the monastery,[50] and from that time the success of the house at Amersfoort was assured. At Delft the brothers were compelled by circumstances to exchange their rules for those of the third rule of St. Francis. In 1433, they joined the Augstinians Regular. Before 1436, the house was again occupied by Brethren of the Common Life, who remained there as such until Delft became Calvinistic. The house at Hoorn perished without leaving records of perceptible influence, which may also be said of the house at Berlikum. As for the institution founded at Albergen in 1406, it was changed into a monastery of the Windesheim Congregation in the year 1447.[51] Albergen evidently was too small a place to support a brethren-house. After the year 1447, it became the policy of the brothers at Deventer and Zwolle to recognize no houses founded in small towns. When the institution at Gouda for example asked for such official recognition, it was refused, as Gouda was said to be too small and too poor a place.[52] Not until 1456, that is, eleven years after the foundation of the house at Gouda, was it accepted as a member of the organization.[53]

At Culm in Poland (Culm became a part of Poland in 1466), near the frontier of Prussia, the brethren were confronted with difficulties of an entirely different nature. They had been invited by a certain Balthasar, a native of East Prussia, who, attracted by the fame of the school at Zwolle, had left his home in search of western culture. It was no small matter to migrate to so distant a country; nevertheless the brethren readily had granted Balthasar's request. Three men were sent in 1472. The country around Culm was not so pleasant a sight as the green pastures along the Yssel, or the smiling fields near Zwolle. The town itself contained but a few inhabitants, and not a single carpenter among them. A little hut was given to the brethren — very shabby, and unfurnished, but it was love which prompted the owners to give it to them. Others there were, however, who vaguely wondered what those three foreigners wanted in lonely Culm. The brethren responded: "We have come here to instruct your children in the 'sciences' and virtues, as we are doing in the bishopric of Utrecht." Indescribable were the hardships which the brethren underwent. It was not long before the mendicant monks began to attack them, who themselves were not even keeping their own vows. Other monks there were not. The three brethren remaind there for two years; then they could hold out no longer. Two of the three, together with the rector of the school they had founded at Culm, returned to Zwolle, but not in despair. The harvest was great, they said, and the laborers few. They should send some experienced brethren together with a few students, and liberally provide them with funds. After some deliberation the request was granted. Several brethren were sent from time to time, and large sums of money. A flourishing school was founded, which in cooperation with the labors of the brethren finally resulted in the moral and intellectual uplift of a considerable part of East Prussia and Poland.[54]

Great as were the difficulties which the Brethren of the Common Life had to face, the sisters were as a rule still more hardly pressed. We must never lose sight of the fact that they were living in an age when the superiority of the monastic state was almost universally recognized. As long as those disciples of Groote upon whom part of the master's spirit seemed to have descended, remained near them, they were able to hold their own. But about the year 1400 the majority of the communities were compelled to adopt the third rule of St. Francis, particularly those so far removed from the Yssel valley that they lost contact with the houses at Deventer and Zwolle.[55] Although the Brethren and Sisters of the Common Life were not hostile to monasticism, they were always and everywhere fighting the battle of self-preservation against the various monastic orders. A great many of the noblest monks in the Low Countries, Germany, and Northern France had proceeded from the ranks of the new brotherhood, and yet the whole institution was a living protest against the decadent monasticism of the fifteenth century. Groote's brotherhood was one of the chief causes of that phase of the Reformation which in certain regions involved the disappearance of monasticism, and everywhere in the West produced a growing desire for more personal faith, more religion in the schools, more knowledge of the Bible, a saner method of discipline, and a reaction against all manner of empty formalism, including the return to the use of the people's language, be it Dutch, German, French, or English.

4. General Characteristics

How did the Brethren of the Common Life usually pass their time, and what were the most characteristic features of their organization? Their constitutions which were practically uniform in Germany, and nearly so in the Low Countries, together with a number of chronicles, treatises, and biographies, enable us to gain a fairly accurate knowledge of their daily work, habits, and ideals.

"Our house was founded," the brethren of Deventer and Zwolle wrote, "with the intention that priests and clerics might live there, supported by their own manual labor, namely, the copying of books, and the returns from certain estates; attend church with devotion, obey the prelates, wear simple clothing, preserve the canons and decrees of the saints, practise religious exercises, and lead not only irreproachable, but exemplary lives, in order that they may serve God and perchance induce others to seek salvation. Since the final end of religion consists in purity of heart, without which we shall see perfection in vain, let it be our daily aim to purge our poisoned hearts from sin, so that in the first place we may learn to know ourselves, pass judgment upon the vices and passions of our minds, and endeavor with all our strength to eradicate them; despise temporal gain, crush selfish desires, aid others in overcoming sin, and concentrate our energy on the acquisition of true virtues, such as humility, love, chastity, patience, and obedience. Toward this end we must direct all our spiritual exercises: prayer, meditation, reading, manual labor, watching, fasting — in short, the harmonious development of our internal and external powers."[56]

"Whereas the fear of the Lord is necessary to those who wish to overcome evil, it is expedient for each of us to meditate on such subjects as induce man to fear the Lord, like sin, death, judgment, and hell. But lest continued fear might engender dejection and despair, we shall have to add more hopeful subject matter for meditation, such as the kingdom of heaven, the blessings of God, the life of Jesus Christ, and his passion. These subjects we shall arrange in such a way that on Saturdays we shall meditate on sin, Sundays on the kingdom of heaven, Mondays on death, Tuesdays on the blessings of God, Wednesdays on the final judgment, Thursdays on the pains of hell, and Fridays on the passion of Christ."[57]

The constitutions further state that the brethren were to rise between three and four o'clock in the morning (later shortly before five), preparing themselves at once for prayer and the reading of certain prescribed selections. All the members of the house were expected to attend the daily mass, and were exhorted to free their mind from all distractions, "thus preparing themselves, as it were, for a spiritual communion."

Since it was considered most beneficial for all men to perform some manual labor every day, the brethren would be expected to spend several hours a day in copying religious books, or else in performing other tasks. But lest the spirit suffer from neglect, they should occasionally utter short prayers, called "ejaculations." The brethren were to consume their meals in silence, in order that they might pay proper attention to the reading of a selection from the Bible. After supper they could do as they pleased in their own rooms till eight o'clock. At eight all guests would have to leave the house. The doors were shut fast, and silence was observed till half past eight, when they went to bed.

On Sundays and holidays certain passages in the Scriptures were read and explained; and in this connection there was opportunity for general discussion, when each member of the house could freely express his opinions, as long as he did not indulge in impractical disputes and argumentations. The school boys and other people were invited to attend the discussions which were held in the vernacular.[58] The influence thus exerted upon the common people by the brethren is incalculable. For not only were there a great many among them whose fame as orators brought people long distances to hear them, but it was their combined, their continued efforts, which must have brought tangible results, considering the great number of holy days they observed. Not one of them was as famous as a Brugman, Wycliff, Hus, or Savonarola, but they formed a vast organization. Their voices were seldom heard on the streets, for they wished to avoid publicity. Nevertheless, their influence, though not always manifested visibly, reached the minds of thousands, while the books they circulated reached still larger numbers. They continued their labors in an orderly way. Like the persistent drops of water, which in the course of time even form impressions on the most solid rocks, so did the efforts of the Brethren of the Common Life affect the most perverse sinners. One could always rely on their addresses. The brethren were always ready to help the sick and comfort the

afflicted. And the school boys could always get a room in their
dormitories, no matter whether they were able to pay for them
or not. By avoiding notoriety and scandal, by preaching reform
to all men and women without stressing unduly the faults of the
clergy, the brethren labored — unnoticed by those historians
who record only the interruptions against the course of nature,
against peaceful reform and bloodless revolution, thereby ignoring the great movement which throughout the fifteenth and sixteenth centuries helped to change the medieval mind into the
modern mind.

The most interesting feature about the brethren's labors as
preachers was their informal addresses. On Sundays and holy
days the people were accustomed to assemble in the room des-
ignated for this purpose. A chapter of the Bible was read in the
people's language which contained some practical advice or
instruction. Those passages in particular were selected which
in very plain words taught the people how to "extinguish vice,
acquire virtue, despise worldly things, and fear the Lord."
Thereupon all members of the house, in so far as they were
gifted by nature to act as spiritual guides of the masses, would
be expected to exhort the people, either separately in their
respective rooms, or in addressing the whole assembly in turns.
But they were not to preach, the constitutions[59] state — merely
to exhort and instruct. Confession of sins, and mutual correction were looked upon by the brethren as very helpful means
of combatting evil.

As time went on the Brethren of the Common Life found it
necessary to appoint rectors, procurators, librarians, and several
other office-holders. In the constitutions of the houses at Deventer and Zwolle the duties of the rector, procurator, librarian,
tailor, and nurse were carefully outlined; several other offices
were treated together in one chapter, though later they were
more elaborately discussed in the constitutions used by the German houses, belonging to the "Colloquium of Münster."[60]

The houses of the Brethren of the Common Life in the Low
Countries used to send representatives to their annual meeting,
called "Colloquium Zwollense." Another means of preserving

discipline and unity were the annual visitations by two rectors, preferably those of Zwolle and Deventer.[61] The houses in Germany, of which the one at Münster was the chief, also were visited in the same manner.[62] There also were held monthly meetings in each house, where divers matters relating to discipline, religious exercises, or manual labor could be discussed. Each house should, if possible, have four priests and some other members of the clergy. If somebody applied for admission, the brethren were required to examine his physical condition, and his mental equipment; he should be asked from which country he had come. He would be asked, also, whether he could write, and loved to read books. In case he was found to be in good health and of sound mind and habits, he would be allowed to remain in the house for two or three months, whereupon he might be promoted to a further trial of ten or twelve months. After this lapse of time he might become a Brother of the Common Life, having first sworn before a notary public and in the presence of some witnesses that he renounced all claim to any property of his own. Members could be expelled in case of ill-behavior. The brethren were exhorted to preserve mutual love, peace, and harmony, and although none of them would be expected to take the vows of chastity and obedience, nevertheless they all should strive to cultivate these virtues.[63] The virtue of humility in particular was highly extolled by the brethren at Deventer and Zwolle. No member of the brotherhood was to have any property of his own, as it had been ceded by him to the house on being admitted as a member there. They were to spend a part of their income to meet current expenses, and the remainder for the relief of the poor.[64] As for the other regulations found in the various constitutions, they need not be commented upon here.[65]

The Brethren and Sisters of the Common Life may well be called practical mystics, in distinction from such men as John Ruysbroeck. Love for their neighbor impelled them to work among the people in the cities. Their highest aim was the reformation of the Church, which could most effectively be done, they thought, by educating the youths of the land, and by instructing the common people in the essentials of the Christian religion. They paid much attention to their "spiritual natures," or their "inner selves." Formed in the image of God, as they believed, and assured by Christ that the kingdom of heaven is found within the human heart, they continually strove to explore their inner lives, to unite their inner selves with God or Christ, and thus regain their lost heritage. They were also much given to meditation.

As Christian mystics they constantly aimed to imitate the lives of Christ, and the apostles. They loved to seek parallels between Christ's life and their own, for their religion was one of action, of deeds. Groote had instructed them to read the Gospels and the lives of the Church Fathers in preference to other books, as the former contained biographies. Paul's Epistles and the various books of the Old Testament were by no means neglected by them, however. As they read the Acts of the Apostles, the thought must often have struck them that it was not at all necessary for a good Christian to seek refuge in a monastery. At any rate, their desire to win ever more souls for Christ kept them in the cities. "We have decided," the Brethren of the Common Life at Zwolle wrote 1415, "to live in cities, in order that we may be able to give advice and instruction to clerics and other persons who wish to serve the Lord."[66] One of the most successful ways by which the brothers at Deventer won the hearts of young men, was the church drama.[67] Theodore Herxen, as we saw above, devoted several treatises to the "art of drawing boys to God." Both the Brethren and the Sisters of the Common Life were particularly fond of finding practical lessons in the selections read from the Scriptures at their meals. These lessons they tried to remember for the purpose of applying them on specific occasions, and for the sake of mutual exhortation. Another feature of their practical mysticism was the collection of excerpts from writings perused by them. These were called "good points" or "rapiaria."[68] Special notebooks or slips of paper were at all times kept in readiness in order to improve their knowledge.[69]

The Brethren and Sisters of the Common Life, in conscientiously following Christ, gloried in self-denial, poverty, humility, and obedience, but if we bear in mind the circumstances under which they had founded and sought to develop their institution, we may say that their outlook upon life was quite free from excessive asceticism. True, they lived very soberly: their meals were extremely simple, their clothing at first scarcely respectable. But whatever may have been their worst form of mortifying the flesh, their asceticism was of a mild nature.[70] And as time went on, experience taught them that stinting the body does in no way enhance the beauty of the soul, or the dignity of the spirit. Consequently, we find that after the year 1400, they dressed more properly, used more wholesome meals, reduced the number of hours devoted to copying books, took more exercises in the open air, lived less estranged from "worldly" people, and also acquired more respect for learning as a final end.[71]

.5 The Brethren as Educators

It has often been asserted by scholars of late that the Brethren of the Common Life paid little or no attention to education. On the other hand one also frequently reads statements to the effect that they even made their living by teaching. Once again the sources should be consulted, rather than the conflicting opinions of modern scholars. In the first place, then, let it be understood that the brothers at Deventer never had a real school of their own there, nor did any of their members teach in the cathedral school of that city until several years after the death of Radewijns.[72] There were two schools at Deventer during the days of Groote and Radewijns.[73] From 1378 till 1381, they were both supervised by William Vroede, Groote's friend, who upon Groote's advice brought about certain reforms in these two schools.[74] As rector of the cathedral school he was succeeded by John Lubberts (1381-1385),[75] and not by Florentius Radewijns, as some writers believe.

At Zwolle John Cele was rector of the city school from 1375 1417.[76] His educational labors, which were imitated at Deven-

ter, together with the assistance freely accorded to the school
boys by the Brethren of the Common Life and the other disciples of Groote at Deventer and Zwolle, were causes which made
the schools of Zwolle and Deventer famous long before the days
of Hegius. It will be remembered that under the administra-
tion of Cele the attendance at the school at Zwolle rose to 1200.
The hearty welcome extended by those pious matrons and the
kind-hearted brethren must have acted as a very powerful mag-
net for the boys who had come from Poland, the interior of
Germany, the upper Rhine valley, and the distant shores of
Flanders, where on their return they extended the influence of
the school. The brothers themselves received their interest in
education from Groote and Cele. Groote had always laid stress
on the importance of offering a better education to future pas-
tors. Hence his friendship with the teachers at Deventer and
Zwolle. The brethren, in inheriting most of Groote's ideals,
soon shared his views on the need of a better education, particularly for those boys who intended some day to join the ranks
of the clergy. Groote's chief aim had been the reform of the
Church; the surest and quickest way to reach that happy end
in his opinion was the training of young men. This training
should by no means exclude the study of literature, pagan or
classic as well as Christian; while grammar, rhetoric, logic,
mathematics, and philosophy were to retain their places in the
curriculum. Cele materialized Groote's plans at Zwolle, aided
as he was by the brethren in that city. Not long after his death
the reform inaugurated by him spread to Deventer and many
other places where Groote's disciples had founded brethren-
houses.

At Amersfoort the brethren never had a school of their own,
and for more than a century after the foundation of their home,
none of them seem to have taught in that city. We find, however,
that in 1529, one of the brothers was forbidden to teach school
by the city council, at least until the quarrel between him and
the rector of the city school was settled. During the years 1530
and 1531, the magistrates were trying to secure a new rector for
their school, and asked the brothers to pay his salary, "as had

been the custom before."[77]   The brethren, therefore, appear to have been interested in the local school. At Cassel they taught school in their own house. At Culm the brethren, as was indicated above, founded a splendid new school, which helped to introduce the best fruits of Western education into East Prussia and Poland. At Delft twelve poor boys were usually provided by the brethren with food, clothing, and lodging. Whereas during the first period of their history in Delft they sent these boys to the public school for instruction, later on the latter were taught by the brethren themselves. A boarding school was founded at Doesburg, while at Gouda, Ghent, and Grammont they had schools of their own, as well as at Groningen, 's-Hertogenbosch, Liége, Magdeburg, Marburg, Nijmegen, Rostock, and Utrecht. At Mechlin they formed part of the local school-board. Doubtless the brethren in other cities conducted a like work.[78]

The most important schools were found at Deventer, Zwolle, and Münster, where also the most influential brethren-houses had been established. A complete proof of the excellence of these schools was given by John Sturm, the celebrated rector at Strasbourg, when he outlined the plans of his "gymnasium" to the magistrates of the Alsatian metropolis.[79] He did not recommend the schools of Cologne, of Louvain, and of Trier, and preferred Deventer to Utrecht. Nor was Sturm the only teacher who acknowledged the debt he owed to Cele's followers, as will be seen later.

John Cele was succeeded as rector of the town school at Zwolle by Livinius of Middelburg, one of Groote's followers,[80] and he in turn by Herman Kerstken. About the year 1432, John van Dalen was appointed rector; he helped to usher in a second period of prosperity enjoyed by the public school at Zwolle, aided as he was by the Brethren of the Common Life.[81] Again several hundred boys came flocking to Zwolle from all directions.[82] Several buildings had to be erected by the brothers to lodge them, but even these did not suffice. Many kind mothers were induced to open their doors to one or more of them. Their own mothers and aunts had done so in the days of John Cele, when

they themselves had often asked where all those strangers had
come from; and many a pious father had once gone to that same
school, where he had been taught so well that for many years the
maxims of Zwolle's learned teacher were upon his lips, when
friends of his youth would come to visit him![83]

It is no wonder that among all those boys at least a few great
minds were found. And where Groote's ideas were acted upon
with so much tender devotion, where so much love was lavished
upon responsive hearts, and such ideals were expounded as the
Imitation of Christ contained, the school at Zwolle could not
fail to send out once more a host of religious youths. The
names of most of these boys have been lost to memory, and of
the others only a few can be mentioned here. Naturally one
turns first to him who became the most famous educator in
Transapline Europe — to Alexander Hegius.

Hegius was born near the village of Heek in Westphalia in
1433. He was teacher at Wesel in 1474, and from 1475-1483,
taught school at Emmerich, no doubt supported in the usual
way by Brethren of the Common Life, who had a house in each
of these two places, while at Emmerich they had founded two
dormitories for the pupils of the local school. In 1483, Hegius
was appointed rector of the school attached to St. Lebwin's at
Deventer, where he remained until his death in 1498. When
teaching school at Emmerich he had become acquainted with
Agricola, of whom he learned Greek. Gansfort also was an
intimate friend of his, as appears from one of his letters.[84] Anxious to promote the study of the classics, he encouraged his pupils
to learn both Latin and Greek. He himself had been taught
Greek too late to master that language so well as some of his
contemporaries. But he was always eager to learn more, and
diligently read the classics and the Fathers.

Alexander Hegius, though he may be called one of the leading
humanists of the late fifteenth century, as he showed a great interest in the study of the Ancients, was nevertheless too closely
associated with the Brethren of the Common Life to despise the
use of the vernacular, as so many scholars of his time were doing.
As poet, he became the forerunner of the "younger humanists,"

and, although he lacked real poetic enthusiasm, his labors in this direction are nevertheless of historical significance.[85]

His school at Deventer grew to 2200 pupils. This was due in part to the assistance given him by the brethren. At Zwolle he had been instructed in what might be calld the rudiments of Christian education. The ideals of the Christian Renaissance were never opposed to art or learning, as many a manuscript will show us today, written and illuminated as they were by the Augustinian Canons Regular and the Brethren of the Common Life. Before Hegius began the study of Greek, he had managed to attract fifteen hundred pupils to his school at Emmerich. In 1475, he was not yet a humanist in the proper sense of the word. Still his fame had reached the cities of Trier, Cologne, Strasbourg, Liége, Magdeburg, and other centres of learning. His love of poetry, of the Greek language, and of ancient letters in general were not the causes of his early fame. The secret of his success lay deeper than that. It was the favorable circumstances attending the presence of the brothers at Wesel and Emmerich, Hegius' early instruction at Zwolle, and the peculiar bent of his nature which enabled him to become Cele's truest successor. Hegius was not a Petrarch nor a wandering humanist like Agricola or Hermann von dem Busche, to name some of the best types of the true humanists, but he was the greatest educator of Transalpine Europe in the fifteenth century, and the marvelous success he enjoyed as teacher from 1474 till 1498 he owed mainly to the work of two men: Gerard Groote, founder of the Brethren of the Common Life, and John Cele, who inaugurated, upon Groote's advice, the reform which assisted the revival of learning in Northern Europe. This revival till 1455, developed largely independently of the Italian Renaissance and later added the best thoughts of the classics, in so far as they were discovered by Italian humanists, to its great store-house of medieval learning. Hegius, in continuing Cele's work, advocated a reform in the text-books. The *Medulla* was not worth being read any longer, he said.[86] On the last page of his *Invectiva* he gives a list of grammars which should be altered. Throughout this whole essay, in fact, he indicates the need of better text-books.

As for style, he asserted in his *Farrago* that one should appro-
priate the diction of Cicero, Virgil, and Sallust, and imitate the
Italian humanists. The *Disciplina Scholarium*, the *Gemma Gem-
marum*, and the Lexica of Hugutio Brito and John Januen-
sis, should be cast aside as no longer worthy of study.[87]   Here
he does not speak as a true medievalist, but appears to have
absorbed some of the ideas of the Italian Renaissance.

A striking portrait of Hegius was drawn by Butzbach, one of
his last pupils.[88]   It shows him not only a scholar and teacher.
As a true child of the Devotio Moderna, he directed much of his
attention to the relief of the poor, the sick, and the afflicted, a
practice in which he differed from humanists of the Italian type.
When death claimed him,[89] he was followed to the grave by a
mourning crowd of grateful men, women, and children, who
loved and revered him.   All his possessions he had spent in
"helping to extend God's kingdom on earth."   Other humanists
have received greater praise from Erasmus and others, but where
some of his contemporaries were greater scholars, his influence
upon the several thousands pupils sent out by him to reform the
Church in the Low Countries, Germany, and France, was greater
than that of a mere scholar.   For instance, Agricola and Mutian
Rufus did not leave thousands of students behind who eagerly
and unitedly carried out their plans for reform in school, church,
and monastery.   They were not constructive, though great
critics.   Butzbach rightly pointed out the difference between the
thorough reform instituted by Hegius and the ineffective work
of the shifting, homeless humanists of the Erfurt type. "Now-
adays," he says, "one only has to give presents in order to get a
degree.   Knowledge is no longer the first essential."[90]

It was easy enough for the wandering Bohemians of learning
in the early sixteenth century to poke fun at existing conditions.
A negative criticism is easy.   When it came to actual reform,
however, it was the school at Deventer which furnished the required missionaries.   Thus it had been in the early years of the
fifteenth century, and so it remained throughout the whole
life-time of Hegius.   The priors were always glad to get recruits
from Deventer.[91]   While certain contemporaries of his, like the

celebrated Anton Vrye, or Liber, were soon forgotten after their death, Hegius continued to be a living force in the hamlets and cities of the Yssel valley and beyond.[92]

During the rectorate of Hegius, then, Deventer was one of the chief centers of the movement usually referred to as the German Renaissance. The best thoughts of the Italian Renaissance were absorbed at Deventer and Zwolle, and from there some entered Germany, now transformed by the Devotio Moderna, which had become an intellectual movement, though its chief aim remained the restoration of the Church in all its members.[93] An index of how strong an intellectual movement this was, is the fact that many classics were issued from the presses at Deventer before 1500: more than four hundred and fifty works.[94]

One of the best known humanists of the Yssel valley type was Ortwin Gratius, a man of great learning, and sound judgment. Few of his contemporaries were such warm advocates of the revival of ancient learning as he; not many equalled his scholarly equipment; his poems were unusually fine, his Latin quite praiseworthy. Few men have ever been so shamefully and so unjustly attacked as he, not only by his contemporaries but also by later writers. The investigations of three modern historians, however, have vindicated his claim to the title of Christian humanist, scholar, poet, and educator.[95]

Much might be written about other pupils of the Brethren of the Common Life, some of whom taught school while they were members of the celebrated brotherhood. Thus the schools at Deventer and Zwolle not only served as a means of improving intellectual standards among the clergy, but offered preparatory courses for students intending to enter the universities, and also sent out a great number of teachers to other cities. So great was their number that in the Netherlands scarcely a school could be found during the opening years of the sixteenth century, where there was not felt at least some connection with the Yssel valley "gymnasia."[96] In Germany at that time, and throughout the preceding century, if one were to study the origins of each of the early secondary schools throughout the

North and West, he would undoubtedly be able to trace the influence of Deventer and Zwolle. Mention can only be made here of the two chief centers of the German Renaissance, that is, the two schools which contributed most largely to the dissemination of learning in Germany from 1450 till 1520 — the schools of Schlettstadt and Münster.

For several centuries Strasbourg had been the ecclesiastical and intellectual metropolis of Alsace. With Trier, Cologne, Liége, Aachen, and Utrecht it had possessed a sort of educational monopoly in the regions which once had separated Germany from France. But conditions did not always remain thus. Cologne and Trier began to send their most promising sons to little Zwolle, which was only an insignificant parish in the diocese of Utrecht, but the town of Cele's school. It was not long before Alsace developed a similar situation.

A Westphalian teacher, named Louis Dringenberg, who had been trained at Deventer,[97] came to Schlettstadt in 1441. Here for a period of 36 years, he was rector of the public or town school.[98] There were no Brethren of the Common Life in Schlettstadt, which may account for the fact that he was unable to draw such vast numbers of pupils to his school as Cele had done to Zwolle, but this school at Schlettstadt eventually surpassed that at Strasbourg. The reason was given by a learned author: "While thus Strasbourg and most other cities lagged behind, Schlettstadt already possessed a flourishing school. Founded about the middle of the fifteenth century and supervised by the magistrates, its rector was the Westphalian Louis Dringenberg, who had carried hither the spirit and method of the Brethren of the Common Life."[99] More to the point is the following statement by G. C. Knod, another Alsatian scholar of note: "This spirit of pedagogical skill and pious wisdom, as it prevailed in the schools of the Brethren of the Common Life, had also asserted itself in the town school of Schlettstadt. It was the first school conducted by laymen in South-German regions which, in conscious deviation from the clerical institutions, outlined its scope and method after the humanistic fashion."[100]

In several cities the Brethren of the Common Life had schools
of their own, as at Rostock, Ghent, Liége, and Utrecht, while in
almost every city where they had a house one or more of the
members of the brotherhood became school teachers, particularly after the year 1450, when, as time went on, the printed type
made it unnecessary for them to continue their work as copyists.
If one takes these facts into consideration, one can form a better
opinion of the way in which Dringenberg brought this new
"pedagogical spirit of the Brethren of the Common Life" from
Deventer to Schlettstadt. He doubtless adopted much of the
course he had followed at Deventer, where the teachers used
Cele's method of combining sound religious instruction with a
well-selected list of studies, took due care of the pupils' individual needs, preferred kind warnings to harsh punishment,
sought to inculcate a love for individual research by letting
pupils delve among the classics rather than confine themselves
to text-books, and taught the boys the use of their vernacular
as well. This method Dringenberg introduced at Schlettstadt.
His successors continued his method in general.[101]

At Münster the Brethren of the Common Life founded a
house as early as the year 1400. They did not found a school at
that time, but aroused an interest in learning, which was very
great during the second half of the fifteenth century.[102] This
fact has been established by the research of Dr. Bömer, the librarian of the university at Münster.[103] Münster in the fifteenth
century became the great gate-way through which the religious and educational reforms of Groote's followers entered Germany, passing Almelo, Frenswegen, Schüttorf, and Coesveld to
Münster, and beyond to Rostock, Hildesheim, Magdeburg and
even to Cologne and the Upper Rhine valley.[104]

Now it happened, as we saw, that both at Zwolle and at Deventer the schools were reformed and rendered famous mostly
by men who were connected with the brotherhood. At Münster,
when eventually the cathedral school was reformed, it was by
Rudolph von Langen, who had attended school at Zwolle with
Alexander Hegius.

Impressed by the fame of Deventer's school, Von Langen believed that the school of the ancient and celebrated cathedral of his own city should at least equal St. Lebwin's at Deventer in luster. To secure a good rector, it has been said that he asked his old friend Hegius to come, but the sources leave the question undecided.[105]   Von Langen appointed Timan Kemener, a pupil of Hegius, and in the year 1500 a thorough-going reform of Münster's cathedral school began.   His successor, John Murmellius, a native of Roermond, continued the work of educational reform.   He had studied at Deventer and Cologne, and in 1500 we find him teaching school at Münster under the direction of Timan Kemener.   In the cathedral school at Münster he taught till 1507, in the school of St. Martin, from 1507 till 1512, and from 1512 till 1513, again in the cathedral school.

Few men so faithfully followed the policy outlined by Gerard Groote, and first practised by John Cele at Zwolle, Hegius at Emmerich and Deventer, and Dringenberg at Schlettstadt, as Murmellius.   He cared little for mere style and mere eloquence. Education would be a complete failure, he taught, if one concentrated all his energy on oratory and style.[105]   He freely criticized the lives of bad priests and monks, as Groote also had done, and in his attack on the decadent forms of scholasticism so prevalent in his day, he simply repeated what Groote had said.   He did not direct his assaults against philosophy, but against empty phrases, devoid of practical contents.   To roam about the continent in search of fame and honor, as many mere humanists were doing, was a vocation not suited to his character. Not the love of self, he said, but the glory and honor of God should be the final aim of all instruction; all knowledge was useless without the acquisition of virtue.[107]   Whereas many leaders of the Italian Renaissance studied the classics for style only, the men of Deventer, Zwolle, Schlettstadt, and Münster delved into the same mine and found there fine phrases, but greater treasures in wisdom.   When they wrote, they proved themselves good stylists too.   Murmellius, though he died at thirty-seven published fifty works in fifteen years, some of which were wonderful store-houses of pedagogical, literary, philosophical, and historical value.[108]   Considering his distinguished career as a teacher, it is astonishing how he contrived to produce so much.   His text-books were popular in Germany for several generations; one of them passed through seventy-seven editions, and was used in the schools till 1800.[109] His *Pappa Puerorum* was published thirty-two times in less than sixty years.   In editing both classic and Christian writers he became a mighty force in the realm of revived learning.[110]   In laying proper stress on physical and moral improvement, on grammatical constructions, the proper study of art and literature, he aimed at that harmonious development of character which was possessed by the Greeks of old.[112]   His commentary on Boethius shows how well he was acquainted with the classics.   One remarkable feature about his works is the simple, clear style, the absence of pompous expressions.   Better than most scholars of his time he knew how to compress brilliant thoughts into brief sentences — a rare quality in a humanist of the early sixteenth century.   And though he indulged in the use of satire, as was usual at that time, his language remained remarkably free from revengeful or spiteful sarcasm, as was unusual.

Murmellius was assisted and followed at Münster by other noteworthy teachers, such as John Pering, a former pupil of Hegius; Joseph Horlenius, a pupil of Pering; and Jacob Montanus, later a member of the Brethren of the Common Life at Herford, and a friend of Luther.[112]

The fact is, Münster and Deventer sent out so vast a host of really great scholars and teachers that it is quite impossible to enumerate them.   Under their leadership practically all the larger schools in Western Germany were organized and reformed.   Through them the benevolent influence of Cele's work found its way into many a city where no Brethren of the Common Life were found, such as Attendorn, Dortmund, Düsseldorf, Eisleben, Essen, Lübeck, Luneburg, and Minden.[113]   And as the pupils of these teachers in their turn continued Cele's work, the literary productions and the educational reforms of Groote's followers were diffused throughout the land, entering shop and farm-house, chapel and monastery, kitchen and workshop, appealing to the hearts of high and low, of rich and poor, of old and young. Who can calculate or describe the influence which thus radiated from the Yssel valley schools in all directions? Such influence never dies, and readers must have been impressed by the fact that modern education perpetuates the best features of the reformed education of Groote, and Cele, and the Brethren of the Common Life.

CHAPTER IV

The Congregation of Windesheim

THE Brotherhood of the Common Life and the Congregation of Windesheim had a common ancestor in Gerard Groote, but they developed two different types of religious life and teaching. If Groote had lived longer he would have been able to foresee certain difficulties which might have caused serious trouble if the spirit of Christian charity had not operated so powerfully to maintain harmony amidst chaotic conditions. The fifteenth century witnessed terrible scandals in monasteries and secular institutions. Even in distant Rome, the Eternal City, the Holy Father sometimes commanded little respect. If only his friends had lived as piously as did the disciples of Gerard Groote, there would have been no need of the movement called Reformation.

1. Monasteries and Convents Founded
or Reformed by Windesheim

Simultaneously with the development of the Brotherhood of the Common Life came the rise of the Congregation of Windesheim, the center from which proceeded monastic reform, and from which many books were distributed. The Brethren-house at Deventer kept on sending recruits to the new monastery at Windesheim, until Radewijns, the rector of the brethren in Deventer, became somewhat alarmed. At last he sent a letter to John Vos, prior of Windesheim: "Beloved father John in Windesheim, I note that many are inclined to enter a monastery, and only a few come to our brethren-house. And though some at first prefer the brethren-house, where they are contented for some time, sooner or later, having become acquainted with your calm lives and saintly conversation, they are easily impelled to admire you, as happened with John Brinckerinck, who wanted very badly to be invested there."[1]   One feels in perusing the whole of this letter that Radewijns, in common with most men of his day, regarded the monastic state as something more saintly than any other.   Brinckerinck had twice wanted to leave the brethren-house for a monastery.[2]   John Vos himself had been one of the members of the brethren-house, before he had gone to Windesheim.   The monastery, it should be remembered, was erected in order to provide a place of shelter for the brethren in times of need.   Here, amidst those dignified rows of elms and willows and surrounded by smiling pastures, one would be three miles from the nearest city, and beside the silent waters.   Here one could lead a life of rest and contemplation, undisturbed by school children and the bustle of busy streets.   No wonder that so many members of the brethren-house were eager to go to Windesheim!   And no wonder that Radewijns himself would have liked to leave Deventer, if such a course of action had seemed proper to him, for he writes on one occasion: "If it is convenient to you, I shall be glad to visit you, for the last days I have been ill.   I would rather be ill there with you, as one of you, and die there, than at Deventer."[3]   Only duty kept him "in the world."

For several years the brethren at Deventer and Windesheim acted as if they were all members of one house.   Thus, when in 1392, it was thought expedient to erect another monastery, the men at Deventer again sent the required funds.   John Brinckerinck was still a member of their house at that time.   His skill as carpenter was well known among the brethren, for in the previous year he had helped to build the new brethren-house.   Now he was equally ready to exert himself.[4]   John Busch preserved the following letter by Radewijns to prior John Vos: "John Brinckerinck arrived yesterday from the monastery of Marienborn (Mary's Fountain) near Arnhem.   And Henry Wilde and Henry Wilsem would like to know whether the house should have a roof of stone or not.   John Brinckerinck says that if lack of funds compels us to cover it with straw, it will only last eight years.   We have 392 florins with which to finance the construction, and no more than that.   We can arrange that John

Ketel, our cook, give his thousand florins to Marienborn and three hundred of his mother's money. . This money we could use to great advantage ourselves, but charity weighs more with us, though our means are small."[5]

The history of the brethren-house at Deventer and the monastery of Windesheim, until the year 1424, may be compared to two streams from one source, which often unite, and usually flow side by side.[6] Shortly after the founding of Marienborn, came that of "New Light" near Hoorn by the same men, aided by two other disciples of Gerard Groote.[7] Deventer and Windesheim also had common interests at Eemsteyn near Dordrecht, founded in 1382, and protected till 1384, by Groote.[8] This monastery must have joined the other three about the year 1393.[9] Together they formed the Congregation of Windesheim in 1394 or 1395,[10] favored with privileges from both the pope and the Bishop of Utrecht.[11]

Once secure of its position, the new chapter rapidly extended its sway, adding new members at the average rate of one a year.[12] In 1395 or later a monastery near Amsterdam joined.[13] In 1398, Mount St. Agnes, near Zwolle, became a member,[14] followed by Frenswegen in Bentheim east of Overijssel, in 1400,[15] Leyderdorp, near Leiden, in 1403;[16] Briel in 1406;[17] Haarlem;[18] Thabor, in Friesland,[19] and Zalt-Bommel, in Gelderland,[20] in 1407. Then came the incorporation of the celebrated chapter of Groenendaal, in 1413, comprising seven monasteries, of which the monastery of Groenendaal, near Brussels, was the chief.[21] The spiritual force of Windesheim was sweeping across the Low Countries, absorbing and overpowering even the most ancient houses. Soon the Augustinian monasteries in many parts of Germany began to swell the tide. First a few single monasteries joined, then a whole chapter, namely that of Neuss, consisting of thirteen monasteries, of which however the one at Bethlehem near Doetinchem hesitated till 1441.[22] About the same time several other monasteries joined the Windesheim circle, such as Wittenburg, near Hildesheim; Ludingakerke, in Friesland; Sion, in Beverwijk; Richenberg, near Goslar; Sacravallis, near Dalfsen, in Overijssel (which joined in 1430.) Also, another monastery belonging to the chapter of Neuss, namely the one at Reimerswaal, in Zeeland, joined in 1430.

A large number of other communities followed in due time. The story of their reform or their foundation is partly found in the *Chronicle of Windesheim* and partly in Acquoy's work on Windesheim, while several articles which have apppeared since 1880 in various historical magazines in Holland and Germany give further particulars. Suffice it to say here that in the year 1464, the entire congregation counted more than 84 members and about the year 1500 it had more than 100.[23] One wonders how it was possible for these two apparently obscure and certainly not wealthy convents of Windesheim and Diepenveen to cause so great a veneration in the minds of contemporaries. Why did Eemsteyn, where the founders of Windesheim had been instructed, apply for admission. and why did the monks of Groenendaal so gladly submit to the rules of the Windesheim Congregation? Why did the instructed absorb the instructors?

Now the most striking fact about the history of the Devotio Moderna is the way in which from humble, poor beginnings mighty forces developed. Not brain-power or money only caused the movement from Deventer and Windesheim to become a world-force in religion and education. Nor did the privileges given to Groote's followers by bishops and popes have so very much to do with their rapid growth. There were other orders and congregations highly favored by the Church, many of which were swiftly approaching collapse or utter ruin. No, the protection of the Church, though helpful to some extent, was not responsible for the power of Windesheim. When its missionaries journeyed from city to city they carried no papal bulls with them, and they seldom spoke of their privileges. Their mission was to waken a new religious ardor and personal faith, a faith accompanied with "good works."

One of the most interesting examples of this monastic reform is that introduced at Frenswegen in Bentheim, near the Dutch frontier. This monastery had been founded by Henry Crul and Everard of Eza, assisted by the count of Bentheim. Everard of Eza was a learned scholar. When the fame of Groote's preach-

ing had attracted his attention, he had almost immediately left
for Deventer to hear the new preacher. With the intention of
catching Groote in some lapse, he posted himself out of sight
and listened, expecting to come forward and confute him. But
instead of silencing Groote, who had not without reason been
considered one of the brightest stars at Paris, he was completely
won by the master's spirit and powerful arguments. Not long
thereafter Groote passed away, and now Everard wanted to join
the brethren at Deventer; but at that time these brethren were
attacked by many enemies, and Everard was considered one of
them. When he opened the door of the vicarage the brethren
ran away into their rooms for fear. Only after some lengthy
deliberations he was finally accepted as a member. It was he
who warned Radewijns and his followers against the folly of
neglecting their bodily needs, and persuaded them to take
physical exercises in the open air. Thus he was useful to them
in his own way. But soon he left Deventer for Almelo, where
he invited some priests and clerics to live the common life with
him. Finally he decided to found a monastery for them, which
led to the erection of Frenswegen. But what happened? The
men who had so hopefully started upon their new life needed
the guiding hand of a monk from the Yssel country. They
were reduced to the direst poverty; and when a pestilence came,
despair seized upon the remaining few. Windesheim heard of it,
and ordered Eemsteyn to send one of their inmates. In 1400
Frenswegen was incorporated into the Windesheim Congregation. Now for a time all went well, but soon want once more
troubled the small community, and the men seemed unable to
go on. Finally they lost their new rector and for the second
time turned to Windesheim for aid. This time the brethren
sent one of their own men, named Henry Loeder, who had
spent eleven years with them. For twenty-one years (1415-1436)
Loeder was prior at Frenswegen, raising this monastery to a
position of prominence in Northwestern Germany, for he
carried to Frenswegen the ideals of John Vos, the practical
mysticism of Groote, and the enthusiasm he had himself absorbed in the Yssel country during his long stay. Poverty and

manual labor did not seem a hardship any more to the monks at Frenswegen. They worked, read, and loved each other as brothers till the glory of their mutual loves shed its radiant beams across Westphalia, Saxony, Friesland, and the Rhine provinces. Sixteen missionaries were sent out to various monasteries, of whom twelve became priors of as many houses. From far and near people came to seek admission at Frenswegen, and more than one hundred men were invested during Loeder's priorate. He himself was wont to travel from community to community, reviving relaxed discipline and stimulating despondent or negligent hearts into new activity. He was rightly called the Apostle of the Westphalians, Saxons, and Frisians.[24]

Another missionary sent from Windesheim was John Busch, author of the *Chronicon Windeshemense,* in whose life it is evident how the Devotio Moderna spread from Windesheim. Born at Zwolle in 1399, he was for several years a pupil and later an assistant of John Cele, the famous teacher. Busch was a brilliant student, wherefore his parents wanted him to go to Erfurt. "No," said he, "I wish to do some work for God — to reform monasteries." Gerard Calcar, rector of the brethren-house at Zwolle, accordingly sent him to Windesheim, where he was invested in 1419. Here he labored hard to master his lower self. For a time the enemy seemed too strong for him, till one day (the 21st of January, 1421) he thought he heard Jesus say to him: "Now thou art mine, and I am thine." "From that day," says Busch, "my enemy could trouble me no more." In 1424, he was sent as missionary to the monastery of Bödingen; in January, 1429, to Ludingakerke, in Friesland; in August of the same year to Sion, at Beverwijk. From 1431-1434, he lived at Bronopia, near Kampen, whence he went to Windesheim once more. In 1436, or 1437, he was sent to the monastery of Wittenburg, situated about ten miles west of Hildesheim; in 1439, he went to Sülte, near Hildesheim, where in 1440, he became prior. Here he labored with considerable success till, in 1447, he was called to the celebrated monastery of Neuwerk near Halle, where he resided till 1454.[26]

This monastery of Neuwerk was one of the richest in all German lands. Its domains extended over an area of eleven square miles, with a population of twenty thousand inhabitants. When Busch first arrived upon the scene, he found the monks living dissolute lives, having lost all sense of propriety. These monks certainly had not left the outside world in order to serve God more perfectly! They were the kind of persons who deserved the lash of derisive scorn applied by men like Erasmus. Busch was outspoken in condemnation. He was not satisfied with mere criticism, either. To the much needed negative criticism he added constructive suggestions and ideals. John Busch told those monks what Groote had said to the monks of his day. One feels while perusing the account left by Busch himself that he did not possess that warmth and freshness of newly-born religious ardor so characteristic of the founders of Windesheim; but he was sincere, and steadfast. He loathed wantonness, selfishness, pride, and indolence. The ideals of Groote's earliest disciples he carried with him wherever he went, and usually he succeeded in his task. That he had to meet with much opposition cannot be doubted, for men are not prone to exchange a life of ease and luxury for one of self-abnegation. Busch made enemies everywhere, just as Groote had done before him, and every other earnest reformer does. But he persevered, and won. Pope Nicholas V heard of his work, and sent Cardinal Cusa to Magdeburg in 1451, instructed to appoint Busch to supervise the reform of all the monasteries of the Augustinian Canons Regular in Saxony, Meissen, and Thuringia.[27]

Cusa at once ordained that the monastery of Neuwerk should be the head of a number of other monasteries, which together were to be called the Chapter of Neuwerk. This chapter was then to join the Chapter of Windesheim, as had been the case with Groenendaal, near Brussels, and Neuss, on the Rhine.[28] Consequently Busch was sent to Windesheim to obtain the required permission. But when the men at Windesheim considered the enormous estates possessed by Neuwerk, and contrasted the luxurious living of its wealthy inmates with their own spare living, they felt that such monasteries as Neuwerk were not fit places for servants of Christ. Their own lives, though not marred by excessive asceticism, embodied the ideals of their predecessors. They told Busch all this. For wealth and fame they did not care, they said; no matter what the pope would think, or Cardinal Cusa. Only monasteries could join their congregation whose inmates were willing to cast aside the idols of material advancement. Thus Neuwerk had to remain outside the Windesheim circle, but so great was the moral and spiritual influence of Windesheim that this rich and powerful chapter of Neuwerk gave up its own ancient rules and accepted those of the Windesheim Congregation.[29]

In 1454, Busch resigned his position at Neuwerk; in 1455, we find him in the monastery of Wittenburg, near Hildesheim. From this center he reformed four monasteries. Then he went to Windesheim once more; from Windesheim to Diepenveen (1456) ; and thence to Bronopia, near Kampen. Not long thereafter Germany called him back. He accepted the call and went to the monastery of Sülte, near Hildesheim, where he spent twenty years (1459-1479), and reformed twenty monasteries.

Windesheim was transforming not only the Augustinian Canons Regular, however, for we read of the reform of Benedictine monasteries conducted by the missionaries of Windesheim,[30] and of the reform of Cistercian,[31] and Premonstratensian monasteries.[32] From Windesheim the movement spread to other congregations, such as that of Bursfeld, which was Benedictine, for John Dederoth, usually called John von Minden, abbot at Clus near Gandersheim, in the diocese of Hildesheim had become acquainted with John Vos the prior of Windesheim, at the Council of Constance. Inspired by the religious ardor of Vos, Von Minden sought with the help of prior Rembert of Wittenburg to reform his own monastery. He continued his work at Bursfeld, where he became abbot in 1433. Thus the new devotion of the Augustinian Canons Regular passed to the Benedictine order.[33]

Much worthy reform was also accomplished by the monastery of Böddiken in Westphalia ("Kreis" of Büren), which like Frenswegen and Bursfeld also became a great center of renewed religious life.[34] but these examples must suffice here. Böddiken, as a member of the Windesheim Congregation, shone merely as the reflex of the greater light, and the labors of its monks resembled those of their friends at Frenswegen to so great an extent that they need not be recounted.

The work of the sisters of Diepenveen was more than a reflection of that of Windesheim. This convent was founded by the Sisters of the Common Life of Deventer. It was Deventer and not Windesheim which gave Diepenveen its best thoughts and its best leaders. From Diepenveen convents were founded and reorganized, as monasteries were from Windesheim. To its missionaries, therefore, our attention will now turn.

2. Reforms by Diepenveen

The convent of Diepenveen, founded as it had been by the Sisters of the Common Life, always kept in close touch with the sister-houses. Together with the "House of Master Gerard" at Deventer, it continually strove to improve conditions in the existing houses, and to found new ones. With the message of self-renunciation, preached by Groote's disciples, fresh upon their minds and hearts, the leaders at Diepenveen always sent out their most devout sisters as missionaries, for well they knew that these might never return.[35]

One of these missionaries was Fije van Reeden, who had first spent some time in the "House of Master Gerard," from where she had been transferred to Diepenveen by Brinckerinck. Before she had lived there long enough to be invested, her convent was asked to found a new house of the Sisters of the Common Life at Xanten on the Rhine. Fije was chosen as the person best fitted for this task. As matron of the new institution she performed her duties so well that she won the respect of all sisters and of their friends outside the house, and she was so successful that Brinckerinck called her the Apostle of Cleves. Xanten was located in the duchy of Cleves.

But the activities of the Brethren and Sisters of the Common Life were watched by many clerics with feelings of unmistakable hostility. Groote had been persecuted by them, Zerbolt had been impelled to write his *Treatise on the Common Life,* and Brinckerinck had often found it necessary to defend the brethren and sisters at Deventer. At Xanten some clerics bitterly attacked the Sisters of the Common Life as heretics. Here no great leaders of the "New Devotion" were found, and Fije van Reeden accordingly had to appear before the inquisitors at Cologne. The poor woman was frightened beyond measure. She tried to persuade a pious cleric to accompany her to Cologne, but she appealed in vain. No one was found who dared to meet the inquisitors in her company. She therefore appeared all alone before the papal inquisitors, many of whom, filled with "holy anger" against the Brethren and Sisters of the Common Life, for reasons not difficult to divine, maligned and slandered her, saying that she deserved the stake. But in spite of all their efforts they failed to convict her of heresy. Then they tried another plan: they accused her of immorality, but the charges brought against her were not proved and the end of the whole matter was that she went home vindicated. In 1429, she died at Xanten.[36]

There were also some houses of the Sisters of the Common Life which had been founded by Diepenveen and which at a later date were changed into convents. As examples might be named the house at Tienen, in Brabant, and that of St. Truyen, near Tienen. Then there were several convents founded or reformed by the sisters of Diepenveen — probably fourteen or fifteen in all.[37] The story of one of these reforms is interesting and instructive enough to be related here. It is that of the Benedictine convent of Hilwartshausen on the Weser, between Bursfeld and Minden.

Tradition told that in the days of Charlemagne a pious hermit, named Hilwert, lived in a large forest near the place where the Fulda and Werre join. Here the son of a king was killed one day by a wild beast, and shortly afterwards his sister erected a convent on the spot where he had been killed. It was named

Hilwartshausen, or Hilwert's house, after Hilwert, the hermit. At first only king's daughters lived here, later on daughters of dukes and counts were accepted; still later, those of rich nobles were taken in. As time went on discipline relaxed. The nuns had broken all the rules of obedience and restraint, went out hunting and gambling, and sometimes danced all night with monks from neighboring monasteries. At last the scandal reached the ears of their parents and nearest relatives, who with the aid of dukes, counts, and priors endeavored to enforce discipline. For forty years no advance was made. Finally the nuns were compelled to dress in the white garments of the Augustinian order. But what happened? The women ran about the house, frantically exclaiming: "We can not distinguish one from the other any more. They have dressed us as if we were to be buried."

A short time afterwards John Busch came to Hilwartshausen. He was accustomed to see his work crowned with almost immediate results. But although he remained here for eight days, he failed absolutely to improve conditions. What was now to be done? The countess on whose estates the monastery was situated appealed to the prior of Böddiken, which, as has been said, was a member of the Windesheim Congregation. He appointed a pious nun from Fritzlar as prioress, while two other sisters from the same convent were sent to assist her. It soon appeared that he had not made the right choice. The new sisters found it impossible to remain there long. When they left, the inmates of the convent joyfully ran to the windows, crying: "Thank God that we got rid of those devils!"

The prior of Böddiken now decided to try a safer scheme. He went to Windesheim to ask for two or three sisters from Diepenveen. His request was granted only when he promised that the persons entrusted to him were to be returned "without injury either to body or soul." Three sisters were sent, named Stijne des Grooten, Dayken Dyerkens, and Aleid ter Maat. They arrived at Hilwartshausen about the year 1460. As soon as the nuns were aware of their arrival they screamed: "The devils have come." They made such a noise that it was not thought safe to let the reformers enter the building. Only the prioress came to meet them. She led Stijne des Grooten, the leader of the little party, through the building, but could not prevent the sisters from making all sorts of hostile grimaces. One of the nuns, in seeing them approaching, threw herself upon the floor and sought to indicate her feelings of disapproval by grotesque movements of her limbs. This astonished Stijne not a little, but she was unaware of the meaning of the strange spectacle. "What ails this sister?" she asked the prioress in surprise. The latter, not knowing what to say, answered with a forced laugh, whereupon the newcomer, believing the other sister to be troubled by some physical disease, said in a very soft and kind voice to the prioress: "Dear mother, give her some wine to drink; perhaps she will improve then." Thus in her innocence and tenderness of heart she softened the animosity of one of her enemies. A short time afterwards Stijne was appointed sub-prioress. With the greatest circumspection she went to work. First one should try kindness, she reasoned, later, severity. Besides, she knew what it was to love one's neighbors as dearly as oneself; Groote, Radewijns, and Thomas à Kempis had said that one should even strive to be kinder to them than to one's own nature. Stijne had often meditated upon these teachings at Deventer and Diepenveen — now the time had come for her to practise them. Gradually she won the love and respect of the sisters, and they would come to her for help rather than go to their own prioress. Especially the younger ones soon learned to love her as a mother or a dear friend, though still she insisted that they all should perform their proper duties with alacrity. When the hour had come for spinning, she would say: "Come, dear children, let us now do a little spinning. Now you know that we are not allowed to talk, but we may laugh." Then the sisters would group themselves about her and begin working in silence. All of a sudden Stijne would start to smile. The younger sisters, encouraged by her example, would all respond with hearty laughs, "so that for a long period a loud noise was heard in the room, though none of them spoke a word." Thus she gradually taught them that manual labor and even enforced silence did not necessarily imply hardship or misery.

The other two sisters from Diepenveen contributed their share to the reform of Hilwartshausen. Dayken Dyerkens practised each day this well-known maxim of Groote's disciples: "Be harsh to yourself and kind to others." Whenever injustice had been done to her or an act of unkindness, she always sought to repay it with some form of what one might call true Christian service. How much those little deeds of love must have cost her can only be felt by those who have also gone through such experiences. In a very short time she had broken down all barriers of resistance. And her success must appear the more remarkable because she combined the strictest discipline with her unselfish love. One evening she had left the younger sisters alone for a few moments. Now the time had come, they thought, to have a little fun. Accordingly they began to dance, for the moment completely oblivious to the newly introduced monastic reform. But woe to them, when Dayken came back! There was no end to the penances, and never again did they venture to dance when Dayken was out of sight.

The most lovable of the three reformers from Diepenveen was Aleid ter Maat, who was assigned a humbler post than the other two sisters. All day long she was busy in the kitchen, but in the evening she would visit the sick, or else some of the sisters would come and spend a few sweet moments of confidential talk with her. There was no harshness about Aleid. To her they could freely open their hearts, and confess their secret wishes and their sorrows. She reminds us of John Ketel, the pious cook at Deventer, and of Florentius Radewijns. "One suspects," says Dr. Kühler of Amsterdam, "that it was largely due to her lovable character that the monastic reform attempted by the sisters of Diepenveen was so complete a success, though the sources are silent on this point."

Several uneventful years passed before it was found expedient to let the three sisters return to Diepenveen. Not that they had forgotten their "earthly paradise," as they called it. Far from it. Often Dayken Dyerkens would sigh: "Oh, that I might once more see the gates of Diepenveen opened to me, and that I might enter there — how happy I would be!" Finally, after the lapse of six years, her wish was granted. Great was the joy of the three reformers, but equally great the sorrow of the nuns they were to leave. For a good while the new religious fervor at Hilwartshausen was a living force — just as long as the remembrance of the kind words and deeds of the departed sisters remained impressed on the minds of the nuns. But gradually these impressions were weakened, and supplanted by entirely different ones. Discipline relaxed once more. The nuns of Hilwartshausen were not in touch with that great spiritual force which Groote's disciples in the Yssel country successfully maintained. Far away from the Yssel valley, no matter how brightly the new fires of devotion had at first lighted up the whole atmosphere in brethren-house or monastery, the principles of the Devotio Moderna were less effectually assimilated. Well might the more pious nuns at Hilwartshausen exclaim: "If only we had kept those sisters from Diepenveen with us, we would have kept up our first love."[38]

3. General Characteristics

The monasteries of Windesheim and Diepenveen have often been called the "model convents" of the fifteenth century.[39] The reforms introduced by them were the chief cause which for a time at least halted the downfall of monasticism in north central Europe. To Windesheim and Diepenveen the pious abbots, priors, bishops, and princes looked for help, when indolence, greed, and vice threatened to ruin the lives of the monks and nuns. Many an ambitious prior took a journey to the Yssel valley to watch those men and women who so steadfastly clung to Groote's ideals of piety and as a rule they returned with one or more assistants, filled with new hope. Thus Windesheim and Diepenveen helped to reform several hundred monasteries in the Low Countries, Germany, and France. Nearly one hundred of these actually joined the far-famed Congregation of Windesheim, humbly obeying the instructions of the prior superior, and devoutly following the Windesheim rules embodied in the constitution drawn up during the closing years of the fourteenth century — a very remarkable document. Before 1387, the founders of the new monastery had cared little about monastic life in general, or about the rules of the Augustinian order, but in 1394, they decided to form a chapter and to prepare the foundation of a constitution. John Vos and Henry Wilde went to the celebrated monasteries of St. Victor and Ste. Geneviève at Paris to study the rules followed there, but instead of slavishly copying those rules, they studied many others, and finally drew up a constitution which contained elements selected with great care from those used in various monasteries.[40] In 1395, Pope Boniface officially approved of their work. This encouraged the men of Windesheim to compose an *"Ordinarius,"* a *"Kalendrium,"* and a *"Manuale."* Shortly after that a committee was appointed to draw up the Windesheim missales, evangelaria, epistolaria, lectionaria, capitularia, and collectaria, all agreeing to a letter. The brethren must have had great will-power, for nothing so complete had ever been attempted before.[41]

The constitution they adopted prescribed the way they and their successors were henceforth to spend their time. Their lives were not very different from those of the Brethren of the Common Life, while the theological views they entertained coincided absolutely with those of their friends at Deventer, at least during the life of Florentius Radewijns. But as time went on monastic conditions differentiated them from their brethren. The men at Windesheim had left the "world" behind them in order to explore their inner selves in a life of comparative solitude, and this silence and meditation did not fail to react upon their minds. Jealously the monks at Windesheim and in all of the monasteries belonging to their chapter, clung to their old ideals. They began with Groote's enthusiasm fresh upon their responsive hearts and minds; their early acts clearly personified that living faith which abounds in "good works," as James had commanded in his Epistle. Windesheim passed through a golden age, a silver age, and a period of de-

cline. By the opening years of the sixteenth century one would
look in vain for great theologians and great scholars at Windesheim.

After studying the works of Groote, Radewijns, Mande, and
Peters (the last two were the best writers Windesheim produced), one can picture the sort of life the men at Windesheim
led. They loved to read the Bible and the Fathers, and they
devoted much of their time to manual labor of some sort. Their
clothes and meals were quite simple. Certainly there was much
real piety to be found at Windesheim. Not only were the
"sacred writings" copied there with zest,[42] but the monks conscientiously strove to follow in the foot-steps of Christ. They
believed in the blessings of manual labor and of poverty; and
their meals, taken but twice a day, were plain, though wholesome and fairly plentiful. Most of the monks had at one time
been members of the Brethren of the Common Life, and the
clothes they wore differed but little from those used by friends
at Deventer. They too were ascetics to a certain extent. Not
that they starved or mutilated their bodies, but they distrusted
sensuous pleasures as their enemy, and to be free from all external things was their ideal, perhaps also their secret motive
in "fleeing the world." Some of the monks even thought it
wrong to have a hearty talk with their own mothers.

One can easily imagine that it was not the braver, the more
active sort of men that left the brethren-house for the monastery.
There were some great minds among the early inhabitants at
Windesheim, and some splendid men like John Vos of Heusden,
but many were timorous,[44] or carried away by excessive humility
and self-abasement.[45]

There was much about the lives of the monks at Windesheim
that deserves respect. It seems that the loving heart of Radewijns had inspired the men who founded the new monastery
under his supervision — inspired them to emulate his numerous
deeds of charity. Seldom if ever did the poor ask Windesheim
in vain for material assistance. Many a lonely wanderer, after
having crossed the weird outskirts of the Veluwe or the vast
heaths of Overijssel, would hopefully knock at the gate of

Windesheim to ask refuge for the night. Windesheim became famous for its charity.

And Windesheim became famous also as a center of literature and art. The monks belonging to this congregation often spoke about the inner life, but that did not always signify little regard for learning. There were many scholars in the monasteries, and splendid libraries.[46] Though at first the monks at Windesheim copied books chiefly for their own use, they began about the year 1500, to edit work for export to foreign countries.[47]

One of the most remarkable achievements Windesheim could boast of was the correction of the Vulgate. The monks had made up their minds that the Latin Bibles then in use differed too much from each other to be all correct. Consequently they wanted to get a version which should form the standard for all further copies. They had one sent from Paris, one from the monastery of Bethlehem near Doetinchem, and one from the monastery of St. Jansdal near Harderwijk. For several years they compared and copied until finally their standard copy was completed. So well did they perform their task that their copy, according to Hirsche and other authorities, became the basis for the Vulgate adopted officially by the Church at the close of the fifteenth century.[48] In a similar way they brought out editions of the Fathers.[49]

Furthermore, the Windesheim circle not only produced a great mass of manuscripts, but illuminated them beautifully. Many capable artists were developed in these monasteries, both sculptors, and painters. Thus the monastery of Rooklooster in Brabant produced Hugo van der Goes, one of the greatest painters North of the Alps during the second half of the fifteenth century.

Dr. Acquoy says that if one takes a general view of the Windesheim group, he must come to the conclusion that the remarkable moderation displayed by the monks and nuns of this chapter in all their ways of living, and of expressing their thoughts, is highly commendable and truly amazing. The chapter of Windesheim, he continues, was indeed one of the greatest and perhaps the most influential in the whole history of Western monasticism.[50] Several hundred monastaries had for a time at least basked in the gentle warmth of the newly awakened religious life, that was proceeding in all directions from Windesheim and Diepenveen. The missionaries from the Yssel valley had journeyed from place to place, carrying with them the best thoughts of Gerard Groote, the founder, and of Radewijns and Zerbolt, the two first leaders of the Brethren of the Common Life. No new theories had been expounded by them, nor had they at any time hinted at a need of revolutionary changes in church, home, or monastery. A mild form of asceticism clung to the followers of Groote at Deventer and Windesheim until the opening years of the sixteenth century. Windesheim broke with no hallowed traditions; it made much of Mary, the mother of Christ, and believed in indulgences and in the invocation of saints.[51]

But the Windesheim Congregation, in pointing out the uselessness of mere form, and in stressing the need of a personal, living faith, helped unconsciously to prepare the way for a great religious upheaval. For a time it tended to stay the onward march of demoralization among the regular and secular clergy. Its missionaries scattered the works of Groote, Radewijns, Zerbolt, Peters, and Thomas à Kempis across the Continent, so that even today one finds copies of them in libraries and book-stores in most of the larger European cities. Thus the principles of the Devotio Moderna became the spiritual food of many thousands of devout men and women beyond the Low Countries, in Germany, France, and Spain, and would later be crystallized in the lives of great reformers, like Luther, Calvin, Zwingli, and Loyola.

CHAPTER V

The Original Version of the "Imitation of Christ"

FOR MORE than three centuries a multitude of writers have written books and articles on the authorship of the *Imitation of Christ*. So vast is the amount of printed material devoted to this subject that no human being will ever be able to read it all. In the fifteenth century the *Imitation* appeared in print at Augsburg, Cologne, Nuremberg, Paris, Lyons, Rouen, and Venice, ascribed respectively to St. Bernard, Gerson, and Thomas à Kempis. Now that the dispute is about to be terminated, thanks to the discovery of a number of manuscripts at Lübeck, which once belonged to the Sisters of the Common Life in that city, and a copy of Book I by Gerard Zerbolt of Zutphen, we are able to manipulate properly the material at hand, and note how essential it is to study the lives and writings of Groote, Radewijns, Zerbolt, and their followers, before one can understand how the *Imitation of Christ* was composed and how it became the Gospel of the Devotio Moderna.

1. Analysis of the Work

"After the Gospel, the *Imitation* undoubtedly is the book that reflects with the greatest perfection the light which Jesus Christ brought us down from heaven. It eminently contains the Christian philosophy. . . . Nowhere else do we find the same doctrine inculcated with a more persuasive eloquence and simplicity than in the unpretending little volume that all of us have a hundred times perused."

Thus reads the verdict of a notable Catholic author in America.[1] His view is supported by that of thousands upon thousands of other writers in all countries, and belonging to every religious denomination. For rich and poor, high and low, learned and simple — all who for the time being are weary of external, formal observances, or dissatisfied with the dry bones of dogma held out to them by many preachers may find the advice and instruction they need in turning over even the first few leaves of the *Imitation of Christ*. Nobody knows through how many hundreds of editions the little book has passed since the close of the fifteenth century, or into just how many languages and dialects it has been translated.[2] Not a single year passes without adding new editions to the many already existing. Together with the Bible it has found its way into the remotest regions, eagerly devoured by Christian and pagan, by civilized and barbarian. Who knows how many millions of stubborn hearts it has softened, how many aches it has healed, how much hatred it has melted as the sun melts the snow in spring?

In analyzing the teachings of the *Imitation*, one is reminded immediately of Groote's theological and sociological views, which are repeated in the works of Radewijns, Zerbolt, and Peters. The great underlying thought of the *Imitation*, as Hirsche says,[3] is the fact that man is a pilgrim here, an exile. According to Groote and his disciples, man is a sort of prisoner on earth, his prison, the flesh, which besets him on every turn with obstacles, blocking his way back home to the happy state before the fall. Man has to cleanse his blood from poison, his mind from sin, his heart from vice. First vice must be extinguished, ere virtue and love can find room in the human heart.

The *Imitation* therefore distinctly teaches the depravity of human nature: "O how great is human frailty, which is always prone to evil. There is no man that is altogether free from temptations whilst he liveth on earth: for in ourselves is the root thereof, being born with inclination to evil. For through Adam the first man, Nature being fallen and corrupted by sin, the penalty of this stain hath descended upon all mankind."[4] It is man's duty to extirpate sin, to cleanse his blood from poison, his heart and mind from vice: " 'Hope in the Lord, and do good,' saith the Prophet, 'and inhabit the land, and thou shalt be fed in the riches thereof.' " A great many pages are devoted to the problem of fighting various sins: Radewijns, it should be remembered, had made excerpts from Cassianus and David of Augsburg about the principal sins and their remedies; Zerbolt had copied after Radewijns' "rapiarium," when drawing up his *Spiritual Ascensions;* in the *Imitation* also the reader is exhorted to study his daily shortcomings. He is urged to "resist the blood," and to conquer his lower self: "This ought to be our daily endeavor, to conquer ourselves. Who hath a greater combat than he that laboureth to overcome himself? Thou must be lord and master of thine own actions, and not be a slave or a hireling. The perfect victory is to triumph over ourselves." Groote and his disciples carefully explored the inner self. "Know thyself," was one of their maxims; hence we read in the *Imitation*: "The highest and most profitable reading is the true knowledge and consideration of ourselves."[5]

The *Imitation* urges us to fight our passions, and repeatedly elaborates upon the nature and effects of temptation.[6] This also is in accordance with Groote's and Radewijns' writings. On several occasions Groote had been obliged to give counsel to those among his disciples who were dejected on account of their inability to get the better of their temptations, and all the inmates of Radewijns' vicarage had considered the conquest of sin as man's prime duty. They searched every day in religious books for practical help in their constant struggle against evil, writing down the most helpful excerpts they could find in their "rapiaria." In the *Imitation* we meet with many of these excerpts: "O, if men bestowed as much labor in the rooting out of vices, and planting of virtues, as they do in the moving of questions, neither would there so much hurt be done, nor so great scandal be given in the world, nor so much looseness be practised in religious houses (monasteries). Examine diligently thy conscience, and to the utmost of thy power purify and make it clear. . . . Think with displeasure of all thy sins in general, and more particularly bewail and lament thy daily transgressions." There are many shortcomings singled out for a more detailed study, such as the love of "worldly things," and too much familiarity with human beings especially with women.[7] Gossip is a great evil, so is curiosity. The opinions of others are not to be given undue regard: "He enjoyeth great tranquility of heart that careth neither for the praises nor dispraises of men." Fame, therefore, is absolutely worthless, as also are honors, and material possessions. And if one looks for comfort from human beings, one is certain to be disappointed sooner or later.[8] Since man is a pilgrim and exile here on earth, he must not give himself to mirth; he has much more occasion for tears than for laughter, though dejection is not desirable.[9]

"O, if men bestowed more labor in the rooting out of vices, and planting of virtues." The more one's vices disappear, the more room there will be for new virtues; this is the view set forth by Radewijns (d. 1400) in his *Omnes inquit artes,* where he elaborates upon the eight principal vices, and their "remedies." These "remedies" are the new virtues to be introduced into the mind and heart. Zerbolt (d. 1398) used the "rapiarium" of Radewijns in composing his *Reformation of the Faculties of the Soul* and his *Spiritual Ascensions.*[10] The *Imitation* follows these in devoting much space to the "rooting out of vices, and planting of virtues." Above all other virtues rank humility[11] and obedience,[12] which are the "remedies" against pride. Self-renunciation and resignation are ranked high among virtues.[13] The reader is taught that only through suffering,[14] by carrying his cross with him every day, in imitation of Christ, can he reach the heavenly country. One must keep one's eye single, one's attention concentrated upon the final goal: Heaven.[15] It is advisable to avoid society as much as possible, to devote much time to contemplation, to read the "sacred writings" with one's mind freed from temporal cares, and with devotion. Traveling is to be avoided as much as possible, but manual labor is recommended, and poverty deemed essential.[16] On every page of the *Imitation,* it will be seen, one meets with thoughts expressed before by Zerbolt, Radewijns, and Groote.

When the mind becomes clear, and the heart pure, one receives the highest gift from heaven: love. Thus Groote had taught his disciples. Love is more than virtue and more than the mere absence of vice, wherefore the men and women of Deventer could find no words fit to describe the value of love. The *Imitation* in turn makes much of love; in the first place, the love the creature owes to the Creator,[17] and to Christ his savior; in the second place, love for his neighbor.[18] But the love and worship of self is looked upon as an abomination in God's sight.

Groote and his disciples were all mystics. Much of Groote's mysticism found its way into the *Imitation*: " 'The Kingdom of God is within you,' saith the Lord. Learn to despise outward things, and to give thyself to things inward, and thou shalt perceive the Kingdom of God to come in thee. Christ will come unto thee, and show thee his own consolation, if thou prepare for him a worthy mansion within thee. Let not Moses speak unto me, nor any one of the prophets, but rather do thou speak, O Lord God Inspirer and Enlightener of all the prophets; for thou alone without them canst perfectly instruct me, but they without thee can profit nothing. They indeed may sound forth words, but cannot give the Spirit. Unless thou help me, and inwardly inform me, I become altogether lukewarm and ready to fall to pieces. He to whom all things are one, he who reduceth all things to one, and seeth all things in one, may enjoy a quiet mind, and remain peaceable in God. O God, make me one with thee."[19] As mystics, Groote's disciples placed the acquisition of virtue above that of learning, as is indicated in passages like the following: "Be studious for the mortification of thy sins; for this will profit thee more than the knowledge of many difficult questions." But the *Imitation* does not disparage the value of booklearning: "Yet learning is not to be blamed, nor the more knowledge of any thing whatsoever to be disliked, it being good in itself, and ordained by God." Empty phrases, mere style, and scholastic disputes, however, are considered worthless."[20]

As for the views about God and man expressed in the *Imitation*, not a single statement can be found deviating from those taught by Gerard Groote. The Brethren of the Common Life at Deventer built their views upon the teachings contained in the New Testament and the Fathers. Perhaps they failed to grasp the meaning of certain phrases in the Gospels and in the Epistles by Paul, Peter, and James. If they did, they only repeated the errors made by men like Augustine, Jerome, Ambrose, Bernard, Bonaventura, Cassianus, David of Augsburg, and Thomas Aquinas. One important theological question is the salvation of man, and closely connected with it, the conception of heaven and hell, of man's depravity, the value of faith and "good works," and the nature of "grace." That Groote's disciples implicitly believed in the depravity of human nature has been repeatedly indicated above.[21]   But Groote and Zerbolt had taught that man remained in touch with God, for they were real mystics. Since man had been created in God's image, something divine remains in his sinful heart: "For the small power which remains is as it were a spark lying hid in the ashes."[22] Grace can fan this spark into a bright flame, if man so wishes. This inner light will then purge away sin and vice. Thus human nature is sanctified and the small spark of divinity augmented into a flame of pure love. Some of the most powerful literature on this fascinating subject had been written by Gerard Zerbolt in his book entitled, *The Reformation of the Powers of the Soul*. We shall see presently how his thoughts were crystalized in the *Imitation*.

2. Thomas a Kempis

The compiler of the *Imitation of Christ* was Thomas à Kempis, or rather, Thomas Hemerken of Kempen. He was born in the town of Kempen in the diocese of Cologne. The date of his birth is not certain. Some writers claim it must be placed in the year 1379 or 1380; others, in the year 1380 or 1381. His father was called John Hemerken, or John with the little hammer, for he earned his living with his hammer, though he also owned a tract of land. That both Thomas and his brother John à

Kempis were not mere phantoms invented by chronicle writers, is shown by a document written at Kempen in the year 1402, in which the sale of their father's home is attested.[23]

In 1392, the fame of Deventer's cathedral school had reached the duchy of Guelders, in which Kempen was situated. Whether it was due to the presence of the Brethren of the Common Life or to the reforms initiated on Groote's advice, certain it is that many parents were anxious to have their boys educated at Deventer. In Thomas' case there was an additional reason for his going there. His brother John had been an inmate of Radewijns' vicarage, and was now living at Windesheim. In 1392, Thomas arrived at Deventer.[24] "When I came to study at Deventer," he wrote afterwards, "I went to Windesheim, where my brother was living. He told me to visit Florentius Radewijns." Eager to follow John's advice, for John knew the vicar well, Thomas came to Radewijns. He was not a wealthy boy; he could not even pay for his board and lodging. Radewijns took compassion on him, and invited him to stay at his house.[25] Thus fortune smiled upon him from the first day.

Not only did Radewijns provide him with lodging, but he gave him books and paid his tuition at the school of St. Lebwin's. His teacher at that time was a certain John Boheme. One day Thomas brought him the tuition fee. "Who gave it to you?" the teacher asked. "Radewijns," was the boy's reply. "Then take it back to your kind master," said the teacher.[26] It takes very little imagination to see how much the friendship of a man like Radewijns meant to the boys then attending the cathedral school. Thomas must have told his parents about it, and the other boys. His parents in turn probably mentioned his experiences to other parents. In this way even before the close of the fourteenth century the influence of Gerard Groote was being felt in homes far beyond the Yssel valley.

But the brethren-house at Deventer was too small to lodge school boys. Radewijns, therefore, looked around for some other quarters, and sent Thomas to a certain devout woman, doubtless one of Groote's disciples.[27] How long the boy stayed with her we do not know. It seems that after a few years he lived with the brethren again, for he tells of experiences in the brethren-house: "All I earned," he writes, "I gave to the community; the rest I needed was given by Florentius. Here I learned to read and write the Holy Scriptures and books on moral subjects, but it was chiefly through the sweet conversation of the Brethren that I was inspired yet more strongly to despise the world. I took pleasure in their godly conduct. Never before could I recollect to have seen such men, so devout and fervent."[28]

What Florentius Radewijns did reminds us of Groote's work among the school boys at Deventer. He also had often invited them to come to his house, and had given them work to do. Some of these boys became Brethren of the Common Life, though at the time they visited Groote they were living still in private homes. Thomas à Kempis too was first lodged with a pious woman, as soon as Radewijns found a place for him. Later he was asked to become a real inmate of the brethren-house. Perhaps Thomas lived only one year with the brethren at Deventer, as his own remarks seem to prove, but the influence of Radewijns had been shaping his young mind before he re-entered the brethren-house. Later he wrote: "During seven years of my life (1392-1399) I experienced the wonderful compassions of Florentius Radewijns."[29] Add to this that his own brother John had lived with Radewijns, Brinckerinck, and Vos in the brethren-house at Deventer, and the conclusion is justified that when Thomas began to preach and write, he repeated the maxims of Groote and Radewijns, the two founders of the new brotherhood, the two men who inaugurated the Devotio Moderna.[30]

The world has long waited for a comprehensive history of the whole movement inaugurated by Gerard Groote, in which the services of each predominant personalty are clearly pictured, their productions carefully measured, and properly balanced. The moment one fails to grasp the significance of any one of the leaders of Deventer, he cannot understand the others. Hence the only thing to be done is to study Thomas à Kempis in his spiritual heredity and environment.

It must have been near the close of the year 1399, that Thomas à Kempis went to the monastery of Mount St. Agnes.[31] The spot may have seemed sacred to him for the reason that Gerard Groote had visited the place in the summer of the year 1384, pointing out to his disciples this site for their first brethren-house. Here the pious John Ummen had lived, the blind leader of the Brethren of the Common Life of Zwolle, and now a monastery had been erected on this hill of St. Agnes, or *Agnie-tenberg*.

In 1412 or 1413, Thomas à Kempis was ordained priest,[32] and shortly after this began his career as editor, writer, and copyist. In 1425 he was elected sub-prior, for soon the other monks had been impressed by his great religious fervor. Says Tolensis, who spent many years at Mount St. Agnes: "In the church and in the performances of ecclesiastical ceremonies, it is difficult to describe his rapt intention, and I might say inspiration. While he chanted the psalms, his eyes were ever raised towards heaven, and he appeared to be filled with a divine enthusiasm, captivated and carried away by the unutter-able sweetness of the holy psalmody: so that he never stood with his heels resting upon the ground; that is to say, as he meditated, the tips of his toes alone touched the floor, the rest of his body was lifted heavenwards, whither his soul tended with all its desires."[33] When in 1471, he passed away, it was his name which had made the monastery of Mount St. Agnes celebrated above many ancient convents. Even the greatest among the great, like a Wessel Gansfort, had not deemed it below their dignity to have a few moments of conversation with this vener-able mystic. He had written thirty-eight works, among which the *Soliloquy of the Soul*, the *Garden of Roses*, and the *Valley of Lilies* are excellent.[34]

3. The "Rapiaria" Made at Deventer

Thomas à Kempis never could have chosen a better time to "learn to read and write the sacred writings" than in the year 1398-1399. It was in the summer of 1398, that the two institu-tions of Gerard Groote at Deventer passed through the greatest crisis that ever was to threaten their existence. In the brethren-house at Deventer the men had lived a semi-monastic life, undisturbed by quarrels, feuds, and hostile attacks. Then came the terrible pestilence in June, taking the lives of nearly all the experienced members. First in the vicarage of Radewijns, and later in the "House of Florentius," or the real brethren-house, they had for more than fourteen years tried to do what they believed Christ had commanded in the Beatitudes. They had conscientiously endeavored to "despise the world," to "remain unknown," to "offer themselves to God," and to "subdue the flesh."

Let us in imagination visit Deventer. It is early in the month of June that the pestilence has made its appearance in the brethren-house. More than half of the inmates have the disease, while most of the others have hurriedly fled across the Veluwe to Amersfoort, taking many school boys with them. Thomas à Kempis remains at Deventer, where for six years he has followed in the footsteps of his beloved Radewijns. The pious cook in the brethren-house and all the older members have died. Heart-rending letters have been passing between Amersfoort and Deventer. In the brethren-house Thomas has found the spiritual exercises of John Ketel, the cook, and of Lubbert ten Bossche, besides those of the other dead brothers. Zerbolt has just left for Amersfoort, and Thomas finds himself practically the sole possessor of the jealously guarded treasures in the library.[35]

Thomas copied the letter sent by Amilius van Buren to the brethren at Amersfoort, where Radewijns was then staying. In this letter Amilius told the absent rector about the death of Lubbert ten Bossche, or Lubbert Berner, as Thomas calls him. Thomas adds that Van Buren was sitting beside the dying man: "He (Amilius) carefully kept account of all the edifying words which he heard fall from his lips; and after Lubbert's death he faithfully made record of them, writing them in order in a letter. . . and this letter I have determined to insert here." Not satisfied with that, Thomas also copied the letter composed by Lubbert shortly before his death, together with the answer from

Radewijns to the brethren at Deventer. The story of Lubbert's decease is very impressive: "And he answered me, as it were in great amazement: 'Wonderful, wonderful, marvelous, marvelous, yea great and marvelous are the things which I saw when I sat up.' And then he added: 'Call the brethren, call the brethren;' and when I called them, immediately he breathed his last." What is still more remarkable, Thomas copied excerpts from the "devout exercises" of this pious brother. He began with the following sentence: "Thy task shall be to labor to uproot thy vices and to gain virtue."

This is not all. Thomas was the trusted friend of Amilius van Buren, rector of the brethren at Deventer during Radewijns' absence in the summer of the year 1398. Amilius had watched by the bed-side of the dying Lubbert ten Bossche. From his mouth Thomas "received many of those good things concerning the virtues of the brethren," which he wrote down in his *Lives of Gerard Groote, Florentius Radewijns, and their Disciples.* Who knows how much more Thomas might have told us, and how many more brief sayings he might have preserved which now are lost? He shows how well he was acquainted with the kind cook: "He made the kitchen a house of prayer, for he knew that God is everywhere. . . He passed no time unfruitfully, nor for a moment neglected his spiritual exercises." Thomas copied the cook's "devout exercises," most likely from the original itself, so that we owe to his busy hand the preservation of this literary production, together with those of Groote, Radewijns, Ten Bossche, and some other men.

Early in 1398, Thomas à Kempis was living in the old vicarage of Radewijns, and not in the new brethren-house, which was called "House of Florentius." "At that time," writes Thomas, "there was no small number of clerks living in the several houses under the rule and discipline of that most devout Father, and following the holy commandments of their Lord, his counsels and precepts, and also at set times toiling at the work of copying books for the schools. . . . At this time by the aid and counsel of Florentius I also took up my abode in this house and continued in the community for about one year, having Arnold as my companion. Here indeed I learned to write, to read the Holy Scriptures, and books on moral subjects, and to hear devout discourses. . . . All I was then able to earn I gave for the expenses of the community. . . . As he (Arnold) sat with the boys in school he noted not their childish clamor, but as the master delivered his lecture he wrote the same on paper and afterwards read it over to himself or with a comrade. . . . At this time the disciples and most devout pupils of our beloved father Florentius, whose lives I have written above, were still in the flesh, namely Lubbert, Henry (Brune), Gerard (Zerbolt), Amilius, James (of Vianen), and John Ketel, and there were with them some others who had been amongst the first members of the community," in other words, among the Twelve of Groote himself.[36]

What was more stimulating still, Radewijns, whom Thomas had now known for six years, felt that he was about to die. Many a time he sent Thomas to the Sisters in Groote's old home to ask them to pray for him, and Thomas also served as his personal attendant in other ways. Although Radewijns did not die until 1400, often it seemed as if death would snatch him away long before the close of the year 1399. How often must not Thomas have been called to the bed-side of the sick rector! And the latter, more intent than ever on things spiritual, cannot have refrained from filling his pupil's mind with spiritual thoughts. Moreover, the words of a dying man, or of one who believes he is dying, are always doubly impressive; they are always retained longest. On the works of Zerbolt and Ketel the breath of newly departed spirits lay fresh and magnetic; here the books of Groote, the founder, were passed from hand to hand; here Thomas found all the "rapiaria," or excerptbooks, of the leaders, who had lived and labored in the brethrenhouse. In this house Thomas also found the Latin compositions written by some one whose name the sources do not reveal, at least not in connection with the pieces themselves, for they seem to have disappeared very soon. These works, very probably drawn up at Deventer by one or more brethren living in the vicarage of Radewijns, we know that Thomas à Kempis copied and revised between 1398 and 1420, adding some chapters himself; and that they were copied almost immediately in many other monasteries and brethren-houses. Soon they became widely known as the *De Imitatione Christi*, or *Imitation of Christ.*

If two hundred or one hundred years ago a work had appeared in which the lives of Groote and his followers had been clearly portrayed and their literary productions carefully analyzed, probably but few books and articles would have been written on the authorship of the *Imitation of Christ*, for those who are well acquainted with the labors of Groote's disciples at Deventer cannot support the views of authors who claim that this famous book was originally composed in Italy or France. Fortunately, however, the long-disputed question has caused many a writer to discover evidence which otherwise would not have been found. Thus a vast amount of material has been made accessible to a relatively large number of students. And although this material in itself has failed to convince all thinkers that the *Imitation* was composed or put together in the Yssel country, nevertheless it will greatly lighten our task of showing that it was produced there.

"In the first place," writes Sir Francis Cruise, "I may state, with what I am satisfied is incontrovertible certainty, that no manuscript of the 'Imitation of Christ' has ever been produced of an age antecedent to the mature manhood of Thomas à Kempis — that is to say, the first third of the fifteenth century."[37] How much paper has been wasted on this point alone! All the efforts of those who wanted to produce a copy written before 1395 have failed. Loth, for example, found the first book of the *Imitation* in a manuscript at Paris which he believed to have been written in 1406.[38] Hence, he concluded, the work must have been produced before this date. A few years afterwards V. Becker carefully examined the manuscript in question and found that it contained a collection of treatises written in many different hands. If one piece in it had been copied in 1406 or 1410, that by no means implied that all the others were of the same date.

About seven hundred manuscripts are still in existence containing one or more books of the *Imitation,* most of which are undated. The oldest dated one written in France is from the year 1456; Italy can boast of no earlier dated copy than that of 1464. It is exceedingly difficult to estimate the exact age of an undated manuscript, for very often a copyist would write with exactly the same hand at the age of sixty as he had employed forty years earlier. Consequently one must always leave a margin of at least fifty years, wherefore even those copies written in an Italian Renaissance hand, such as the one found in the British Museum at London.[39] may very well have been written fifty years later than some people imagine.[40]

As for the copies bearing a date, or provided with a note of some sort from which the correct date can be deduced, the earliest copy known containing all four books is the one found in the "Codex of Gaesdonck," written in the Augustinian monastery of Bethlehem near Doetinchem, a house of the chapter of Neuss, which joined the Windesheim Congregation in 1430. This was written in the year of 1426.[41] At Brussels, however, a manuscript is found in the Royal Library (no. 10137) which has the first three books, written in the year 1425[42] in the monastery of Windesheim for the monastery of Bödingen.[43] One year earlier, book I was copied in the house of the Brethren of the Common Life at Hulsbergen, near Zwolle,[44] and in 1420 or 1421 the Dutch translation of book I at Windesheim.[45] Then there is the so-called "Mölk codex," or "Codex Mellicensis I," containing also book I of the *Imitation,* which may have been written in 1421, for the codex bears the number XXI (although this number does not follow after this book I, but after the *Contemplatio S. Bernardi de Passione Domini,* wherefore the former piece may have been written much later). In this case it was very probably given by the representatives of Windesheim to those of the monastery of Mölk when they met each other at the Council of Constance.[46] Next in order comes the "Codex Noviomagensis," written at Nijmegen in 1427, also in a monastery of the Windesheim Congregation.[47] But there seems to be another copy, produced in

1426 at Ewick, another house of the Windesheim circle, according to Spitzen.[48] Then there is the "Codex Osnaburgensis," written in 1429, by the Brethren of the Common Life at Osnabrück,[49] and then the "Codex Thevenot" at Paris, written about the year 1430, in the brethren-house at Hulsbergen near Zwolle.[50] The "Codex Roolf" was written in 1431, in the monastery of Bethlehem near Louvain, a monastery of the Congregation of Windesheim.[51] It appears, therefore, that all or nearly all the earliest dated copies of the *Imitation* were written by the followers of Gerard Groote. Moreover, the first German translation of the *Imitation* by Thomas à Kempis was made by the Brethren of the Common Life at Cologne in the year 1434.[52] The Brethren of the Common Life and the monks belonging to the Windesheim Congregation were at first solely responsible for the rapid spread of this remarkable work.[53]

As for the verdict of the contemporary witnesses, this also points to Thomas à Kempis as the author, or editor, for those writers who in the fifteenth century regarded Gerson as the author, did not know who had first ascribed it to him and why. John Busch says that Thomas à Kempis wrote the *De Imitatione Christi*.[54] True, even his opinion is sometimes disregarded; and more than that, one German writer uses it as evidence against the supporters of the Thomas à Kempis, but with arguments that carry little weight.[55] There is, too, the testimony of a certain Herman Rijd, who had talked with Thomas à Kempis himself; also of a great many others.[56] That so many contemporaries are silent on this question need not surprise us, for it was not customary for the Brethren of the Common Life at Deventer to add the names of the authors or the dates to the works they were copying. Moreover, they had all been taught the *ama nesciri*, or "love to remain unknown" by Groote and Radewijns, their spiritual ancestors.[57] And furthermore, they all regarded Thomas à Kempis as the author of the *Imitation;* only, they would have been more exact if they had called him the compiler. As a matter of fact, Herman Rijd actually reported that Thomas compiled, rather than wrote the book.

That Gerson, the famous chancellor of the University of Paris, could not have written the *Imitation* is a well-established fact today.[58] But several writers in France, Italy, and England still favor the conclusion that the *Imitation of Christ* must have been written in Italy about the middle of the thirteenth century. These authors as a rule know very little about the mystical productions of Groote, Radewijns, Zerbolt, Peters, and Mande. They write a great deal about a phantom invented by them, called John Gersen, abbot of a Benedictine monastery in Lombardy, who, they claim, composed the *Imitation*. In some mysterious way this work reached the Yssel valley about the year 1400 or 1410. Thomas à Kempis, they continue, found it there, copied it, and placed it at the head of his other works. They admit that the Brethren of the Common Life and the monks of Windesheim were the first to appreciate its inestimable worth. They argue (1) that only after they had made it known to the world did other people read and copy it, (2) that the thirteenth century was the golden age of monasticism, and that the Cistercians and Carthusians, who are mentioned in the *Imitation,* were true to their vows only in that century, so that no monk after the year 1400, could have pointed to those orders and say: "Observe the Carthusians, the Cistercians, and the monks and solitaries of various orders, how they do every night rise to sing Psalms to the Lord."[59] Furthermore, (3) that the fifteenth century was a time of strife, of civil war, and of disorder, in which a work like the *Imitation* could never have been composed; and (4) that, since it contains no references to Thomas Aquinas or any other scholastics of note, it must have been written before their time.[60]

To these arguments we reply (1) that John Gerson and John Gersen are one and the same person. Both names refer to the chancellor of the University of Paris, who defended the Brethren of the Common Life at the Council of Constance, but was not the sort of mystic to write a book like the *De Imitatione Christi.* His name was usually spelled "Gerson," though it is also quite often spelled "Gersen" in fifteenth century manuscripts or incunabula. (2) And how could a work like the *Imitation,* written about the year 1250, have remained absolutely unknown until the year 1415? If Thomas à Kempis discovered it on its mysterious and hypothetical journey from the plains of Lombardy to Deventer, he must have received it from Groote's disciples, who gave him books to read, but who never referred to the *Imitation* until he himself had copied it. That Thomas à Kempis copied it is beyond question, for his autograph copy, finished in 1441, is still in existence;[61] and that Groote's disciples were the first to distribute it is now admitted. As to the argument about the Carthusians, Groote and his disciples respected that order very highly. (3) Also, they paid very little attention to civil wars. (4) That they refrained from quoting Thomas Acquinas in the *Imitation* is exactly what one should expect.[62]

4. Thomas à Kempis was the Compiler of the "Imitation"

But Thomas à Kempis was not the author of the whole *Imitation*, if we use the term in the modern sense. The first Dutch translation of book I appeared in 1420 or 1421 at Windesheim, as we have said; books I-III, found in the "Kirchheim Codex," "were copied from the autograph of Thomas à Kempis in the bishopric of Utrecht (at Windesheim) in 1425;" and the "Gaesdonck Codex" contains all the four books, copied in 1425, 1426, or 1427. Then we have the autograph copy of Thomas à Kempis at Brussels, with book I-IV, but book IV placed before book III, and followed by eight other works of Thomas himself, with a note at the end to the effect that this manuscript was written by him, and finished in the year 1441. Spitzen asserts that Thomas wrote the whole work in this codex before 1425, since the "Gaesdonck Codex" already has all the four books. He concludes that Thomas must have written the original between 1416 and 1420. Book I-III appeared in 1416 or 1417, and book IV in 1418 or 1419.[63] This view is supported by Paul Hagen of Lübeck,[64] who discovered a Low German translation of parts of books II-IV in the *Stadt-bibliothek* of Lübeck. Bishop F. J. van Vree of Haarlem found a Dutch translation of two chapters of book IV in a manuscript left by the Sisters of the Common Life at Deventer.[65] Van Vree thought it possible that Thomas à Kempis borrowed these two chapters from some work composed by one or more disciples of Groote.[66]   He and other writers, like Malou,[67] Spitzen,[68] Becker,[69] and Bonet-Maury,[70] have made an extended list of extracts from the works of Groote, Radewijns, and their followers which they compared with corresponding passages in the *Imitation*. A few years later Becker, in a series of articles, endeavored to show the futility of all such work. He concluded that all one can prove, is a similarity in thought and construction; and he believed that the *Imitation* is an original work, composed in the monastery of Mount St. Agnes near Zwolle.

Thus matters stood when in 1920, Paul Hagen published an article in the *Beiaard,* called "De Navolging van Christus en Thomas van Kempen," which is the Dutch translation of an article intended for a German periodical.[71]   Hagen briefly commented here on the interesting discoveries he had made, and also gave the present writer some valuable information, explaining to him how he had conducted his researches.

Among the numerous manuscripts in the City Library at Lübeck which originally belonged to the Sisters of the Common Life of that city, there are two which contain a treatise in Low German called *Admonitions tending to Things Internal.* Also, there is a manuscript in the same library in which chapters VI-IX of the fourth book of the *Imitation* are found, all in the same Low German dialect apparently in use at Lübeck in the fifteenth century.[72]   This was not left by the Sisters of the Common Life living in the convent of Michael, but by the beguines in the *Johanneshof,* a house situated near that of the Sisters of the Common Life.[73]   There can be no doubt that these beguines got this literary material from their friends across the street, and that the latter, in turn, had received it from one of the sister-houses of Deventer or Westphalia, for it was the Low Countries that provided those pious women at Lübeck with religious productions of various kinds.[74]   Just as Thomas à Kempis was only one of the many boys who received the teachings of Groote's followers at Deventer, and just as the works he wrote had been preceded by a great many others, so did the sixty-four chapters of the *Imitation,* translated at Deventer and adapted for the use of the sisters at Lübeck, form merely a small portion of the writings produced originally at Deventer and spread abroad by the disciples of Gerard Groote.

What conclusions are we justified in drawing? Those sixty-four chapters in the Low German dialect, which we shall call L, were put together by Thomas à Kempis when he was still living at Deventer, and must be looked upon as the work of Radewijns, Zerbolt, or one of their followers. Now, L differs so much from the other chapters of book III and IV that they must have been written by two different personalities and at different times, even though the whole work seems after all to have been compiled by Thomas à Kempis, as will be shown presently. We find, for example, that in the first twelve chapters in L the word "O" occurs but once, while in the twelve which are lacking in L, it occurs twenty-five times. In the first sixty chapters of L we find it but nine times; but in the few passages missing here and found in the complete *Imitation*, it occurs thirty times. It is well known that Thomas à Kempis in his later life was in the habit of using this interjection. The almost complete absence of the interjection in the L chapters proves that these were copied during the last year spent by Thomas at Deventer, where he was so strongly influenced by the lives and ideals of Radewijns, Zerbolt, Ketel, and Ten Bossche. The interjections used by Thomas à Kempis are often followed by rhetorical questions. Such questions rarely occur in L. Thus we read in Chapter XXI of Book III of the *Imitation* proper: "O when shall it be fully granted me, to consider in quietness of mind and see how sweet thou art, my Lord God?" And in Chapter XXXIV: "O when will that blessed and desired hour come?" In Chapter XLVIII no fewer than ten such questions succeed each other, of which the first and last start with "O when," and the others with "When." Rhetorical questions are very often repeated in other works by Thomas à Kempis, as, in the *Valley of Lilies*, where in Chapter XXVI, eight similar questions are found with the word "O" in six, and the word "when" in eight. Rhetorical repetitions are also characteristic of Thomas à Kempis' own style. When the writer of the L chapters repeats a word as he repeats "in the cross" nine times in Chapter XII of the second book of the *Imitation,* it is because this is strictly necessary; when Thomas à Kempis repeats, as in using "many" in Book III, Chapter XLVIII, he does so rhetorically. A second example of this sort of repetition, which the L chapters do not have, can be found in Book III, Chapter XXI, where "above all" occurs eighteen times, and in addition the word "thou" is used seven times, the word "alone" six times. Here eleven superlatives are employed. Again, that part of Book III, Chapter LVIII which has the word "I" sixteen times, in a series, is not a part of the L chapters.

The difference in style between the L chapters and those added by Thomas à Kempis is further illustrated by the manner in which God is invoked. While L has only nine comparatively short titles by which to invoke God, the whole *Imitation* has forty-one, some of which are quite elaborate and rhetorical. It is worth noting also that every one of the titles found in the *Imitation,* but absent in L, repeatedly occur in the other writings of Thomas à Kempis. He undoubtedly was the person who worked over the Latin equivalent of L, adding the customary interjections, questions, and exclamations, so characteristic of his own works. The material he found at Deventer in the year 1398-1399, is simpler in style and far more powerful than the paragraphs which he added on Mount St. Agnes.

One can also prove that the matter which was added to L was added by a young monk. In 1416, Thomas à Kempis was a young monk. He was the young monk who wrote that "the life of a young monk is a cross," and that once having proceeded, it will not do for him to look behind him. The author of L, on the contrary, must have been a man of ripe experience outside of a monastery. Apparently he had not been a monk in his previous life, or at least not for a long period. Thomas himself wrote especially for monks, as the contents of Book III, Chapter X plainly indicate, whereas L was not addressed to monks only, but to all Christians generally. He who wrote L, even if he was a monk, which appears very doubtful, nowhere so enthusiastically praises monasticism as Thomas à Kempis does. Thomas writes in Chapter X of Book III: "For it is not granted all to forsake all, to renounce the world, and to undertake a life of religious (monastic) retiredness. . . . O sacred state of religious (monastic) servitude. . . ." In Chapter LVI we read: "Truly the life of a good monk is a cross;" this same sentence is also found in Vol. VI of his *Opera*, p. 249.

In the use of dialogue the writer of L far surpasses Thomas à Kempis. In L the Lord is the principal speaker, and he is not interrupted by approbation, whereas, in those chapters of Book II not found in L, the author who is Thomas à Kempis himself, often breaks into the dialogue, and in a wholly unwarranted and inartistic fashion, just as he does in Vol. V of his *Opera*, on pp. 146-150. There he at first addresses Christ, and then speaks to Jesus, Pilate, the reader, and humanity in general, after which he turns to Christ once more. In L the Lord affirms the words of his Son with a short "It is so, my Son" (Chapter XII of Book III) ; whereas in the *Imitation* we read: "O Lord, it is true," in which the author injects his own personality (Book III, Chapter VI, of which this part is lacking in L), and: "O Lord, what thou sayest is true" (in Book III, Chapter XVIII; also lacking in L). In a similar way Thomas throws in some remarks of his own, thus interrupting the Lord, in Book III, Chapter XXIII: "O Lord, do as thou sayest, for this is delightful for me to hear," just as he does in Vol. I of his *Opera*, on p. 4: "Thou hast well said, Lord," and in Vol. IV on p. 199: "O Lord, it is true what thou sayest: all that thou sayest pleases me."

When one comes to analyze the subject matter of L, one sees that Chapters I-XII, XIII-LX, and LXI-LXIV form three independent and original treatises. They are not dependent on the chapters which follow them in the *Imitation* proper. Chapters I-XII of L correspond to Book II of the *Imitation*, which Thomas himself treated as a separate piece of work with a title of its own. Chapters XIII-LX are like forty-eight chapters of Book III, and the way in which they close proves that here the original treatise, called: *Of Internal Consolation*, ends. In L Chapters I-LX appear like one treatise, beginning with the celebrated saying of Christ: "The kingdom of heaven is within you." They close with the following sentence: "Give me a happy departure from this world, and lead me straight-way into the kingdom. Amen." They begin and finish with "the kingdom of heaven." Thomas spoiled this fitting end by adding some material of his own, and by changing the order of some of the chapters. The same can be said of Chapters LXI-LXIV of L, which also form an independent treatise with a title and a fitting close. They constitute the best part of Book IV of the *Imitation;* in form and contents they can be easily distinguished from the preceding and following chapters of Book IV. Their title is: "A Short and Fitting Exercise for the Communion Service," which "exercise" forcibly reminds us of the religious exercises, or *devota exercitia,* of the men at Deventer who left Thomas à Kempis in possession of their literary productions.

Once more then we must ask why the *Imitation* at once acquired such world-wide circulation, leaving the other productions by Thomas à Kempis far, far behind? He did indeed place it at the head of his other works, thereby showing that he regarded it as his own work. And John Busch called Thomas its author. The *Imitation* in its present form, therefore, may be termed the work of Thomas à Kempis, using this term in its early sense, for he composed a portion of the work himself, and worked over into it some "devout exercises" of Radewijns and Zerbolt, which he later adopted for the use of novices at Mount St. Agnes.

5. Gerard Zerbolt Wrote the Original Version of the "Imitation"

Radewijns and Zerbolt were very closely associated with each other in the brethren-house at Deventer, as we have seen. The latter became a leading scholar and author, but the former continued to act chiefly as an adviser and moderator. While Zerbolt sat in the library studying profound questions of law and theology, his friend was giving counsel to some poor or sick followers in the city.[75] Tremendous was the knowledge of human nature acquired by Radewijns, but he did not possess the facilities for presenting his knowledge to the world in great literary works. That he left for Zerbolt to perform, while young Thomas à Kempis gradually learned to copy the excerpt-books.

It is remarkable to note how many fifteenth century editions of the *Spiritual Ascensions* by Zerbolt were published and how closely this mystical production resembles the first book of the *Imitation*. The first edition was printed in or about 1486 at Deventer — a significant fact. The second edition appeared two years later in Cologne, the third before 1490, at Basel, the fourth in 1490, at Lübeck, the fifth between 1483 and 1493, in Strassburg, the sixth about 1495, in Paris, the seventh and eighth about a year later in Paris, the ninth about 1498, in Cologne, the tenth in 1499, at Montserrat, the eleventh about 1500, in Strassburg, and the twelfth about 1500, in Cologne.[76] We do not know exactly when the edition of Sorg at Augsburg made its appearance, but the leading authorities give the year 1490. The only original work by Radewijns, on the other hand, was not published till the nineteenth century, and even that composition is largely a collection of sayings by earlier writers.

A striking example of the powerful influence which Zerbolt exerted upon great leaders may be seen in the words of Professor Martin Luther at the University of Wittenberg. He was in the middle of his course of lectures on the Epistle to the Romans by the Apostle Paul, somewhere in the academic year 1515-1516. After some ten years of struggling against the forces of evil in mind and body he finally broke with the theology accepted at that time by the leading clergy in the Roman Catholic Church. He concluded that man can perform no good works without divine assistance.

This significant statement of Luther is found in his Lecture on Paul's Epistle: "Nowhere have I found so clear an explanation of original sin as in the little treatise of Gerard Groote: 'Blessed is the man,' where he speaks as a sensible theologian, and not as a rash philosopher," the quotation making reference to the *Spiritual Ascensions* of Gerard Zerbolt, which begins with: "Blessed is the man." Paul had written in the third chapter of his Epistle to the Romans: "Therefore we conclude that a man is justified by faith without the deeds of the law." What were the conclusions drawn by Luther? All our thoughts, and all our deeds are sinful. Even in our very noblest thoughts and our best works the stain of sin mars every effort we make to improve our character. Man can do nothing without grace; he is depraved, owing to the fall of Adam. "And what is original sin?" Luther asks. "According to the subtle arguments of the scholastic theologians, it is the absence of original justice. . . . According to the Apostle and the simple teachings of Jesus Christ, it is not merely the deprivation of a function in the will, not merely the withdrawal of light from the intellect, or power from the memory, but it is the loss of all rectitude and all efficacy in all our faculties, both of the body and the soul, of the interior and the whole of the exterior man. It is besides the inclination to do evil, the dislike of good, the aversion to light and wisdom, the love of error and darkness, the departure from and abomination of good works, and the approach to evil. Hence, as the Fathers have justly remarked, this original sin is the fuel itself of concupiscence, the law of the flesh, the law of the members, the disease of nature, the tyrant, the original disease. . . . Here you have that hydra with its many heads, that imperishable monster with which we here below are struggling till death. Here you have that untameable Cerberus, that invincible Antaeos. I have found no one to give such a clear explanation of original sin as Gerard Groote in his little treatise: 'Blessed is the man,' where he does not speak as a rash philosopher, but as a sound theologian."[77]

Luther can fully agree with only one earlier writer, and this writer Gerard Zerbolt of Zutphen, a Brother of the Common Life at Deventer. Luther had studied for one year with the Brethren of the Common Life in the great city of Magdeburg (1497-1498), where no doubt he had heard something about Gerard Groote, the founder, and Gerard Zerbolt, the first librarian of the brotherhood. In the year 1532, he wrote to the rector of the Brethren of the Common Life at Herford: "If all other things were in as good condition as the brethren-houses, the Church would be much too blessed even in this life. Your dress and other commendable usages do not injure the Gospel, but are rather of advantage to it, assailed as in these days it is by reckless and unbridled spirits who know how to destroy, but not to build up."

What had fascinated Luther, together with thousands of other scholars, was the remarkable method used by Zerbolt and other devout brothers. They believed not only in the fall of man but also in the rise of man. Zerbolt had prepared an elaborate system of exercises for the recovery of lost faculties in the mind and body of man. That is why his masterpiece was later named *Spiritual Ascensions*. His other great mystical book was entitled, *On the Reformation of the Faculties of the Soul*. The *Imitation of Christ* was likewise devoted to the problem of uprooting vices and the acquisition of virtues. Strange though this may seem to certain readers, this splendid program of fighting sin appealed as much to Luther as it did to Ignatius Loyola, the founder of the Jesuits. The latter was swept off his feet by the *Imitation*, as is well known. As a result his followers until this day always must carry with them a copy of this book wherever they go. But what is less well known is Luther's admiration for Zerbolt's great book and for the Brethren of the Common Life. He did, however, misunderstand Zerbolt's view on the depravity of man. Zerbolt explicitly taught that man was not totally depraved.

From the Netherlands the chief literary productions of Groote's followers spread throughout the Holy Roman Empire and France, and invaded Spain and Italy besides. It would be a very complicated task to follow the trail of even the *Imitation* alone, on its journey from place to place, and often from home to home. One remarkable incident, however, should be recorded here. In the Benedictine monastery of Montserrat, near Barcelona, in Spain, lived a pious abbot, named Garcia of Cisneros, nephew of Cardinal Ximenes of Cisneros. He had heard the fame of the Imitation, Gerard Zerbolt, and the brethren, wherefore he took a trip to France, and came back with a collection of mystical writings. In January, 1499, he set up a press at Montserrat. At once he began to print 800 copies of the *Spiritual Ascensions* of Gerard Zerbolt.[78] This work and the *Rosary* of Mombaer seem to have impressed him very much, for about this time he composed a work which he copied very largely after these two. He called it *Ejercitatorio de la vida expiritual, or Spiritual Exercises.* In 1500, he printed 1,006 copies of this work, 800 in Spanish, and 206 in the Latin translation. Several times it was reprinted in Latin, and both French and Italian translations were made.[79]

The *Spiritual Exercises* of Garcia of Cisneros have been carefully analyzed by P. H. Watrigant, a Jesuit scholar. The result of his investigation shows that Garcia of Cisneros copied the general outline of his course of spiritual exercises from Zerbolt. The aim he pursues is the same as that sought by Zerbolt. Chapters XLIX-LII of the work are almost verbally reproduced from Chapters XXVII-XXX of the *Spiritual Ascensions by* Gerard Zerbolt of Zutphen.[80] His chief source was Zerbolt, but he also made use of the *Imitation,* Mombaer's *Rosary,* Gerson, Richard of St. Victor, and Bonaventura. Garcia borrowed rather heavily from Mombaer. "Almost all the practical hints, and nearly everything relating to the general method simply are extracts from the *Rosary.*"[81] The latter work was written by a monk in the Windesheim Congregation and based largely on Zerbolt's books.

The Devotio Moderna had become a movement of consequence. Doubtless, many other men soon followed Garcia's example in Spain and Italy, and many students carried home with them from Paris works like the *Imitation* and the *Spiritual Ascensions.* The main reason why the work of Cisneros is mentioned here is that it had a great influence on the life of Ignatius Loyola, founder of the Jesuits.

Loyola was still a soldier when on the 21st of March, 1522, he knocked at the gate of the monastery of Montserrat, where Cisneros had died in 1510. Here he spent three days in a narrow cell, and confessed all his sins to Father Xanones. On March 24 he laid aside his armor forever, put on a hair-cloth, and issued forth as a pilgrim and servant of God. He intended to go to Barcelona, but on his way he met some kind people who were going to the convent of St. Lucia at Manresa, situated only a few miles from Montserrat; there they secured a room for him. As the pestilence was raging at Barcelona, Loyola was obliged to remain at Manresa, and not only a few days, but nearly a whole year.

At Manresa, Loyola went through nearly the same experiences as had Luther in the monastery at Erfurt. Tormented by the burden of sin and the fear of future punishment, he groaned, struggled, fasted, and prayed for forgiveness. He confessed his sins every day, but this very confession increased his fears, and then he would wrestle again, and again, till at last hope wiped the drops of sweat from his weary brow. Luther fought from July, 1505, until October, 1512, while Loyola finished his battle in about half a year. There were several books that Loyola devoured at Manresa, chief among which were the *Imitation*, the Life of Christ by Ludolph of Saxony (d. 1378), *the Flower of the Saints,* containing legendary accounts of martyrs, and the *Spiritual Exercises* of Garcia of Cisneros. The *Imitation* made such an overpowering impression upon him that after reading it he cared little for any other work. From day to day he read only in the *Gersoncito*, as he called the *Imitation*.[82] In fact, when he finished his *Spiritual Exercises*, in 1525, he placed the *Imitation* before the Gospel: "On the second day of the week and thereafter, it will be very profitable to read a selection from the *Imitation* or the Gospels, or the 'Lives of the Saints.' "[83] Afterwards, when the official Latin translation appeared, which was first printed in 1545, this sentence was changed to read: ". . . from the Gospel or some other pious book, like the 'Imitation,' or the 'Life of the Saints.' " For Loyola did not mean to say that the *Imitation* was a better work than the Gospel. He probably meant that it was easier to understand.[84] But his extraordinary liking for this masterpiece of the Devotio Moderna linked him at once with the other disciples of Gerard Groote. It has often been intimated that what the Bible became for Luther, the *Imitation* was for Loyola. The little work did indeed to a very large extent mould his whole life and all his plans.[85]

Loyola loved the *Imitation*. He just as anxiously strove to circulate it as Luther did the Bible. Every one whom he wished to honor he presented with a copy. We involuntarily ask why this little mystical production from the Yssel country appealed to him so soon and so powerfully? It really contains nothing new, reasons Professor H. Böhmer of Marburg. Nevertheless, in some way it changed Loyola's whole outlook upon life. Henceforth he no longer sought refuge in formal, external observances. He now tried to enrich his inner life. The mysticism of Groote's followers had gripped him, and it held him fast. Gradually his whole inner life became purified; his will, feelings, thoughts, prayers, and actions were simultaneously spiritualized; after that time he was a new man. It was then that he first thought of composing a course of religious exercises.[86]

The *Spiritualia Exercitia* of Loyola may be termed one of the last fruits of the Devotio Moderna.[87] The method of contemplation and most of the material for the meditations Loyola borrowed from the *Life of Christ* by Ludolph of Saxony, who wrote his work before Groote's conversion. In some way, however, Loyola copied in an unmistakable manner after Zerbolt and Mombaer. He could not have read Zerbolt before 1526, for till then he only knew Spanish, but still he must have been acquainted with its contents. The pious folk at Manresa probably had received some copies of Zerbolt's *Spiritual Ascensions* from the neighboring town of Montserrat. However this may be, Loyola borrowed quite systematically from Zerbolt. No one can disguise the fact that there is a great analogy between the plan of the *Spiritual Ascensions* of Gerard and the general arrangement of the "Exercises" of Ignatius Loyola. And when one enters upon a more detailed comparison, he notices that the ascetic of Manresa resembles the Dutch author more closely than his compatriot of Montserrat. For in addition to the points which he has in common with both, he resembles Gerard in several important particulars which Cisneros has left out. Striking examples of the instructions given in the

Spiritual Ascensions and the *Exercises,* relate to the examination of the conscience and the exact notion of true devotion. In the two masterpieces of Gerard of Zutphen and Ignatius we everywhere meet with a practical spirit which is not found to the same degree in the work of Garcia of Cisneros. This practical spirit is clearly demonstrated in the nature of the wholesome spiritual exercises: that one should regulate his manner of living in accordance with the divine plan. We also find this practical spirit in the objects of the exercises: our vices must be eradicated and new virtues acquired. Again, this same practical spirit is displayed in the method of procedure. Gerard of Zutphen and Ignatius employed it with greater discretion and moderation than did Mombaer.[88]

Protestants in general would have been much more friendly to the *Imitation* if it had come out at once in the garb which Zerbolt originally gave to it. He not only composed Book I but also the treatise upon which the second and third books were based. This treatise the present writer published in English translation in his edition of the *Imitation* (1927). It was the first English translation of this powerful piece of mystical literature. The *Imitation* received its title and most of its appeal from Book I. In its original form it reflected perfectly the attitude of the Brethren of the Common Life toward the duty of the average Christian in the world of affairs. These pious men did not condemn monasticism but preferred to live in semi-monastic institutions. They kept the three monastic vows and they were very friendly with the monastic orders, especially after Zerbolt had convinced the Franciscans and the Dominicans that they were thoroughly orthodox. At the Council of Constance (1414-1418) they were ably and successfully defended by Gerson, the Chancellor of the University of Paris. Moreover, from Pope Eugene IV they received valuable privileges. Again, Cardinal Cusa was so impressed by their useful labors that near the end of his life he left a large sum of money for the founding of a home for twenty young men, who were to study with the Brethren of the Common Life at Deventer. This house survived the storms of the Reformation.[89]

Nevertheless, the Brotherhood of the Common Life, as Zerbolt showed in his brilliant treatise, *On the Common Life*, had a tendency to side with those who favored a reduction of asceticism in all directions. Thomas à Kempis, as we shall see, frowned upon Zerbolt's bold ideas in the realm of politics. He naturally did not have much interest in legal studies, but Zerbolt was an expert in those. Consequently, Chapter II of the *Imitation* mentioned a person who knew less about the law than others did. Thomas à Kempis retained this interesting passage. Neither he nor Zerbolt showed heretical inclinations. They freely utilized the works of medieval saints and doctors, and praised them for their work. Luther and Calvin, on the other hand, showed little respect for them.

It has recently been demonstrated that Radewijns and Zerbolt were deeply interested in a mystical treatise by the Franciscan friar, David of Augsburg, entitled, *Profectus Religiosorum.* Radewijns strongly urged his disciples to read that inspiring book, and it is mentioned in the introduction to the original constitution of the brethren-house at Deventer.⁹⁰ The two famous works by Zerbolt contain large sections copied almost verbally from this treatise. In the *Treatise of Spiritual Exercises* by Radewijns numerous quotations have also been found.⁹¹

About the year 1840 a teacher at the Gymnasium in Eutin, in what was once known as Oldenburg, found an interesting manuscript containing the Eutin Copy of Book I of the *Imitation.* This book is after all the only one of the four in the *Imitation* which deserves the title subsequently given to the four books collectively. The German instructor in question was fascinated by the fifteen chapters which follow the first book of the *Imitation.* There are altogether forty chapters, of which the first twenty-five form Book I of the *Imitation.* In 1845 he published a treatise on the subject, in which he stated that here we have the original version of Book I of the *Imitation.*⁹² He was absolutely right, but later authorities disowned his claim, which led to the neglect of the manuscript until 1927.

Now we know that Chapter XXIX in the composite work was largely copied from Chapter LXI of Book III of the *Profectus*

Religiosorum by David of Augsburg, and that all of the forty chapters owe much to the same writer, though still more to Radewijns and Zerbolt. According to one learned professor in the University of Nijmegen, the first twenty-five chapters were copied from an earlier treatise by Gerard Groote. Zerbolt was the copyist.[93] But other writers in the Netherlands made different assertions, pointing to errors of judgment in the numerous articles by this admirer of Groote.[94] The latter, however, had done an immense amount of research work, and we are greatly indebted to him for the publication of four versions in parallel columns, including Book I of the *Imitation* as it appeared in the autograph of Thomas à Kempis. These four versions clearly reveal the influence of Radewijns and Zerbolt upon Thomas à Kempis.

The Eutin Copy deserves careful study. Its first twenty-five chapters form a mystical treatise far superior to Book I of the *Imitation* as the literary world has known it ever since the middle of the fifteenth century. This composition may well be considered the finest flower of Christian mysticism, and it ranks next only to the New Testament in the Bible. Here indeed we find the very heart, the Gospel, of the Devotio Moderna. It was written in the brethren-house at Deventer, either by or under the influence of Radewijns and Zerbolt. Why a work of such immense religious power should have lain neglected so long in a German monastery and later in an insignificant high school at Eutin may seem a veritable mystery. Its superiority to the poor copy by Thomas à Kempis can be seen in the following comparison:

Verse 3 in Chapter I cannot fail to arrest the eye of the observer: While Thomas à Kempis asks to meditate upon the life of Christ, the Eutin Copy insists that the reader do not stray from his subject, which is the imitation of Christ. As we have seen, Thomas very often wandered away from his theme, and he delighted in fanciful discursions, interrupting God or Christ at inopportune moments. He was the author of a book entitled, *Meditations on the Life of Christ.* Consequently, he changed the third verse in the *Imitation* to suit his own taste. He liked meditation better than action.

In the fourth verse of the Eutin Copy, unlike that by Thomas, we are told that "he who has the spirit of Christ will find the hidden manna." Thomas speaks of having the spirit, and other copies of the spirit of God, whereas the subject introduced is the doctrine of Christ. Consequently, the reader of Christ's words is expected to have His spirit in order to understand these words.

The tenth verse contains a sensational revelation. In the Eutin Copy we find the correct Latin phrase: "*Si scires totam bibliam,*" while Thomas à Kempis, unlearned as he was in the Latin tongue, inserted a Germanic phrase: "*Si scires totam bibliam exterius.*" That is a literal translation of the Dutch idiom, so well known to Thomas. Another version reads: "*Si scires totam bibliam corde.*" That corresponds to our own English: "If you knew the whole Bible by heart."

In the nineteenth verse Thomas refers to a proverb, which is not mentioned in the Eutin Copy. In the next verse the latter adds a lengthy statement about the main theme in the *Imitation*, which Thomas chose not to copy here: "Conform yourself to the invisible things and the better life, and thus you will imitate Christ, for every action of His is for us an instruction." Then follows a text from the Book of Job, which is to be found also in the Lübeck edition of 1489. This is most signicant, for it was in the home of the Sisters of the Common Life in Lübeck that Book II and Book III of the *Imitation* were read in the original version, though in Low German translation. Eutin is not far from Lübeck, and the whole region between the Yssel Valley and Lübeck was thoroughly affected by the spirit of the Devotio Moderna.

In the first verse of Chapter II the Eutin Copy contains another important statement not accepted by Thomas. In the fourth verse Thomas talks about a person who knows all things in this world but does not possess love, while the Eutin Copy mentions only the knowledge about Christ. The title above Chapter II is here: "*De Cognitione sui.*" Thomas, on

The third page of the *De Libriis Teutonicalibus*
by Gerard Zerbolt of Zutphen

the other hand, has *"De Humili Sentire sui ipsius."* He again has strayed from his subject in the fourth verse of this chapter, while the author of the Eutin Copy continues to adhere to his chosen task: the imitation of Christ. The latter has nothing to correspond to verses 7-10, but adds material later on in the chapter that is missing in the printed version. It is becoming clear to us now why Thomas could have been so bold as to assert that he wrote the *Imitation.* He certainly made numerous far-reaching changes in Book I. Both versions, however, have the famous and characteristic phrase: *"Ama nescire,"* or *"Ama nesciri."* Thomas has the latter, which seems more to the point. Yet the Eutin Copy is not without merit, for it reads: *"Ama nescire ad quae non teneris et gaude pro nihilo reputari."*

As a matter of fact, we note a tremendous difference between the view of Zerbolt and that of his pupil, Thomas à Kempis. The former wrote: "If you wish to know or learn anything profitable, then love to know nothing about those things that do not concern you, and rejoice in being considered of little value." The pupil was more drastic and less sensible. He changed Zerbolt's profound words into these: "Love to be unknown." Zerbolt would hear of no such thing, for he was a scholar and recognized the hand of God in all forms of scholarship. In the fourteenth century there were indeed numerous mystics who took pride in the fact that they were dealing with things unknown. One work was entitled, *The Cloud of Unknowing,* and the House of Harper in recent years published an English version of this remarkable book. It was not the type that Zerbolt and Groote were recommending for their lay pupils.

In Chapter III Thomas added verses 3-6, in which he discussed topics studied in the schools. Since he himself attended none of the higher institutions of learning, he spoke disparagingly about "genus and species." The author of the Eutin Copy, on the other hand, was a real scholar, such as Zerbolt was, and he did not wish to belittle the work done in the universities. Very well known are these words of Thomas à Kempis in verses

3 and 4: "What does it avail to cavil much about dark and hidden things, concerning which we shall not be reproved in the day of judgment, because we did not know them? It is a great folly. . . . to give our minds to things that are curious."

Zerbolt was too great a scholar to argue that his readers should not be interested in "things that are curious." He had naturally heard certain fearful clergymen talk about the need of avoiding the study of scientific subjects. The latter were of the opinion, as was Thomas à Kempis, that laymen must not pry into God's secrets. Zerbolt also was not the author of verses 10-22 in Chapter III, where Thomas à Kempis wanted all things reduced to one. The latter favored the process of generalization, so appealing to simple minds. He praised those who did not exhibit "deep search after learning." No wonder, for Thomas had never attended a university and was afraid of science.

What is still worse, Thomas wrote in verse 14: "Quanto aliquis magis sibi unitus et interius simplificatus fuerit." As has been pointed out by Professor J. van Ginneken of the Catholic University at Nijmegen, and repeated in the handsome volume entitled, *The Following of Christ: The Spiritual Diary of Gerard Groote*,[95] Thomas wrote "sibi" for "tibi," and he mistook "simplificatus" for "similatus." He also missed the words "de te."

Even more startling is the absence in the Eutin Copy of these famous remarks by Thomas: "Tell me where are all those doctors and masters with whom you were well acquainted while they lived and flourished in learning?" Zerbolt had too much respect for these men with doctor's and master's degrees to treat them with such words of scorn. Thomas writes in verse 30: "Oh, how quickly passes the glory of this world." That is strictly Biblical and respectable, but Zerbolt had to utilize the services of doctors and masters in the affairs of his brotherhood. We know of one learned Benedictine abbot, who aided him in his work.[96] And how could Zerbolt have talked so glibly about learned abbots as did Thomas when he wrote in verse 28: "Now others possess their prebends"? Thomas showed much concern over the fate of those who "perish through their vain learning in this world," but the Eutin Copy maintains a discreet silence here (verse 32).

In this connection it might be noted that in verse 11 of Chapter II Thomas suggested that nobody be puffed up because of great knowledge in some art of science, while Gerard Zerbolt warned against pride without complaining about having accomplished something great in art or science. The title of Chapter II is equally revealing. While Zerbolt speaks of self-knowledge as being the main topic, and makes much of studying a person's own thoughts and character, the humble Thomas shows his dislike for the idea of obtaining knowledge, even of the person himself.

The title of Chapter V is in itself enough to prove that Gerard Zerbolt was the author of the original version as found in the Eutin Copy. There he copied the exact words he had used in a separate treatise devoted to the same subject. His title was "De Lectione Sacrae Scripturae." Thomas changed these words into the following: "De Lectione Sanctuarum Scripturarum." Zerbolt was the author of an interesting pamphlet entitled, *An Liceat Libros Divinos Tranferre in Vulgare.* Only one copy of this composition escaped the destruction of the sixteenth and seventeenth centuries. This copy was discovered by the present writer in the year 1920. He was the first to publish it.[97] The first sentence in this treatise begins with these words: "Quoniam sunt nonnulli minus sacram scripturam intelligentes."

The first verse in the copy in Eutin reads: "Veritas in sacris scripturis inquirenda est, non eloquentia." The corresponding verse by Thomas à Kempis has: "Veritas est in scripturis sanctis quaerenda: non eloquentia." Here again we note the contrast between the words "sancta" and "sacra." The third and fourth verses by Thomas discuss the problem of preferring useful ideas above profound thoughts, while the reader is advised to read "devout books" rather than profound literature. That is in keeping with the pious mind of Thomas à Kempis. Gerard Zerbolt, on the other hand, has nothing to say about these matters. In verse 5 Zerbolt says that the reader must not be offended by the simplicity of the author or the book he reads, while Thomas speaks of the authority of the writer. In verse 10 Zerbolt again has the telling phrase "sacra scriptura," and this time Thomas does not mention the sacred writings at all. Thomas in verse 11 refers to the "words of the saints." Zerbolt shows no interest here in saints. Over against "lectione sacrae scripturae" by Zerbolt in verse 9 Thomas has "lectione scripturarum." Moreover, Zerbolt does not have the two verses (7 and 8) in which Thomas says that human beings will pass on while the truth of God remains forever.

It was of course perfectly natural for Zerbolt to devote a whole chapter to the subject of reading sacred literature. He had said in his treatise on the reading of sacred books in the vernacular that laymen ought not to read books that were too difficult or obscure. That is why in the present book he told the reader not to complain if his reading material seemed too simple to him. He also made much of the fact that the truth is more important than the style of a book. Again, he spoke eloquently about the need of reading a book in the same spirit as that in which it was written. Thomas à Kempis would probably have seen no need at all of writing a chapter on the reading of sacred books, but, having been provided with such a chapter by Zerbolt, he kept and changed it to suit his own tastes. It is also interesting to note the title of Chapter IV in the Constitution of the Brethren of the Common Life at Deventer, published for the first time by the present author: "De Studio Sacrae Scripturae." This title is almost identical with that of Chapter V in the *Imitation* by Zerbolt.

Chapter VI is of great importance, as it urges the reader not to become too familiar with other persons. In recent years a number of Dutch historians have overlooked this feature in the Devotio Moderna. For example, a learned Dutch scholar at the University of Leiden went so far as to say that when Erasmus indulged in neurotic friendships with other monks, he resembled the leaders of the Devotio Moderna. Since he had nothing else of importance to say about the Devotio Moderna in his study of Erasmus, he certainly left us a sad picture about the influence of this great movement upon the mind of the famous Dutch humanist.[98] Zerbolt and Radewijns, as well as Thomas à Kempis, would have resented such thoughtless interpretation on the part of a modernistic professor. In the Eutin Copy we read the same sentiments as those presented by Thomas. Even more convincing are the verses in Chapter VIII: "On Shunning too much Familiarity." Erasmus must have paid little heed to that chapter when he was a monk.

It is not clear why the author of the Eutin Copy in Chapter VII did not discuss, as Thomas did, the fate of those who are considered "poor in this life." Thomas told them not to be ashamed of their condition, while the original version ignored the poor people. In the latter work there is also no reference to the desirability of loving only God and the angels, rather than human beings. Zerbolt no doubt felt that a person should love his neighbor as himself, as Christ had stated. In his opinion it would not do to go so far as Thomas and condemn all forms of human affection (Chapter VIII, verse 6).

Most interesting is the plagiarism indulged in by the author of the Eutin Copy in verse 5 of Chapter VIII. While he copied literally from Daivd of Augsburg, as the scribe did also in Chapter XXIX, that is the fourth chapter added by a scribe to the first twenty-five, Thomas carefully revised the original version. Thomas said that a man should merely commend all women to God. Zerbolt was not so inhumane, and he suggested that one should either love all women equally or else keep at a distance from all of them.

It is interesting to note the difference in the word order adopted by the two writers in question. Thomas often follows an arrangement that resembles somewhat the order in Dutch sentences. He puts the verbs farther to the end of the sentence, while Zerbolt has another type of sentence structure. For example, the first verse in Chapter VIII reads in the copy at Eutin: "Ne revele cor tuum omni homini." Thomas, on the other hand, has: "Non omni homini revele cor tuum." In Zerbolt's treatise on the reading of the Bible in the vernacular we find this statement: "Quam si illud expenderent in rebus terrenis." Thomas would probably have put the verb at the end of the sentence.

Another difference between Thomas and Zerbolt is the way in which Thomas wanders away from his subject while Zerbolt meticulously goes right on with his theme. This is a matter of great importance, since we are now dealing with the book which caused the great fame of the four put together in the form of the *Imitation* as we now know it. The first book begins with these words: "He who follows me shall not walk in darkness, says the Lord." Zerbolt, who was very consistent and scholarly, stuck to his subject and at the end of Book I he wrote these significant words: "Follow the Lord." Thomas, on the other hand, rambled on with no thought about literary perfection. He ended the first book in this manner: "The more violence you do to yourself, the more, also, you will grow in virtue."

The title of Chapter IX shows that Thomas was not satisfied with a discussion of obedience but had to add to the original version these two words: "And Subjection." In verse 4 he wrote: "Go where you will, you will find no rest save in humble subjection to the rule of a superior." That sentiment was too strong for Zerbolt and Radewijns, who had refused to accept monasticism for themselves. Consequently, the Eutin Copy does not contain this verse. The same is true of verses 7-10, which mention the desirability of excessive obedience and humility. Instead of this we have the important political theory of the rights of the individual, not brought up by Thomas: "If you have an opinion which is better than the yoke of your prelate, nevertheless for the sake of obedience relinquish your idea and accept the order of your superior, in so far as it is good. But if the commands of the prelates are contrary to the precepts of God, we are not obliged to obey them but rather those of God." Such bold language naturally did not appeal to the humble monk, but Zerbolt had written in his *Treatise on the Common Life* that he and his associates were free to carry on as they saw fit regardless of the criticism leveled against them by venerable prelates. Groote had used almost exactly the same words as those we have just quoted. He had gone so far as to say that it was not necessary to obey the Pope unless the latter were in the right.[99]

In Chapter XI Thomas inserted his eighth verse, which reads: "If we were perfectly dead to ourselves, and not entangled within our own breasts; then should we be able to taste divine things, and to have experience of heavenly contemplation." In the brethren-house at Deventer this sentiment was not entirely overlooked, but the scholarly mind of Zerbolt was too much immersed in legal affairs to ignore the value of worldly wisdom. Extreme forms of asceticism were not nearly so popular in Deventer as they were at Windesheim. Deventer was the home of practical mysticism, but Thomas felt more at home in his monastery than in the brethren-house. To the original version of the *Imitation* he added statements that seem logical to a monk but not fashionable in great Hanseatic cities. He also added verse 13, in which he spoke of *"religio,"* the Latin for monasticism. On the other hand, he eliminated the references made in the Eutin Copy to the devil who is going around and roaring like a lion, seeking whom he may devour. He also refused to copy the phrase so familiar in the brethren-house: *"bona exercitia."* Furthermore, he left out the reference to those who welcome temptations in order to achieve new victories (Chapter XIII, verses 3 and 9).

The title of Chapter XII in Zerbolt's version reads this way: "De Adversitate." But Thomas has "De Utilitate Adversitatis." We see here a difference in the respective attitudes toward the suffering of adversity. While the Brother of the Common Life is less ascetically inclined than the average monk, he must give expression to his own state of mind by leaving out the idea that adversities are in themselves useful. At the end of Chapter XII Zerbolt adds two significant verses, which Thomas must have disliked. Zerbolt says that temptations force us to know ourselves better. In his famous book on spiritual ascensions he made much of self-knowledge, and here in his first book of the *Imitation* he again emphasized the need of studying our inner selves and our thoughts.

In verse 8 of Chapter XIII Zerbolt presented some interesting observations about certain monks. He knew that Groote had at one time entered a Carthusian monastery, but that at the end of his life he had cautioned his followers against adopting severe rules, like those of the Carthusians. Now Zerbolt was sitting in the house of the Brothers of the Common Life in Deventer. He was thinking about the Carthusians and he wrote: "The more saintly a man is or the place in which he resides, the stronger will be the temptations he will have to deal with: The Carthusians and the cloistered folks and the real monks sustain the greatest tempations." He was pointing' toward the monks as a bystander; he was not one of them himself. Now what did Thomas do with this passage? He wrote: "There is no order so saintly nor a place so secluded that there are no temptations nor adversities."

The fourteenth chapter adds further contrasts between the two versions under discussion. While the Eutin Copy in verse 3 presents a famous text from the Gospel about a man who out of the good treasure of his heart produces good works, Thomas omits the quotation and establishes for himself a greater degree of independence. In his ninth verse he refers to differences of opinion which lead to dissensions. Again he speaks of "religious persons," meaning monks, and again the Eutin Copy ignores the monks. The title of Chapter XV makes us wonder why Thomas wishes to increase the gap between the two versions. Whereas he speaks of works done out of love, the other version is entirely negative in referring to evils to be avoided. Once more we must point to Thomas' habit of wandering from his subject. He adopted a new title for the chapter, though the old one conformed absolutely to the contents of the opening verse which begins as follows: "For no worldly thing, and for the love of no man, is any evil to be done." In this chapter the older version mentions "fraternal love" and "fraternal charity," for a brother was known as a *"frater."* He was not a *"religiosus."* Thomas omitted both phrases, as might have been expected of a man who was once a *"frater"* and later a *"religiosus."*

The "*frater*" who wrote Chapters XV and XVI had much to say about going out to help the poor and afflicted: he quoted the Apostle who wrote: "Bear each other's burdens." That verse was not literally copied by Thomas who ascribed it to God directly. The title of his seventeenth chapter reads significantly: "Of the Monastic Life." The Eutin Copy could not very well carry such a heading, and here we read: "Of the Life of the Congregation." In the second verse Thomas referred only to monks, but the older version has at the end of the first verse the phrase, "discordia fratrum," meaning discords among the Brethren of the Common Life, and in the next verse it discusses a congregation which may live either in a spiritual or a secular atmosphere. Thomas of course had to drop the remark about the secular environment, for that was the realm in which the Brethren of the Common Life labored by preference. However, in verse 3 the Eutin Copy has one reference to the monastic life. Verses 9-12 by Thomas are not to be found in the Eutin Copy. Here we read: "You came to serve, not to rule. You must know that you were called to suffer and to labor, not to be idle and gossip. Here therefore are men tried as gold in the furnace." That was true of the monastery, but the Brethren were too busy helping people in the cities to devote themselves to suffering and to the serving of a monastic superior.

Whereas the title of Chapter XVIII in the Eutin Copy has simply, "Of the Examples of the Fathers," Thomas wrote, "Of the Examples of the Saintly Fathers." In verse 5 the former begins thus: "The elect of God all hated the worldly things." Thomas said nothing about the elect of God but merely mentioned the fact that "they hated their lives in this world." In verse 12 he remarked that the saints were poor in things of this world, which statement is missing in the other version. The latter also lacks verses 18-24, in which the typical expressions of Thomas appear four times: "*O quantus,*" "*O quanta,*" "*Och teporis*" and "*Utinam.*" It was exactly this type of literature, as we saw, that he added to the second and third books of the

Imitation. Moreover, the word *"Och"* is Dutch, not Latin. Zerbolt would have scorned to use it.

Thomas took far more liberties with the first book than with the others, for after his departure from the "fraterhuis" at Deventer he sensed the profound difference between the Brotherhood of the Common Life and the monastic orders. Consequently, when he came to Chapter XIX with its simple title of, "On the Good Life," he felt impelled to change it into these words, "On the Exercises of a Good Monk." In the first verse the "good man" became the "religious man," meaning the monk. Verses 19-26 do not appear in the Eutin Copy, for Thomas wanted to add some remarks about exercises fitted for monks. Similarly, he added verses 38-43 to Chapter XX, which are devoted to a depreciation of worldly things. Again, in Chapter XXII he inserted verses 9-11, 19-20, and 24-29. His favorable opinion of asceticism was neatly expressed in two verses (35 and 36) of Chapter XXIII, where he wrote: "Chastise your body now with penitence, that then you may have a sure confidence."

Near the end of Chapter XXIV Thomas presented this new material (verses 40 and 41) : "If until this day you had always lived in honors and delights, what would all that profit you, if you were to die this moment? All is therefore vanity, except to love God and to serve Him only." Verses 31-35 are also his original work. In the last chapter we note further revisions. Verses 11-24 are all by Thomas and missing in the Eutin Copy. This section begins with these words: "Nor did he have a mind to search curiously any further, to know what would befall h'im." Thomas was again urging the reader not to become too much interested in secular things. In verses 29-31 he referred twice to monks, but both statements are missing in the older version. Gradually he was leading up to a very important remark that has caused much misunderstanding among the European authorities.

We must carefully weigh his words in verse 35, for the whole paragraph is wanting in the Eutin Copy, as is perfectly natural: Thomas was an Augustinian monk, and he remembered the words of Groote in connection with the founding of the new monastic organization. Groote's disciples had been asking him what order they should join, and he had replied, "Not the Carthusians, nor the Cistercians, for their rules are too strict for you." But as for the Augustinian Canons Regular, that was another matter. They formed a highly venerable order, and their asceticism was very mild. Consequently, we are not a bit surprised to hear Thomas remark: "Observe the Carthusians, the Cistercians, and the monks and nuns of various orders, how they do every night rise to sing psalms to the Lord!" Yes indeed, they were used to rigorous discipline and mortification of their bodies, which elicited the admiration of Thomas à Kempis. If he had been in Groote's place, he might well have told the men and women to become Carthusians. Groote had spent a few years himself in a Carthusian monastery, and he knew what was expected of his associates. Naturally he could not have composed the verse just quoted, although one Dutch writer has repeatedly asserted that he wrote the whole of Book I of the *Imitation*. Why should a Carthusian monk say to his colleagues, "Look at those Carthusians"?

In short, the original version of Book I of the *Imitation*, published for the first time in the year 1940, reveals the intellectual and religious climate in which its author labored. What the present writer surmised in 1919 was proved to be a fact in 1940. The momentous years at Deventer when Zerbolt and Radewijns instructed Thomas à Kempis were fruitful in many ways. Zerbolt saved the Brotherhood of the Common Life through his brilliant treatise on the nature of his congregation. His two mystical treatises were just being acclaimed as masterpieces. He was the leading scholar in his brotherhood for a period of fifty years, and until the *Imitation* was finally put together, his *Spiritual Ascensions* was the outstanding book of spiritual exercises in the Devotio Moderna. He combined sound scholarship with religous fervor, and he cautioned his colleagues against excessive mortification of the flesh. Radewijns agreed with him in setting the brotherhood apart from the monastic world, while maintaining the highest moral stand-

ards possible. In this manner these two instructors of Thomas
à Kempis provided him with choice material which he saw fit
to adjust to the monastic ideal. The immortal work would have
reflected the Christian philosophy far more successfully if he
had not tampered with the ideals of his great teachers. But
when the original text has become available in modern languages
it may be expected that the Gospel of the Devotio Moderna
shall illuminate the world as its diluted copy never could have
done.

Conclusive proof for the authorship of Book I of the *Imitation by* Gerard Zerbolt of Zutphen may be found in the very
first chapter. Thomas à Kempis has the following statement
known as verse 20: "Endeavor therefore to withdraw your heart
from the love of visible things and turn to the invisible things."
The version in the Eutin Copy reads: "Endeavor therefore
to withdraw your heart from all love of visible things. . . . and
thus you will imitate Christ, for every act of His is an instruction for us." In the treatise which Zerbolt wrote for the Brethren of the Common Life entitled, *Super Modo Vivendi*, he
wrote: "Every act of Christ is an instruction for us, as St.
Augustine says." The Latin text is given here for the con-
venience of the reader: Book I of the *Imitation*: Ut sic Christum
imiteris, quia omnis actio (eius) nostra est instructio. *Super
Modo Vivendi*: Sexto omnis Christi accio nostra est instructio
secundum Augustinum.[100]

These few words quoted above contain a wealth of illumina-
tion. In the first place, they indicate what is the correct title of
the whole book in the English translation. In recent years a
number of scholars have hit upon the following title, borrowed
from the opening words of the first chapter: *The Following of
Christ*. If they had been acquainted with the version by Zerbolt, they would have noted his reading, *imiteris*. The whole
idea of Book I is an actual imitation of Christ, which is more
than a mere following. It is a great pity that Thomas à Kempis
saw fit to eliminate the beautiful passage by Zerbolt, as quoted
from St. Augustine. He was nearing the end of the first chapter. There was but one verse left. Why could he have been

so blind as not to realize that Zerbolt was building up a powerful argument for the imitation of Christ? Zerbolt suggested that every action of Christ was an example and an instruction. Christ's disciples should imitate every action insofar as it was humanly possible.

Illuminating also is the difference between the versions of Zerbolt and Thomas à Kempis near the beginning of Chapter I. Once more we shall give the Latin originals:

ZERBOLT:	THOMAS à KEMPIS
Summum igitur nostrum studium sit in vita Iesum imitari, quia eius doctrina omnes instructiones sanctorum praecellit et qui eius spiritum haberet. . . .	*Summum igitur studium nostrum sit in vita Iesu Christi meditari. Doctrina Christi omnes doctrinas sanctorum praecellit et qui spiritum haberet . . .*

What do we find here? Once more we have the Latin word for imitating Christ, and once more Thomas à Kempis refuses to use it. Zerbolt is very meticulous with his style, and he does not want to confuse his readers. He speaks again about the instruction we get from Christ, but Thomas à Kempis again omits this thought. Zerbolt emphasizes the imitation of Christ, as he should. He has only reached the third verse of the first chapter. Why should he wander away from his main theme? Poor Thomas was not so wise and so learned as Zerbolt. He did not want to copy everything as he had found it in the library of the brethren-house at Deventer. He no doubt was under the impression that he was making some sort of an improvement. Unfortunately that was not the case. And so it happened that the first six thousand editions of the *Imitation* were marred by his amateurish meddling. It seems almost incredible that scholars in Europe failed to note the incongruities in the work by Thomas à Kempis. When in the year 1845, a German writer of no mean ability made the contents of the Eutin Copy known to the world and told the truth about Book I of the *Imitation,* he could get no hearing. For more than another hundred years the imperfect rendering was printed and read by millions of devout Christians, who would have been edified far more had they read the powerful version by Gerard Zerbolt. In the year 1927, the present writer published in the *Nederlandsch Archief voor Kerkgeschiedenis* a remarkable work by Gerard Zerbolt. It is entitled, *Scriptum pro Quodam Inordinate Gradus Ecclesiasticos et Praedicationis Officium Affectante.* Chapter III has the following heading: "De Vicioso et Inordinate Appetitu ad Sacerdocium." What was more natural for Zerbolt than to prepare a similar title for a chapter in the *Imitation?* That he certainly did. Chapter VI of the *Imitation* has this heading: "De Inordinatis Affectionibus." The first verse corresponds neatly to the chapter heading: "Quandocumque homo inordinate aliquid appetit . . ." Here we have two typical concepts of Zerbolt. In the first place, the idea of a person's having excessive desires to possess something. In the second place, we note that the sinner has a bad appetite. Both of these phrases Thomas à Kempis took over from Zerbolt.

Very interesting is the contrast between Zerbolt's discussion of predestination in Chapter XIII of Book I of the *Imitation* and that by Thomas à Kempis (verse 27). Zerbolt merely says that a person's whole life is ordained according to the foreknowledge of God. Thomas à Kempis presents here the full-fledged Calvinistic doctrine of predestination, which led Father Joseph Malaise in his edition of the *Imitation* to write (p. 271) : "The third of the three verses, interpolated by à Kempis after verse 23, has left him open to the accusation of holding the heretical doctrine of Predestination." On the other hand, Zerbolt, in his version of Chapter XVIII, has plain references to predestination which Thomas à Kempis omits. Zerbolt also favors some belief in predestination near the end of his treatise, *Scriptum pro Quodam* (p. 231 in the version published by the present writer). He says that God equips each person with talents he needs for his vocation, just as He endows all animals with certain faculties. His argument reminds us of the theories expressed by him in Chapter XVIII of the *Imitation.*

Another curious development is the voluminous writing by J. van Ginneken. Being a brilliant speaker and linguist, and at one time the Rector of the Roman Catholic University at Nijmegen, he attracted much attention with his thesis that Gerard Groote was the author of the *Imitation*. He admitted that the Eutin Copy was the work of Zerbolt, who had merely acted as a copyist. He felt that Zerbolt had not only copied Book I, but also the next two books.[101] There is much similarity between the Eutin version of Book I and the version of Books II and III as discovered by Paul Hagen in Lübeck. Van Ginneken noted that himself, and he was right. But he was unable to convince his own colleagues that his main thesis was correct. They continued to believe that the present writer had come closer to the truth in the year 1921, when he paid a visit to Paul Hagen's home in Lübeck and spent a week there studying the manuscripts left by the Sisters of the Common Life in that city and their neighbors across the street. In the year 1489, a copy of the *Imitation* was published in that city which contains the same rendering of the last passages of Chapter I as those by Zerbolt and to be found in the Eutin manuscript copy. There is a good reason for this similarity.

Van Ginneken even went so far as to publish a Dutch translation of Book I of the *Imitation* as based upon a Latin version he ascribed to Gerard Groote. This work was subsidized by the famous institute in Amsterdam known as the *Koninklijke Nederlandsche Akademie van Wetenschappen*, thus showing the high reputation Van Ginneken enjoyed. A new edition appeared in the year 1945, which was used by the present writer. The latter feels called upon to make a few remarks which indicate how a person may be led by a false theory to draw strange conclusions.

Van Ginneken's thesis was that Groote had written a diary, as the original sources indicate. This diary is the *Imitation of Christ*. Now we happen to know that Groote burned his diary, and it is very doubtful that he had two copies at his disposal. The *Imitation* is a composite work, and certainly not a diary. The first book was issued under its proper title. The four do not form a book that corresponds to the title intended for only the first book. Neither Zerbolt nor Thomas à Kempis realized that some day the four books would be bound together and called the *Imitation of Christ*. Thomas actually placed Book IV in front of Book III, showing his own ignorance of the fact that Book II and III have very much in common and differ very much from Book IV.

Van Ginneken got himself into some difficulties with his thesis. The copy of Book I which he ascribed to Groote does not contain the fourth chapter. Nevertheless, Van Ginneken provided one which he borrowed from Thomas à Kempis. He also did not worry much about a passage in Chapter XIII quoted from St. Gregory, who is mentioned there by name (verse 28). This passage was taken over by the editor of the translation, published in 1937, by the America Press. It should be noted, however, that Book I of the *Imitation,* as originally composed, did not carry the names of any of the Church Fathers. Thomas à Kempis did not go that far, either. Zerbolt did mention such names in his other works, but the *Imitation* was a special kind of book.

Another difficulty is caused by verse 35 in Chapter XXV of Book I. Van Ginneken reasoned that Groote wrote that book while doing penitence and penance in a Carthusian monastery. Verse 35 starts as follows: "Look at the Carthusians, the Cistercians." Thomas à Kempis no doubt added that passage, since the Eutin Copy does not contain it. He himself was an Augustinian monk and could well exclaim about the holiness of the Carthusians. But how could Groote have composed it? The manuscript which Van Ginneken used has a note at the top, stating that it was written in a Carthusian monastery in the Rhine Valley. Van Ginneken should have noted that this was proof of copying, not the original authorship of Book I. In short, a monk in a Carthusian monastery in the Rhine Valley made the particular copy of the version which Van Ginneken erroneously ascribed to Gerard Groote.[102]

We must conclude that the Eutin Copy of Book I of the *Imitation* and the Low German version of Books II and III as found by Paul Hagen in the City Library of Lübeck point definitely to Gerard Zerbolt as the author. The version by

Thomas à Kempis contains too many errors to be considered the original of much better compositions. Gerard Zerbolt was the only writer, in the movement called the Devotio Moderna, before 1450, who had produced "big sellers" in a class with the *Imitation*. Gerard Groote was not the type of a writer who could stir the hearts of millions the way Zerbolt could. We have in Book I of the *Imitation* as written orginally by Zerbolt a number of typical phrases to be found in other works by Zerbolt. The latter was the librarian in the brethren-house at Deventer when Thomas à Kempis lived in the same city and joined the brotherhood.

Thomas à Kempis wrote about his teacher, Gerard Zerbolt: "He was our librarian at Deventer. . . . He loved sacred books above all the riches of the world. . . . He said that we cannot do without them any more than without the sacraments of the Church. . . . He collected from the writings of the doctors various aromatic spices, to be used against the diseases of vices and for the curing of the languors of the souls: as appears particularly in two of his books which begin respectively with, 'A certain man,' and 'Blessed is the man.'" Those are the two great mystical treatises we have discussed above.

Dier de Muden, who used to wear the tunic left by Zerbolt and wrote a fine account of Zerbolt's life, made this startling remark: "He gathered from the sacred writings those which were useful for our House and other persons: for he composed or dictated numerous books." In other words, the two most reliable sources plainly indicate that Zerbolt wrote much more than just those two books generally ascribed to him. Moreover, the Sisters of the Common Life in Lübeck had in their library a translation of the book by Zerbolt entitled, *Spiritual Ascensions*. The dialect used for this purpose was the same as that employed in the translation of Books II and III of the *Imitation*. It should be noted here that both translations were made from the original Latin of Zerbolt, and that no great liberties were taken in either case. Those who have seen and read these interesting manuscripts in the dialect of Lübeck know exactly

how this work was performed.   Dr. Paul Hagen, the city librarian, did not labor in vain.

In short, the facile pen of Gerard Zerbolt gave to the *Imitation* such power that his assistant now known as Thomas à
Kempis could not reduce it to the level of mediocrity.   Today the
world is once more in a state of flux, similar to the transition
witnessed in the period from 1375 to 1525: the Age of the
Renaissance.   No doubt the *Imitation* as originally composed
by Zerbolt will calm the hearts of many devout Christians who
are puzzled by the evils of wars, strikes, divorces, and all manner of personal crimes.[103]

NOTES TO INTRODUCTION

1. The Grebbe is a small river to the west of the Veluwe.
2. W. L. Bouwmeester, *De ontwikkeling van Nederlands landschappen*, (The Hague 1911), p. 334.
3. Ch. Petit-Dutaillis, *Charles VII, Louis XI et les premières années de Charles VIII* (1422-1492), in: E. Lavisse, *Histoire de France*, Vol. IV2, (Paris 1902), pp. 115, 147.
4. W. Denton, *England in the Fifteenth Century*, (London 1888), pp. 118-123.
5. K. Lamprecht, *Deustsche Geschichte*, vol. IV, (Berlin 1896), pp. 435-488.
6. H. Pirenne, *Histoire de Belgique*, Vol. I, (Brussels 1902), pp. VIII-IX, 27, 30, 32, 156-158, 161-169, 244-245; Vol. II (Brussels 1903), pp. 178-180, 380-383, 394-395.
7. H. Pirenne, *Hist. de Belgique*, Vol. I, pp. 326-327, 336. — K. Lamprecht, *Deutsche Geschichte*, Vol. III (Berlin 1895), pp. 310-312.
8. H. Pirenne, *Hist. de Belgique*, Vol. I, pp. 156-161.
9. Ch. Petit-Dutaillis, *op. cit.*, p. 170.
10. H. Pirenne, *Hist. de Belgique*, Vol. III, pp. 266-267.

NOTES TO CHAPTER I

1. J. van Ginneken, *Geert Groote's Levensbeeld*, pp. 80-83. This writer devoted many years of study to the life of Groote and the institutions founded by him. He made useful suggestions for which all scholars will be very grateful, but unfortunately he was never able to produce a well-organized history of the Devotio Moderna. His scattered articles on the *Imitation of Christ* and his biography of Groote leave much to be desired. Nevertheless, we shall frequently refer to those passages of his which contain trustworthy information. At the present time the chief sources for the life of Groote are still the same four which the present writer mentioned so often in his first book, *The Christian Renaissance*, namely, the story by Thomas à Kempis, the narrative by Dier de Muden, the first chapters in John Busch's *Chronicle of Windesheim*, and the work by Petrus Horn. Although we do possess an older account on Groote, composed in rhymed verse in 1421, and still another dated somewhat later, these two are too vague to be considered on a par with the four just mentioned, notwithstanding Van Ginneken's arguments to the contrary. We shall refer to these poetical works as the *Frenswegen Hymnus* and the *Windesheim Hymnus*. They were both published in 1942 by Professor T. Brandsma in *Ons Geestelijk Erf*, pp. 5-51. On these six sources see R. Post, "De onderlinge verhouding van de vier oude vitae Gerardi Magni en haar betrouwbaarheid," in *Studia Catholica*, XIX (1943), 9-20. Post is absolutely justified in defending Thomas à Kempis against both Van Ginneken and Professor W. J. Kühler. The latter devoted two articles to these old sources, mentioned in our Bibliography.
2. J. van Ginneken, *op. cit.*, pp. 80-88.
3. J. van Ginneken, *op. cit.*, pp. 94-96.
4. P. Horn, *Vita Gerardi Magni*, pp. 333-334. — J. Badius Ascensius, *Vita Thom. Malleoli*, Ch. VIII.
5. R. R. Post, *De Moderne Devotie*, p. 11. — J. van Ginneken, *op. cit.*, pp. 108-109.
6. P. Horn, *Vita*, p. 334.
7. G. Groote, *Epistolae*, ed. W. Mulder, No. 23, pp. 105-106.
8. J. van Ginneken, *op. cit.*, pp. 99-100. — G. Groote, *De Matrimonia*, Ch. XVIII, ed. M. H. Mulders, pp. 74-76. The editor in pp. 98-107 of his admirable work, *Geert Groote en het huwelijk*, presents a useful discussion of Groote's views on matrimony. In his opinion Groote was mistaken in following the Apostle Paul and St. Augustine. The present writer is of the opinion that Groote knew something about the value of continence that was not fully appreciated by Mulders.

196   The Brethren of the Common Life

9. J. D. van Doorninck, *De Cameraarsrekeningen van Deventer*, Vol. III, Part I (Deventer, 1888), nos. 339, 541, 615, 625, 636. — J. van Ginneken, *op. cit.*, pp. 110-111.

10. G. Dumbar, *Kerkelyk en Wereltlyk Deventer*, Vol. I, p. 548. — R. Dier de Muden, *Scriptum*, p. 3. — Thomas à Kempis, *Vita Gerardi Magni*, Ch. II.

11. Thomas à Kempis, *Vita*, Ch. III.

12. Thomas à Kempis, *Vita*, Ch. IV. — J. van Ginneken, *op. cit.*, pp. 113-130.

13. J. van Ginneken, *op. cit.*, pp. 163-165. We observe here that Groote also gave away a valuable farm.

14. G. Dumbar, *Kerkelyk en wereltlyk Deventer*, Vol. I, pp. 507-510, 549-550. — J. de Hullu, *De statuten van het Meester-Geertshuis te Deventer*, pp. 63, 75 — J. van Ginneken, *op. cit.*, pp. 162-163.

15. R. Dier de Muden, *Scriptum*, p. 5. — W. Moll, *Kerkgeschiedenis van Nederland*, Vol. II, Part II, pp. 119-120. — J. G. R. Acquoy, *Het Klooster te Windesheim*, Vol. I, pp. 27-28. Professor J. van Ginneken's arguments against the chronology established in my work, *The Christian Renaissance*, are not conclusive. More reliable is the account presented by W. Mulder: "Ter chronologie van het leven van Geert Groote," in *Historisch Tijdschrift* XII (1933), pp. 141-167, 271-297, 329-361. Illuminating also is the conclusion drawn by R. R. Post in his book, *De Moderne Devotie* (1940), pp. 11-13, 148.

16. Thomas à Kempis, *Vita Gerardi Magni*, Ch. VII, § 1-2. See also: Ch. VI, § 1 of this same work, and D. A. Brinkerink, *Biographieën van beroemde mannen uit den Deventer-kring* (1901), p. 413.

17. H. Pomerius, *De origine monasterii Viridis Vallis*, p. 289.

18. A. Auger, *Etude sur les mystiques des Pays-Bas au Moyen-Age*, p. 171. Cele did not commence his teaching career in 1377, but about the year 1374. See: M. Schoengen, *Jacobus Traiecti alias de Voecht narratio de inchoatione domus clericorum in Zwollis*, p. 6, note 3.

19. Thomas à Kempis, *Vita Gerardi Magni*, Ch. VIII, § 1.

20. R. Dier de Muden, *Scriptum*, p. 5.

21. M. Schoengen, *Jacobus Traiecti alias de Voecht narratio*, p 5, note 2. Thomas à Kempis, *Vita Gerardi Magni*, Ch. XV, § 1. — Thomas à Kempis, *Vita Florentii*, Ch. VI, § 2. — J. Busch, *Chronicon Windeshemense*, p. 252.

22. Thomas à Kempis, *Vita Gerardi Magni*, Ch. XV, § 1.

23. The sermon preached by Groote on that day has been preserved in several manuscripts; it was called *Sermo contra Focoristas*, and has been printed by A. Clarisse and his son J. Clarisse, in: *Archief voor Nederlandsche Kerkgeschiedenis*, Vol. I, Leiden 1829, pp. 364-379; Vol. II, Leiden 1830, pp. 307-395; Vol. VIII, Leiden 1837, pp. 5-107. For the date when this sermon was preached see: A. and J. Clarisse, "Over den geest en de denkwijze van Geert Groote," in: *Archief voor Ned. Kerkgesch.*, Vol. I, p. 385, note 6. As for its celebrity see: K. Grube, *Gerhard Groote und seine Stiftungen*, pp. 35, 96. — J. van Ginneken, *op. cit.*, pp. 305-320. See also J. G. J. Tiecke, *De Werken van Geert Groote*, pp. 135-144.

24. D. A. Brinkerink, *De vita venerabilis Ioannis Brinckerinck*, p. 324. — D. A. Brinkerink, *Biographieën van beroemde mannen uit den Deventer-kring* (1901), p. 417. — *Frensweger manuscript*, p. 7.

25. P. Horn, *Vita Gerardi Magni*, p. 342.

26. D. A. Brinkerink, *Biographieën van beroemde mannen uit den Deventer-kring* (1902), p. 24. — D. A. Brinkerink, *De vita venerabilis Ioannis Brinckerinck*, p. 324.

27. Thomas à Kempis, *Vita Florentii*, Ch. XI, § 1. — D. A. Brinkerink, *Vita venerabilis Ioannis Brinckerinck*, p. 324.

28. Thomas à Kempis, *Vita Flor.*, Ch. XI, § 1. The church of St. Lebwin at Deventer was named after Lebwin, an English missionary who had tried to convert the Saxons and Frisians north and east of the Yssel. For the history of this church see: G. Dumbar, *Kerkelyk en Wereltlyk Deventer*, Vol. 1, pp. 235-441.

29. Thomas à Kempis, *Vita Gerardi Magni*, Ch. VIII, § 3. — D. A. Brinkerink, *Biographieën* (1901), p. 417. — P. Horn, *Vita Gerardi Magni*, p. 348. The edict was promulgated between August and October 21, 1383; see: W. J. Kühler, *De prediking van Geert Groote*, p. 224.

30. D. A. Brinkerink, *Biographieën* (1901), p. 417. A letter by William de Salvarvilla to Pope Urban VI, asking for a license from the pope for Groote is found in the *Opera* of Thomas à Kempis, behind the *Vita Gerardi Magni*. This letter was written on the 21st of October, 1383. See J. van Ginneken, *op. cit.*, pp. 315-335, 344-355.

31. J. van Ginneken, *op. cit.*, pp. 346-348.

32. D. A. Brinkerink, *Biographieën* (1901), p. 417. — Th. à Kempis, *Vita Gerardi Magni*, Ch. IX, § 2. — M. Schoengen, *Jacobus Traiecti alias de Voecht narratio*, p. 15, note 1.

33. He translated the seven penitential psalms (Psalm 6, 32, 38, 51, 102, 130, 143), and 63 other psalms. See: R. Dier de Muden, *Scriptum*, p. 6. — P. Horn, *Vita Gerardi Magni*, p. 349. — W. Moll, *Geert Groote's dietsche vertalingen*, pp. 2-77, 107-112, 113-148, 149-180, 181-220. For the glosses see: W. Moll, *Geert Groote's dietsche vertalingen*, pp. 42-44, 55-59, 62-67. See also N. van Wijk, *Het getijdenboek van Geert Groote* (1940).

34. R. Dier de Muden, *Scriptum*, p. 10. — Th. à Kempis, *Vita Gerardi Magni*, Ch. XVI, § 4. For the history of his bones see: G. Dumbar, *Kerkelyk en Wereltlyk Deventer*, Vol. I, pp. 507-510. — J. G. R. Acquoy, *Het klooster te Windesheim*, Vol. I, p. 57.

35. E. Underhill, *Ruysbroeck*, pp. 66-67, 184, 88.

36. D. A. Brinkerink, *Biographieën* (1901), p. 419.

37. P. Horn, *Vita Gerardi Magni*, p. 358.

38. Th. à Kempis, *Vita Gerardi Magni*, Ch. XIV.

39. *Ibid.*, Ch. XII, § 1.

40. Th. à Kempis, *Vita Gerardi Magni*, Ch. XVIII, § 10; Ch. XI.

41. G. Groote, Prologue to his translation of certain church hymns, in: W. Moll, *Geert Groote's Dietsche vertalingen*, p. 53: "Want die woerde sijn ende dienen omme die sinne, ende die sinne niet omme die woerde."

42. G. Groote, *Epistolae*, ed. W. Mulder, pp. 138-139. Ram, p. 74.

43. G. Groote, *De Simonia*, pp. 27-29.

44. The *Horologium* was written by Suso, a German mystic.

45. G. Groote, *De Simonia*, pp. 28-30.

46. W. Moll, *Geert Groote's sermoen over de vrijwillige armoede*, p. 430: "Dat hij om dergelijke reden ook ongezind was monnik te worden, meen ik voor zeker te moeten aannemen."

47. G. Groote, *Epistolae*, ed. W. Mulder, pp. 50-51.

48. G. Groote, *Raadgevingen aan eene Kluizenaarster*, pp. 434-437.

49. For eight other examples see: G. Groote, *Epistolae*, ed. J. G. R. Acquoy, p. 77.

50. See p. 22. — G. Groote, *Epistolae*, ed. J. G. R. Acquoy, p. 77: "Etiam, secundum meum videre, non auderem vobis consulere quod intraretis religionem, licet non confidam nec confidendum sit mihi, quia ignorans viam Dei. Desiderium meum est secundum cor meum, ut maneatis in mundo et non sitis de mundo." See also Mulder's edition, pp. 229-230.

51. G. Groote, *De Simonia*, p. 2.

52. G. Groote, *Protestatio de veridica Evangelii praedicatione*, ed. Th. à Kempis, *Opera*. ed. Somm., p. 782.

53. Groote divides all sources of the Christian religion of his time into four classes: (1) The Bible, which is infallible; (2) the writings of the recognized leaders of the Christian church, who had been inspired by the Holy Ghost; (3) the determinations of the doctors; (4) visions of various kinds.

54. G. Groote, *Sermo contra focaristas*, part 3, p. 65.

55. G. Groote, *Epistolae*, ed. W. Mulder, p. 147.

56. G. Groote, *De locatione ecclesiarum*, p. 129.

57. G. Groote, *Sermo contra focaristas*, 3rd part, pp. 71-73.

58. G. Groote, *Sermo contra focaristas*, 3rd part, p. 61.

59. *Ibid.*, pp. 64-65, 73.

60. *Ibid.*, pp. 68-69, 106, 82, 69, 90, 70, 54, 62.

61. G. Groote, *Epistolae*, ed. W. Mulder, p. 104.

62. *Ibid.*, p. 102.

63. *Ibid.*, p. 101.

64. G. Groote, *Epistolae*, ed. J. G. R. Acquoy, pp. 21-23; ed. Mulder, p. 188.

65. G. Groote, *Epistolae*, ed. J. G. R. Acquoy, p. 28; ed. Mulder, p. 133.

66. W. Preger, *Beiträge zur Geschichte der religiösen Bewegung in den Niederlanden* (1350-1400), pp. 62-63, p. 23.

67. G. Groote, *Epistolae*, ed. Mulder, pp. 134-136.

68. *Ibid.*, p. 150. — J. Busch, *Chronicon Windeshemense,* p. 261.

69. The *Frenswegen Hymnus* in lines 176 and 177 gives a misleading impression by stating no precise facts but instead a vague accusation:
Contra proprietarios, focaristas, hareticos.
His extat adversarius et malleus gravissimus.

The *Windesheim Hymnus* has only one line (119) and presents an opinion by some observer who was not familiar with actual happenings:
Haereticorum his malleus velut alter Hieronymus.

70. Professor Lindeboom in 1941 published a learned treatise on the episcopal edict which ended Groote's preaching: "Geert Groote's preeksuspensie," in *Meded. der Ned. Ak. van Wetensch., Afd. Letterkunde.* New Series, Vol IV. In this work he came to the conclusion that Groote must have done far more than merely annoy the clergy through his sermon before the Diocesan Synod of 1383. He correctly surmised that Groote's semi-monastic institution in Deventer, the home of the Sisters of the Common Life, caused more hostility among the religious orders than did his own doctrines or his attacks upon heresies. See pp. 18-35. Illuminating are also two articles by L. Smit entitled, "Geert Groote over de Kerk," in *Studia Catholica,* X (1934), 257-268, 367-377. Smit observes that Groote was not interested in the visible phenomena of the Church but more in the spiritual power as revealed in the saintly lives of its members. See p. 260. Groote, unlike Thomas Aquinas and the Catholic authorities of his time, thought that even the worst heretics still retained a goodly measure of faith. See p. 369.

71. See Fid. v.d. Borne, "Geert Groote en de Moderne Devotie in de geschiedenis van het ordewezen," in *Studia Catholica,* XVI (1940), pp. 397-414; XVII (1941), pp. 120-133, 197-209; XVIII (1942), pp. 19-40, 203-224. This learned Catholic scholar (p. 404, p. 19) is of the opinion that the present writer had emphasized too much the attacks by the mendicant orders upon Groote's followers. Being a Franciscan himself, he naturally would come to such a conclusion, which is partly justified; but in another work, *The Youth of Erasmus,* the friendship between the mendicant orders and the Brethren of the Common Life has been fully discussed. St. Francis of Assisi, like Groote, consciously sought to imitate Christ. Father v.d. Borne realized that perfectly, and in his excellent articles he has shown that Groote was interested primarily in the problem of sanctification. On p. 122 he quotes these words of Groote: "Quidquid enim meliores nos non facit vel a malo non retrahit, nocivum est." On p. 222 he refers to the well-known phase of the Devotio Moderna which was inherited from Groote: *"Christus-beschouwing."* Still more to the point is the interesting book by K. de Beer, *Studie over de Spiritualiteit van Geert Groote* (1938).

72. G. Groote, *Epistolae,* ed. W. Mulder, No. 20, pp. 74-75. The first adequate treatment of Groote's attitude toward heretics appears in the doctoral dissertation of William Spoelhof: *Concepts of Religious Nonconformity and Religious Toleration as Developed by the Brethren of the Common Life,* 1374-1489, Ch. II and Ch. III. Dr. Spoelhof has shown that several authorities in the Netherlands have signally failed to comprehend the cardinal features of Groote's message.

73. Sister G. Feugen of the University of Nijmegen has circulated in mimeographed form a treatise found in Ms. No. 4768 of the National Library in Vienna, which was written by a pupil of Gerard Groote, named "Frater Symon van Deypenheim, sacrae theologiae doctor indignus." He wrote that he would be glad at all times to defend Groote, and in his treatise he discussed the five points at length. Particularly illuminating is the reference in the third point to Thomas Aquinas, for it has often been said that Groote had little respect for the Angelic Doctor. Groote's learned follower said this: "Tercium, quod secundum sanctum (Sister Feugen has "sanctam") Thomam de Aquino ille peccat mortaliter, qui scienter ac voluntarie audierit missam fornicatoris presbiteri per evidenciam facti ut dictum est. Hoc manifeste beatus Thomas declarat in Quodlibeto undecimo, questione VIII."

74. L. Smit, *op. cit.,* pp. 260-262.

75. L. Smit, *op. cit.,* pp. 375-376.

76. J. van Ginneken, *op. cit.,* pp. 281-283.

77. J. van Ginneken, *op. cit.,* pp. 312-313.

78. G. Groote, *De simonia,* pp. 8-9.

79. G. Groote, *Sermo de paupertate,* pp. 434-436.

80. D. A. Brinkerink, *Biographieën* (1901), p. 422. — Th. à Kempis, *Vita Gerardi Magni,* Ch. XI, §. 3.

81. These passages are: Matthew XIX, 10-12; Luke XIV, 20; I. Corinthians VII, 26, 27, 35; Augustine, *Nona confessio:* "Convertisti me ad Te, ut neque uxorem quaererem."

82. G. Groote, *De Simonia,* p. 28.

83. G. Groote, *De matrimonio*, pp. 25-27.
84. *Ibid.*, pp. 76-78.
85. G. Groote, *Zed. toespraak*, p. 306.
86. G. Groote, *Epistolae*, ed. Mulder, No. 29, pp. 129-130.
87. G. Groote, *Zed. toespraak*, p. 307.
88. *Ibid.*, ed. G. Bonet-Maury, p. 96.
89. G. Groote, *Zedelijke Toespraak*, pp. 299-300.
90. G. Groote, *Epistolae*, ed. Mulder, p. 53.
91. Th. à Kempis, *Vita Gerardi Magni*, Ch. XVIII, § § 5-6.
92. M. Schoengen, *Die Schule von Zwolle*, p. 76.
93. G. Dumbar, *Het kerkelyk en wereltlyk Deventer*, p. 304. — M. Schoengen, *Die Schule von Zwolle*, p. 26.
94. Th. à Kempis, *Vita Gerardi Magni*, Ch. X, § 1.
95. The translation in our text is taken from: Th. à Kempis, *Works*, Vol. III: *The Chronicle of the Canons Regular of Mount St. Agnes*, edited by J. P. Arthur, p. 163. For the authentic text in the original Latin, see Willem de Vreese, *Geert Groote De Simonia ad Beguttas* (1940), pp. 41-48.
96. The translation given in our text is found in: Th. à Kempis, *Works*, Vol. III, pp. 213-217.
97. Th. à Kempis, *Vita Gerardi Magni*, Ch. I, § 2.

98. J. Busch, *Chronicon Windeshemense*, p. 46.
99. J. Busch, *Chronicon Windeshemense*, pp. 41, 245.
100. H. Pomerio, *De origine monasterii Viridis Vallis*, p. 290.
101. D. A. Brinkerink, *Biographieën* (1901), p. 412.
102. *Memoryboek der oude Zusteren te Weesp*, in: *Archief voor Nederlandsche kerkgeschiedenis*, Vol. X (Leiden 1839), p. 188.

NOTES TO CHAPTER II

1. The document is found in: J. de Hullu, *De statuten van het Meester-Geertshuis te Deventer*, pp. 63-76; a shorter one in: G. Dumbar, *Het kerkelyk en wereltlyk Deventer*, Vol. I, pp. 549-550.
2. J. de Hullu, *Statuten*, pp. 67-68.
3. Th. à Kempis, *Chron. Mont. Agn.*, Ch. XI. He died in 1400 at the age of 50; hence he was born in 1350.
4. M. Schoengen, *Die Schule von Zwolle*, p. 18. — J. H. Gerretsen, *Flor. Radewijns*, p. 49.
5. J. H. Gerretsen, *Flor. Radewijns*, p. 49.
6. Th. à Kempis, *Vita Flor.*, Ch. VI, § 2. — D. A. Brinkerink, *Biographieën*, (1902), pp. 1, 23.
7. Th. à Kempis, *Vita Flor.*, Ch. IV, § I; Ch. XI, § 1. — Dier de Muden, *Scriptum*, p. 12.
8. E. Barnikol, *Studien*, p. 32.
9. D. A. Brinkerink, *De vita venerabilis Ioannis Brinckerinck*, p. 324: "Quorum XII illi familiarius adhaerebant, ita ut unanimi consensu, spe vite liberioris, voto se castitatis astringernt, licet unus ex illis postea iret post sathanem." — D. A. Brinkerink, *Biographieën* (1902), p. 24: "Meyster Gerijt die hadde ynt irste XII discipele, die onsen lieven Heren hoer reynicheid laveden ende alle vuerige manne woerden ende columpne der deuchden, behalve ene; die viel weder of en sterf quader doet."
10. P. Horn, *Vita Gerardi Magni*, p. 362.
11. The present writer does not see why we should have to reject the account by Busch. For nowhere is he so trustworthy as in his narrative relating to Groote's activities as founder of the new brotherhood. When Groote preached at Zwolle, it was his custom to stop at the house of Busch's grand-father (see: M. Schoengen, *Jac. Voecht narratio*, p. 6, note 6); Busch was one of Cele's best friends, while Groote's confessor, named Henry of Höxter, told him a great many details about Groote's last years: J. Busch, *De ref. mon.*, p. 703: "Dominus Henricus Huxaria, qui fuerat eius confessor, hec mihi sepius enarravit et plura alia."

12. J. Busch, *Chronicon Windeshemense*, p. 254. This is probably not an exact duplicate of the conversation.

13. J. Busch, *Chron. Windeshemense*, p. 254. — D. A. Brinkerink, *Biographieën*, (1901), p. 420.

14. J. Busch, *Chronicon Windeshemense*, p. 256. — W. J. Kühler, *Johannes Brinckerinck*, p. 19. — *Frensweger handschrift*, pp. 22-27.

15. P. Horn, *Vita Gerardi Magni*, p. 362: "Vitam tamen communem discipuli eius post mortem illius de consilio et beneplacito ipsius inceperunt." — D. A. Brinkerink, *Biographieën*, (1901), p. 420: "Ende no sijnre doet soe waert die eerweerdige meystere her florens die overste, ende doe woren sij daer allentelen wat toe gecomen." —— R. Dier de Muden, *Scriptum*, p. 13: "Dominus Florencius custodivit pecunias secum habitancium. Videns autem quod tam plene essent conversi ad Dominum et tam tractabiles et flexibiles, fudit pecunias eorum in unum et fecit eas esse omnium, que fuerant per partes singulorum; et ita deinceps ceperunt vivere in communi." There is one other account which ought to be of some interest to us. In Ms. no. 75 G 58 of the Royal Library at the Hague we find a treatise by Gabriel Byel or Biel, rector of the Brethren of the Common Life at Butzbach near Mainz (see: G. Coeverinex, *Analecta*, part II, ed. G. van den Elsen and W. Hoevenaars, p. 128), called: *Tractatus de communi vita clericorum*. The rector tells his readers on fol. IIb of this treatise that Groote was unable to find good monasteries for his followers. For that reason he withheld many of them from entering a monastery. Finally he resolved to follow Augustine's example by founding a society or congregation, instructing his followers to live the "common life."

16. J. Busch, *Chronicon Windeshemense*, pp. 263-264.

17. Th. à Kempis, *Vita Ger. Magni*, Ch. XVI, § § 2-3.

18. Thomas à Kempis very plainly states that Groote urged his disciples to build a monastery and join the Augustinian Canons Regular (*Vita Ger. Magni*, ch. XV, § 3). Acquoy overlooked this fact; see: W. J. Kühler, *De prediking van Geert Groote*, pp. 231-232.

19. D. A. Brinkerink, *De Vita venerabilis Ioannis Brinckerinck*, p. 326.

20. D. A. Brinkerink, *De vita ven. Ioannis Brinckerinck*, p. 327: "In quottidianis igitur anxietatibus constituti magister Gerardus et sui, maturo et deliberato consilio concluserunt, se monasterium ordinis regularium S. Augustini velle construere, sub cuius alis et umbris ceteri sine approbata apostolica regula, sed in seculari habitu simplici aut clericali degentes protegerentur." — P. Horn, *Vita Gerardi Magni*, pp. 362-363: "Habuit eciam in proposito edificandi monasterium clericorum ordinis canonicorum regularium, volens quosdam de ydoneis clericis sibi adherentibus ad religionis habitum promovere, ut aliis devotis essent in exemplum et contra senientem mundum in refugii castrum religione munitum."

21. Th. à Kempis, *Vita Flor.*, Ch. XVI, § § 2-4.

22. *Ibid.*, Ch. XIV, § 3.

23. Th. à Kempis, *Vita Flor.*, Ch. I, § 1.

24. Th. à Kempis, *Vita Flor.*, Ch. XIV, § 3; Ch. XV, § 3; Ch. XIV, § 2.

25. R. Dier de Muden, *Scriptum*, p. 22. — Th. à Kempis, *Vita Flor.*, Ch. XX, § 1.

26. Th. à Kempis, *Vita Flor.*, Ch. XI, § 2, § 1; Ch. XXIV, § 3. — R. Dier de Muden, *Scriptum*, p. 21.

27. *De magistro Everardo de Eza*, in: Ms. no. 8849-8859, Royal Library, Brussels, fol. 80a.

28. Th. à Kempis, *Vita Flor.*, ch. XI, § 2, § 3.

29. Fl. Radewijns, *Omnes inquit artes*, fol. 1a-4b.

30. Fl. Radewijns, *Tractatulus de spiritualibus exercitiis*, p. 384.

31. Fl. Radewijns, *Omnes inquit artes*, fol. 82a-83b.

32. Fl. Radewijns, *Tract.*, p. 384-387.

33. Fl. Radewijns, *Tractatulus*, p. 389. — *Omnes inquit artes*, fol. 23b.

34. Fl. Radewijns, *Tractatulus*, p. 389. — *Omnes inquit artes*, fol. 23b: "Tota sacra scriptura est propter virtutes; et si homo haberet virtutes et inconcusse servaret, non indigeret scriptura quantum ad se, ut dicunt Augustinus et Crysostomus, quia multi sine codicibus sancte vixerunt in solitudinibus."

35. Fl. Radewijns, *Omnes inquit artes*, fol. 6a-17a. — *Tractatulus*, pp. 405-406, 409, 414.

36. Fl. Radewijns, *Tractatulus*, pp. 411-417.

37. *Ibid.*, p. 423.

38. About one half of the *Omnes inquit artes* is devoted to the life of Christ (fol. 28b-62a, and also fol. 62a-77a).

39. R. Dier de Muden, *Scriptum*, p. 13.

40. W. J. Kühler, *Johannes Brinckerinck*, p. 13.

41. R. Dier de Muden, *Scriptum*, pp. 7-8.

42. Found in: G. Dumbar, *Het kerkelyk en wereltlyk Deventer*, Vol. I, pp. 616-620.

43. G. Dumbar, *Het kerkelyk en wereltlyk Deventer*, Vol. I, pp. 603-610. — *Analecta Daventria*, Vol. I, p. 224, p. 16.

44. G. Dumbar, *Het kerkelyk en wereltlyk Deventer*, Vol. I, p. 629. — R. Dier de Muden, *Scriptum*, pp. 38-39. — G. Dumbar, *Analecta Daventria*. Vol. I, p. 238. — Ms. no. 70 H 75, Royal Library, The Hague, fol. 13b-14a: "Nos Godfridus Toorn, Rodolphus de Muden et Otgerus Johannis presbyteri et custodes domus magistri Florencii in Daventria notum facimus . . . empta est cum domibus in ipsa edificatis de pecuniis deputatis ad primum usum: ad hoc ut in ipsis habitent devoti clerici vel scolares."

45. Th. à Kempis, *Vita Flor.*, Ch. XV, § 2. — R. Dier de Muden, *Scriptum*, p. 24.

46. J. de Hullu, *De Hervorming in Overijssel*, p. 91.

47. J. Badius Ascensius, *Vita Thomae Malleoli*, Ch. IX. The translation given in our text is from: Th. à Kempis, *Meditation on the incarnation of Christ*, ed. D. V. Scully, pp. XXVII-XXVIII.

48. Thomas à Kempis, *Vita Arn. Scoonhoviae*, Ch. II.

49. J. Lindeborn, *Historia episcopatus Daventriensis*, p. 98.

50. W. J. Kühler, *Joh. Brinckerinck*, p. 21.

51. M. Schoengen, *Jacobus Traiecti narratio*, p. 500.

52. See J. van Rooij, *Gerard Zerbolt van Zutphen*, p. 24.

53. Th. à Kempis, *Vita Ger. Sutph.*, § 2.

54. D. A. Brinkerink, *Biographieën*, 1902, pp. 336-337.

55. Th. à Kempis, *Vita Ger. Sutph.*, § 4.

56. Th. à Kempis *Vita Ger. Sutphan.*, § § 5-6.

57. See my article in the *Ned. Arch. voor Kerkgesch.*, 1921, pp. 109-114; p. 118, note 7. It was published by the present writer in 1923. See Bibliography.

58. See my article on the *Super modo vivendi* in the *Ned. Arch. voor Kerkgesch.*, 1921, p. 107, p. 115.

59. *Ibid.*, pp. 115-116.

60. F. Jostes, *Die Schriften des Gerhard Zerbolt van Zutphen*, p. 7.

61. Revius gave a few extracts from this treatise (J. Revius, *Daventria illustrata*, pp. 41-58).

62. A. Hyma, *The Christian Renaissance*, pp. 440, 441.

63. In Ch. LXVII of the *De Spiritualibus Ascensionibus* and ch. XXXIX of the *De Reformatione Virium Animae* the blessings of manual labor are extolled, and Ch. LXVIII of the *De Spiritualibus Ascensionibus* deals with the relations with one's superiors, equals, and inferiors.

64. See pp. 154-157.

65. R. Dier de Muden, *Scriptum*, p. 48.

66. R. Dier de Muden. *Scriptum*, p. 13: "Ista fuit causa movens ad instituendum religiosos, quia simplici communi vita timebant sustinere persecutiones ab emulis, ut sic, aliquibus existentibus religiosis, multi fratres devoti non professi religione tuerentur seu laterent sub professis religionem."

67. J. Busch, *Chronicon Windeshemense*, p. 267; cf. J. G. R. Acquoy, *Het klooster te Windesheim*, Vol. I, pp. 64-65. The bishop, named Floris van Wevelinkhoven, signed his letter of permission on July 30, 1386; see J. G. R. Acquoy, *Het klooster te Windesheim*, Vol. III, pp. 262-264.

68. J. G. R. Acquoy, *Het klooster te Windesheim*, Vol. I, pp. 67-68.

69. *Privilegia et Statuta Capituli Generali Windesemensis*, in: Ms. no. 78 D 55, Royal Library, The Hague, pp. 105, 205.

70. See J. G. R. Acquoy, *Het klooster te Windesheim*, Vol. I, p. 72.

71. J. Busch, *Chron. Wind.*, p. 342.

72. J. Busch, *Chron. Wind.*, p. 94.

73. D. A. Brinkerink, *Biographieën*, 1902, p. 26.

74. On the 21st of January, 1408, the dedication took place, and in 1412 it joined the general chapter of Windesheim (W. J. Kühler, *Joh. Brinck.*, p. 67, p. 72).

75. M. Schoengen, *Jacobus Traiecti narratio*, p. 14, 6-9.

76. *Ibid.*, p. 9, note 2; p. 280.

77. *Ibid.*, p. 9. For a biography on John Ummen see: W. J. Kühler, *Joh. Brinck.*, p. 34. — M. Schoengen, *Jac. Traiecti narratio*, p. 7, note 2. — D. de Man, *Strichtige punten*, p. 196.

78. M. Schoengen, *Jacobus Traiecti narratio*, pp. 219-220, and 28, 59.

79. Ten letters, addressed by Groote to Cele, are still in existence. They were edited by W. Preger, and in 1933 by W. Mulder.

80. M. Schoengen, *Die Schule von Zwolle*, p. 83.

81. M. Schoengen, *Die Schule von Zwolle*, p. 97.

82. W. Preger, *Beiträge*, p. 14.

83. J. Busch, *Chron. Wind.*, p. 213.

84. W. Preger, *Beiträge*, p. 14.

85. J. Busch, *Chron. Wind.*, p. 206.

86. J. Busch, *Chron. Wind.*, p. 206.

87. See: M. Schoengen, *Die Schule von Zwolle*, p. 107.

88. J. Busch, *Chron. Wind.*, p. 208.

89. M. Schoengen, *Die Schule von Zwolle*, pp. 75-76. — J. Busch, *Chron. Wind.*, p. 207.

90. J. Busch, *Chron. Wind.*, p. 207.

91. J. Busch, *Chron. Wind.*, p. 206, p. 217.

92. *Ibid.*, p. 220. — J. H. Hofman, *De bockerij van St. Michiel te Zwolle*, pp. 387-389.

NOTES TO CHAPTER III

1. See p. 64.

2. Ch. V.

3. R. Dier de Muden, *Scriptum*, p. 60.

4. *Ibid.*, p. 55, p 53.

5. R. Dier de Muden, *Scriptum*, p. 54.

6. R. Dier de Muden, *Scriptum*, p. 52.

7. *Ibid.*, p. 59, p. 61.

8. G. Dumbar, *Analecta Daventria*, Vol. I, p. 117.

9. *Ibid.*, p. 118.

10. *Ibid.*, p. 114.

11. See my article in: *Ned. Arch. voor Kerkgesch.*, 1921, p. 125, note 1.

12. See Ch. VIII.

13. G. Dumbar, *Anal. Dav.*, Vol. I, p. 173.

14. *Ibid.*, pp. 173-175.

15. At least this is the impression I have from the many times I heard that remark when a school boy there.

16. G. Dumbar, *Analecta Daventria*, Vol. I, p. 177.

17. A list of these rectors is found in: G. Dumbar, *Het kerkelyk en wereltlyk Deventer*, Vol. I, p. 620.

18. G. Dumbar, Anal. Dav., vol. I, p. 167, p.. 228. — *Het kerkelyk en wereltlyk Deventer*, vol. I, p. 610.

19. M. Schoengen, *Jac. Voecht narr.*, pp. 49-51.

20. M. Schoengen, *Jac. Voecht narr.*, p. 42.

21. M. Schoengen, *Jac Voecht narr.*, pp. 64, 69, 70, 72, 76, 78.

22. D. A. Brinkerink, *Van den doechden der vuriger susteren*, pp. 314-315.

23. M. Schoengen, *Jac Voecht narr.*, pp. 108-112, 428.

24. *Ibid.*, p. 127.

25. M. Schoengen, Jac. Voecht narr., pp. 279-404.

26. G. Dumbar, *Het kerkelyk en wereltlyk Deventer*, Vol. I, p. 626 — W. F. N. van Rootselaar, *Amersfoort* (777-1580), Vol. I, p. 449. — Amersfoort, *Geschiedkundige bijzonderheden*, Vol. II, pp. 7-8.

27. R. Dier de Muden, *Scriptum*, pp. 54-55. — G. H. M. Delprat, *Verhandeling over de broederschap van G. Groote*, p. 120. — M. Schoengen, *Jac. Voecht narr.*, p. 18, n. 5, where a bibliography for the history of this house is given.

28. G. H. M. Delprat, *Verhandeling over de broederschap van G. Groote*, pp. 119-120.

29. M. Schoengen, *Jac. Voecht narr.*, pp. 482 and 32; on p. 32, n. 5, is a bibliography.

30. *Ibid.*, p. 484, pp. 30-31; p. 30, n. I has a fairly good bibliography.

31. *Ibid.*, pp. 78-79; p. 78, n. 3 has a bibliography.

32. M. Schoengen, *Jac. Voecht narr.*, p. 84, n. 3.

33. M. Schoengen, *Jac Voecht narr.*, pp. 84-85, p. 84, n. 8. — R. Dier de Muden, *Scriptum*, p. 76. — *Chronicle of the brethrenhouse at Doesburg*, p. 6.

34. H. O. Feith, *Het klerkenhuis en het fraterhuis te Groningen*, pp. 10-12. — M. Schoengen, *Jac Voecht narr.*, p. 101. — M. van Rhijn, *Wessel Gansfort*, p. 30, p. 30, n. 5. — E. H. Roelfsema, *De fraters en het fraterhuis te Groningen*, pp. 30-31.

35. M. Schoengen, *Jac. Voecht narr.*, p. 485, p. 99, p. 99, n. 5. — H. Gysbertszoon, *Kronyk van het fraterhuis te Gouda*, pp. 10-13, 14, 16. The house was not recognized, however, till 1456: H. Gysbertszoon, *Kronyk*, p. 7, p. 22, p. 45.

36. J. J. Dodt van Flenburg, *De stichtingsoorkonden van het Utrechtsche fraterhuis*, pp. 90-92. — G. H. M. Delprat, *Verhandeling over de broederschap van G. Groote*, p. 151. — S. Muller, *Catalogussen, Stads-archief*, part I, p. 123.

37. H. D. J. van Schevichaven, *Oud Nijmegens kerkan, kloosters, gasthuizen, stichtingen en openbare gebouwen*, p. 100. — G. H. M. Delprat, *Verhandeling*, p. 161. Information on the Dutch houses is to be found in M. Schoengen, *Monasticon Batavum*, Vol. II, (1941). Unfortunately the section devoted to the Brethren of the Common Life is poorly done. See the review by M. A. Nauwelaerts in *Studia Catholica*, XVIII (1942), 228-232.

38. R. Doebner, *Annalen und Akten der Brüder des gemeinsamen Lebens im Lüchtenhofe zu Hildesheim*, pp. 95, 98-100, 103, 105, 111, 115-116, 271.

39. R. Dier de Muden, *Scriptum*, p. 54. — K. Loeffler, *Neues über Heinrich von Ahaus*, p. 234. — L. Schmitz-Kallenberg, *Monasticon Westfaliae*, p. 56.

40. K. Loeffler, *Heinrich von Ahaus*, 1909, p. 778. — *Neues über Heinrich von Ahaus*, p. 238. — *Gedächtnisbuch Kölner Brüderhaus*, p. 5. — *Das Fraterhuis Weidenbach zu Köln*, pp. 104-105.

41. K. Loeffler, *Heinrich von Ahaus*, p. 782. — E. Barnikol, *Studien zur Geschichte der Brüder vom gemeinsamen Leben*, pp. 47, 63, 71. — Ms. No. VII, 3305, Staatsarchiv, Münster, pp. 3-5, 69-71. — Ms. No. VII, 3307, Staatsarchiv, Münster, p. 130. — L. Schmitz-Kallenberg, *Monasticon Westfaliae*, p. 34. — A. Wolters, *Reformations geschichte der Stadt Wesel*, p. 13. — R. Doebner, *Annalen*, pp. 3 and 259, 263, 264, 266, 281, 286, 307, 315. — A. Hulshof, *Verslag van een onderzoek te Rostock*, pp. 38-41. — O. Scheel, *Martin Luther*, Vol. I, pp. 70-97. — E. Barnikol, *Luther in Magdeburg und die dortige Brüderschule*, pp. 12-13. — G. H. M. Delprat,*Verhandeling*, p. 183 — O. Meyer, *Die Brüder vom gemeinsamen Leben in Würtemberg*. — M. Schoengen, *Jac. Voecht narr.*, pp. 134-135. See also the doctoral dissertation by my student, Dr. W Landeen: *The Devotio Moderna in Germany*.

42. J. Lindeborn, *Historia sive notitia episcopatus Daventriensis*, p. 115. — *Letter by Pope Eugene IV*, in: Ms. no. 16515, Royal Library, Brussels, fol. 2b.

43. The "House of Master Gerard"; see p. 19. — The "Lammenhuis," founded in 1390: H. F. Heussen and H. van Rijn, *Oudheden en gestichten van het bisdom Deventer*, vol. I, p. 305. — The "Buyskenshuis,"¹ founded in 1405: H. F. Heussen en H. van Rijn, *Oudh. en gest. van Dev.*, Vol. I, p. 309. — The "Kerstkenhuis"; for a bibliography on this house see: D. de Man, *Hier beginnen sommige stichtige punten*, p. 58, note d. — The "Brandeshuis"; for a bibliography on this house see: D. de Man, *Hier beginnen sommige stichtige punten*, p. 87, note a.

44. See: M. Schoengen, *Jac Voecht narr.*, p. XV.

45. H. F. Heussen en H. van Rijn, *Oudheden en gestichten van Deventer*, Vol. II, pp. 196, 197, 480, 24, 517, 427, 574. — *Oudheden van Utrecht*. Vol. II, pp. 443, 629. — W. Moll, *Kerkgeschiedenis van Nederland*, Vol. II, part 2, p. 176. — M. Schoengen, *Het Weduwenhuis te Doesburg*, pp. 388-390. — *Jac. Voecht narr.*, pp. XV, 69, 48, 77, 81, 82 n. 2, 89, 129, 145, 197, 208. — S. Muller, *De moderne devotie te Utrecht*, pp. 25-30. — R. Doebner, *Annalen und Akten*, pp. 263 (Ahlen), 258-260 (Borken), 264 (Büderich), 259 (Calcar), 260 (Coesfeld), 256-258 (Dinslaken), 75-78 (Eldagsen), 259 (Essen), 259 (Volkmarsen), 261 (Groll), 261 (Herford), 256

(Schüttorf), 259 (Wesel), etc. — L. Schulze, *Brüder des gemeinsamen Lebens*, (1897), p. 487; (1914), p. 262.

46. D. de Man, *Hier beginnen sommige stichtige punten*, pp. LIII, 35, 45, 90, 56, 85.

47. M. Schoengen, *Jac Voecht narr.*, p. XV.

48. J. G. R. Acquoy, *Het klooster te Windesheim*, Vol. III, p. 75. — W. F. N. Rootselaar, *Amersfoort* (777-1580), Vol I, p. 451. — Amersfoort, *Geschiedkundige bijzonderheden*, Vol. II, p. 9.

49. W. F. N. van Rootselaar, *Amersfoort* (777-1580), Vol. I, p. 461, p. 477.

50. *Ibid.*, p. 486.

51. H. F. van Heussen en H. van Rijn, *Oudheden en gestichten van het bisdom Deventer*, Vol. I, p. 210. — M. Schoengen, *Jac Voecht narr.*, p. 18, note 5. — J. G. R. Acquoy, *Het klooster te Windesheim*, Vol. III, p. 127. — M. Schoengen, *Jac. Voecht narratio*, p. 37. — *Privilegia, capituli Windesemensis*, fol. 320a-321b.

52. H. Gysbertszoon van Arnhem, *Kronyk van het fraterhuis te Gouda*, ed. A. H. L. Hensen, p. 27.

53. See note 35.

54. M. Schoengen, *Jac Voecht narratio*, pp. 134-138, pp. 493-496.

55. W. Moll, *Kerkgeschiedenis van Nederland*, Vol. II, part 3, p. 96.

56. Constitution of the house at Zwolle, in: M. Schoengen, *Jac Voecht narr.* pp. 240-241. — Constitution of the house at Deventer, in Ms. no. 73 G 22, Royal Library, the Hague, fol. 1b-2b. Published by A. Hyma in *The Christian Renaissance*, pp. 441-474.

57. *Constitution of the house at Zwolle*, pp. 241-242. — *Constitution of the house at Deventer*, fol. 2b-3d. The selection and arrangement of the subject matter was the work of Florentius Radewijns, for not only does the prologue of the constitution in use at Deventer explicitly state that the written rules of this constitution were the same as those practised in the house at Deventer before, but in the extracts we have of Radewijns' rules, the same subjects are arranged exactly in the same way as found in the written constitution. See: D. J. M. Wüstenhoff, *Florentii parvum et simplex exercitium*, p. 96. It was not Theodore Herxen, rector of the house at Zwolle, therefore, who composed the chapter on meditation, as Schoengen believes (M. Schoengen, *Jac Voecht narr.*, p. CXL), but Florentius Radewijns.

58. *Zwolle Const.*, pp. 246-247. — *Dev. Const.*, fol. 10a-b, pp. 447-448. — Theodore Herxen composed a series of Dutch sermons, filling two bulky volumes, made especially for the citizens of Zwolle. Of the brethren at Gouda we read that they frequently addressed the people in the vernacular. One of the brethren would read a passage from the Scriptures, while another would explain and comment upon this passage: H. Gysbertsz. van Arnhem, *Kronyk van het fraterhuis te Gouda*, p. 44.

59. *Zwolle Const.*, pp. 247-248. — *Dev. Const.*, fol. 10b-11a.

60. R. Doebner, *Annalen und Akten*, pp. 225-226, 227-231, 233-235. — G. Boerner, *Die Annalen und Akten*, pp. 76-86; and p. 87.

61. *Zwolle Constitution*, pp. 259-260. — *Deventer Constitution*, fol. 26a-28a, pp. 459-460. — M. Schoengen, *Jac Voecht narr.*, pp. LVI-LVIII. — M. A. G. Vorstman, *Stukken betreffende de Broeders des Gemeenen Levens*, pp. 79, 81, 115, 133.

62. R. Doebner, *Annalen und Akten*, pp. 214-215.

63. *Zwolle Const.*, pp. 265-266, p. 268. — *Dev. Const.*, fol. 37b-38a, 40a-b, pp. 466-467, 468-469. — *Hildesheim Const.*, pp. 235-236.

64. *Zwolle Const.*, pp. 266-268. — *Dev. Const.*, fol 38a-40a. — Cf. *Hildesheim Const.* pp. 238-239.

65. The Sisters of the Common Life also had constitutions. The first one, drawn up by Groote in 1379, was followed in due time by more elaborate ones, among which the one used at Münster has recently been made more accessible in printed form (see: W. E. Schwarz, *Studien zur Geschichte des Klosters Marienthal*, pp. 112-126).

66. M. Schoengen, *Jac Voecht narr.*, p. 277.

67. D. de Man, *Stichtige punten*, pp. 16-17.

68. R. Dier de Muden, *Scriptum*, p. 65. — D. de Man, *Stichtige punten*, p. LV, p. 129 — J. G. R. Acquoy, *Het klooster te Windesheim*, Vol. II, pp. 301-302.

69. D. de Man, *Stichtige punten*, p. LV, p. 37, note b, p. 51, note a.

70. Th. à Kempis, *Vita Luberti*, § 36. — R. Dier, *Scriptum*, p. 64. — W. J. Kühler, *Joh. Brinckrinck*, pp. 34 and 36 — D. de Man, *Stichtige punten*, pp. LI-LII, p. LIV. — J. G. R. Acquoy, *Het klooster te Windesheim*, vol. II, p. 290, note 7. — M. Schoengen, *Jac. Voecht narr.*, p. 223.

71. A. Hyma, *The Youth of Erasmus.*

72. J. H. Gerretsen, *Florentius Radewijns*, pp. 67-70.

73. M. Schoengen, *Die Schule von Zwolle*, p. 19.

74. M. Schoengen, *Die Schule von Zwolle*, p. 11, note 1, and p. 19.

75. M. Schoengen, *Die Schule von Zwolle*, pp. 17-18.

76. See p. 45.

77. W. F. N. *Rootselaar, Amersfoort*, Vol. II (1898), p. 12.

78. E. Barnikol, *Luther in Magdeburg*, p. 56 — P. Opmerus, *Martyrum Batavicorum*, p. 152 (quoted in: D. van Bleysweyck, *Delft*, p. 520). — D. van Bleysweyck, *Delft*, p. 519. — S. W. A. Drossaers, *Archieven van de Delftsche statenkloosters*, p. 322. — *Chronicle of the Brethren-house at Doesburg*, pp. 38, 46, 84. — *Henric van Arnhem's Kronyk van het fraterhuis te Gouda*, p. 40. — H. F. von Heussen and H. van Rijn, *Oudheden van Deventer*, Vol. I, p. 216. — J. van Waasberge, *Beschrijving van Geraartsbergen*, Vol. II, p. 37. — *Provincial archives, Groningen*, 1511 no. 23. Cf. J. Lindeborn, *Historia episcopatus Daventriensis*, p. 132; G. Bonet-Maury, *De opera scholastica fratrum vitae communis*, p. 80. See particularly: Gysberti Coeverincx, *Analecta*, part II, ed. by G. van den Elsen and W. Hoevenaars, p. 82. — L. Halkin, *"Le Collège liégeois des Frères de la Vie Commune,"* in *Fédération archèologigue et historique de Belgique* (1940), pp. 299-311. — L. Kückelhahn, *Johannes Sturm*, pp. 9, 10-13. — G. Bonet-Maury, *De opera scholastica*, p. 90. — E. Wintzer, *Die Schule der Kugelherren in Marburg*, pp. 161-163. — H. D. J. van Schevichaven, *Oud-Nijmegens kerken*, pp. 101, 103-105. — G. C. F. Lisch, *Geschichte der Buchdruckerkunst in Mecklenburg*, p. 36. — B. Lesker, *Die Rostocker Fraterherren*, pp. 147-148. — A. Dekker, *De Hieronymusschool te Utrecht*, pp. 8-59. — W. Moll, *Kerkgeschiedenis*, Vol. II, part II, p. 245. — S. Muller, *Catalogussen, Stads-archief*, part I (1913), p. 123. — M. Godet, *La Congrégation de Montaigu*, p. 3. — The Brethren of the Common Life conducted a very flourishing school at Hulsbergen, according to Dr. Moll (W. Moll, *Kerkgeschiedenis*, Vol. II, part II, p. 244). At Harderwijk also they had a very good school: H. Bouman, *Geschiedenis der voormalige Geldersche Hoogeschool*, Vol. I, pp. 6-11.

79. *Consilium Joannis Sturmii*, in: G. Bonet-Maury, *De opera scholastica*, p. 90: "Leodii, Daventriae, Zwollae, Vuasaliae literarum exercitationes habent, eisque unum assignatum locum, distributum suis ordinibus, atque ex illis ludis feliciora et plura plerumque prodeunt ingenia quam ex vicinis, ut vocant, Academiis." See also M. Schoengen, *Monasticon Batavum*, Vol. II.

80. I. J. van Doornink, *Bouwstoffen voor een geschiedenis van het onderwijs in Overijssel*, part IX (1888), p. 98. — M. Schoengen, *Die Schule von Zwolle*, pp. 110-111.

81. M. Schoengen, *Die Schule von Zwolle*, pp. 119-121.

82. M. van Rijn, *Wessel Gansfort*, p. 37.

83. See p. 45.

84. W. Dillenberger, *Al. Hegius*, pp. 483-484. H. E. J. Vandervelden, *Agricola*, p. 80. P. S. Allen, *Opus ep. Erasmi*, Vol. I, p. 580, n. 23. — J. Butzbach, *Auchtanium*, p. 231. See also A. Hyma, *The Youth of Erasmus*, pp. 105-114.

85. L. Geiger, *Renaissance und Humanismus*, pp. 391-392 — D. Reichling, *Murmellius*, p. 11.

86. A. Hegius, *Dialogi* (1503), fol. 82b.

87. D. Reichling, *Murmellius*, p. 13.

88. J. Butzbach, *Auctarium*, p. 238.

89. He died on December 27, 1498.

90. P. S. Allen, *Opus ep. Erasmi*, Vol. I, p. 118. — J. Lindeboom, *Bijb. humanisme*, p. 77. — H. E. J. Vandervelden, *Agricola*, p. 81, p. 144.

91. J. Butzbach, *Auctarium*, p. 220, p. 236.

92. J. Lindeboom, *Bijb. hum.*, p. 70.

93. Cf. J. Lindeboom, *Bijb. hum.*, p. 121. — W. Moll, *J. Brugman*, Vol. II, p. 79.

94. D. Reichling, *Murmellius*, p. 9.

95. Cf. D. Reichling, *Ortwin Gratius*, pp. 60-81. — L. Geiger, *Renaissance und Humanismus*, p. 429. — L. Geiger, *Reuchlin*, pp. 248-252. — J. Lindeboom, *Bijb. humanisme*, pp. 106-108.

96. J. G. de Hoop Scheffer, *Geschiedenis der Hervorming in Nederland* (1870), p. 28.

97. J. Geny, *Geschichte der Stadtbibl. zu Schlettstadt*, p. 18.

98. G. C. Knod, *Aus der Bibl. des B. Rhenanus*, p. 4. — J. Knepper, *Jacob Wimpfeling*, p. 6.

99. Charles Schmidt, *Histoire Littéraire de L'Alsace*, Vol. I, p. XIV.

100. G. C. Knod, *Aus der Bibl. des B. Rhen.*, pp. 5-6.

101. G. C. Knod, *Aus der Bibl. des Beatus Rhenanus*, p. 7-12. — J. Knepper, *Das Schulwesen in Elsass*, p. 330.

102. J. B. Nordhoff, *Denkwürdigkeiten*, p. 122. — D. Reichling, *Murmellius*, p. 27. — *Die Reform der Domschule zu Münster*, p. 32. — A Parmet, *Rudolph von Langen*, pp. 67-69.

103. Cf. A. Bömer, *Das lit. Leben in Münster*, p. 43. See also: D. Reichling, *Die Reform*, p. 27.

104. See: K. Löffler, *Das Fraterhaus Wiedenbach in Köln*, p. 101, p. 103.

105. D. Reichling, *Die Reform*, p. 20. — A. Bömer, *Der Münstersche Domschulrektor Timann Kemner*, p. 184. — D. Reichling, *Murm.*, p. 1, p. 3, 45, 69.

106. D. Reichling, *Murmellius*, p. 44.

107. *Ibid.*, pp. 42-43.

108. See: D. Reichling, *Die Reform*, p. 65.

109. L. Geiger, *Ren. und Hum.*, p. 397. — D. Reichling, *Murmellius*, p. 47.

110. See: D. Reichling, *Murmellius*, pp. 46, 48-69, 88-94, 98-115. On pp. 132-165 a list of his works is given.

111. D. Reichling, *Die Reform*, p. 69-70, 74-75. — D. Reichling, *Die Humanisten J. Harlenius u. J. Montanus.*

112. See: A. Egen, *Der Einfluss der Münsterschen Domschule auf die Ausbreitung des Humanismus.* For all the schools in Germany see W. Landeen, *The Devotio Moderna in Germany.* Doctoral dissertation, University of Michigan.

113. *Idem.*

NOTES TO CHAPTER IV

1. J. Busch, *Chronicon Wind.*, p. 43.

2. W. J. Kühler, *Brinckerinck*, pp. 23-24.

3. J. Busch, *Chron. Wind.*, p. 44.

4. D. A. Brinkerink, *Vita. Brincr.*, p. 327.

5. J. Busch, *Chron. Wind.*, p. 343.

6. See J. G. R. Acquoy, *Windesheim*, Vol. II, pp. 7-10. Cf. M. Schoengen, *Narratio*, pp. LXIII-LXIV.

7. J. Busch, *Chron. Wind.*, pp. 343-344; cf. J. G. R. Acquoy, *Windesheim*, Vol. II, pp. 8-9.

8. J. Busch, *Chron. Wind.*, p. 344.

9. J. G. R. Acquoy, *Windesheim*, Vol. II, pp. 9-10.

10. J. G. R. Acquoy, *Windesheim*, Vol. II, p. 10.

11. *Ibid.*, vol. II, p. 13.

12. *Ibid.*, Vol. II, p. 13.

13. J. Busch, *Chron. Wind.*, pp. 344-345. — J. G. R. Acquoy, *Windesheim*, Vol. III, p. 26; Vol. II, p. 13 n. 1.

14. J. Busch, *Chron Wind.*, p. 348. — J. G. R. Acquoy, *Wind.*, Vol. III, p. 34.

15. J. Busch, *Chron. Wind.*, p. 345. — J. H. Richter, *Frenswegen*, p. 16.

16. J. Busch, *Chron. Wind.*, p. 349. — J. G. R. Acquoy, *Wind.*, Vol. III, p. 38.

17. J. Busch, *Chron. Wind.*, p. 350.

18. *Ibid.*, p. 350.

19. *Ibid.*, p. 351. — J. G. R. Acquoy, *Wind.*, Vol. III, p. 54.

20. J. Busch, *Chron. Wind.*, p. 351. — J. G. R. Acquoy, *Wind.*, Vol. III, p. 62.

21. J. Busch, *Chron. Wind.*, pp. 352-353. — J. G. R. Acquoy, *Wind.*, Vol. II, pp. 16-18.

22. J. Busch, *Chron Wind.*, pp. 365-366, p. 401. — C. Block, *Chronicle*, ed. J. G. C. Joosting, p. 48. — *Ordinationes Windeshemense*, pp. 15, 20.

23. J. Busch, *Chron. Wind.*, pp. 366, 482. — J. G. R. Acquoy, Wind., vol. III, pp. 92, 94, 55.

24. Ioannis ab Horstmaria, *Chronica*, fol. 2b-3a, 5b-6a. — J. H. Richter, *Frenswegen*, pp. 16-17, 19-21. — J. Busch, *Chron. Wind.*, pp. 165-172, 175-179.

25. V. Becker, *Een onbekende kronijk*, p. 388. — J. G. R. Acquoy, *Wind.*, Vol. I, p. 291 n. 3.

26. J. Busch, *Liber de ref. mon.*, pp. 393, p. 395-397, 708, 402, 404, 406, 706, 420, 432, 452, 433.

27. *Ibid.*, pp. 452, 457.

28. *Ibid.*, pp. 457-459.

29. *Ibid.*, pp. 459-460.

30. *Ibid.*, pp. 455, 555-568, 730, 784, 498, 431-432, 539-544, 613-615.

31. *Ibid.*, pp. 562-565, 568-572, 588-597, 617-618, 629-632.

32. *Ibid.*, pp. 505-507, 514-517.

33. K. Grube, *Die Legationsreise des Cardinals Nikolaus von Cusa*, p. 394.

34. See: P. E. Schatten, *Kloster Böddiken.* — L. Schmitz-Kellenberg, *Monumenta Budicensa.*

35. W. J. Kühler, *Brinckerinck*, p. 313.

36. W. J. Kühler, *Brinckerinck*, pp. 313-316.

37. *Ibid.*, pp. 317-319.

38. *Ibid.*, pp. 326-335; here the whole story of the reform at Hilwartshausen is found.

39. W. Moll, *Kerkgeschiedenis*, Vol. II, part II, p. 227.

40. J. G. R. Acquoy, *Windesheim*, Vol. I, pp. 205-206.

41. *Ibid.*, pp. 207-211.

42. *Ibid.*, Vol. II, pp. 300-301.

43. *Ibid.*, Vol. II, p. 280.

44. *Ibid.*, Vol. I, p. 184.

45. *Ibid.*, Vol. II, pp. 284-295.

46. *Ibid.*, Vol. II, 198-199.

47. *Ibid.*, Vol. II, p. 143.

48. J. Busch, *Chron. Wind.*, pp. 311-312, XIX, note 1.

49. J. G. R. Acquoy, *Windesheim*, Vol. II, p. 209, p. 214.

50. J. G. R. Acquoy, *Windesheim*, Vol. II, pp. 229-230, 236-38.

51. *Ibid.*, Vol. II, pp. 258-262.

NOTES TO CHAPTER V

1. A. J. Thebaud, "Who Wrote the Imitation of Christ?" in: *American Cath. Quart. Rev.* 1883, p. 650.

2. O. A. Spitzen, *Thomas à Kempis*, p. 2. — E. Waterton, *Thomas à Kempis*, p. 22.

3. Hirsch, *Prologomena*, Vol. III, pp. 44-62.

4. Book I, Ch. 22 (p. 43/30-31 of Pohl's edition); Book I, Ch. 13 (p. 22/15-19); Book III, Ch. 55 (p. 250/8-10).

5. I, 25 (p. 53/6-9); III, 19 (p. 178/6-7); I, 3 (p. 10/1-6); III, 38 (p. 213/26-28); III, 53 (p. 244/25-26); I, 2 (p. 8/8-10).

6. I, ii (p. 19/7-15); III, 5 (p. 151/23-26); I, 13 (p. 36/24-29); II, 9 (p. 76/29-31, p. 77/3-14); III, 35.

7. I, 3 (p. 10/19-24); IV, 7 (p. 109/22-25, p. 109/27-110/1; II, 10 (p. 77/26-27); III, 4 (p. 150/2-5); III, 56 (p. 252/27-253/1); I, 8; III, 45 (p. 225/6-7); III, 53 (p. 244/10-11).

8. I, 8 (p. 15/24-27); I, 10; I, 20 (p. 35/18-36/7); III, 54, (p. 248/24-31; III, 58 (p. 256/29-257/27); II, 6 (p. 69/7-15); I, i (p. 6/17-18); I, i (p. 6/15-16); I, 18 (p. 31/2-3); I, 25 (p. 55/29-31); II, 6 (p. 69/20-22); II, 7 (p. 70/9-11); II, 9; III, 26 (p. 194/10-13); III, 45 (p. 223/9-11).

9. I, 12 (p. 20/25-26); I, 17 (p. 29/6-7); I, 23 (p. 47/31-48/1); II, i (p. 60/23-30); III, 53 (p. 244/13-15); III, 59 (p. 261/23-24); I, 21 (p. 39/6, 13-16); III, 57.

10. See p. 59.

11. III, 14, 13, 20, 51; IV, 15, 18.

12. I, 9; II, 11; III, 13. I, 7; I, 12 (p. 21/1-3); I, 20 (p. 36/12-18); II, 10 (p. 78/15-24); III, 7 (p. 158/11-30).

13. I, 17 (p. 28/29-31); II, 12 (p. 82/7-8); III, 32, 37; III, 39 (p. 215/19-22); IV, 8.

14. I, 24 (p. 51/3-4, 9-12); II 12 (p. 88/3-5).

15. II, 12; IV, 8; II, 4, 6; III, 11, 15, 44, 53.

16. I, 17, 20; I, 5; I, 23 (p. 46/12-13); I, 19 (p. 34/2-7); I, 7 (p. 14/15).

17. I, 1 (p. 6/11-13); III, 34, 42, 46, 50; IV, 7, 8, 9, 15. I, 17 (p. 29/7-8); II, 1, 7, 11; III, 6; IV, 1, 3, 11, 17.

18. I, 13 (p. 23/3-5); I, 14, 15, 16, 25: II, 3 (p. 64/17-23); III, 25 (p. 192); III, 45 (p. 225/4-6). III, 27 (p. 195/8-10).

19. II, 1 (p. 59/5-6, 9-11, 14-16); III, 2 (p. 144/27-145/4); III, 40 (p. 216/15-17); I, 3 (p. 9/8-13).

20. III, 43 (p. 220/20-22); I, 3 (p. 10/12-14); I, 1 (p. 6/2-11); I, 3 (p. 8/25-28); III, 3 (p. 146/5-7); III, 43; III, 44 (p. 149/9-11).

21. See pp. 59-81.

22. See Chapter 55 of Book III.

23. V. Becker, *L'auteur de l'Imitation*, p. 4 — K. Hirsche, *Prologomena*, Vol. III, p. 264 — J. Mooren, *Th. à Kempis*, pp. 113, 32, 227, 230-231.

24. H. Rosweyden, *Vindiciae*, p. 123.

25. Th. à Kempis, *Vita Joh. Gronde*. Ch. I.

26. Th. à Kempis, *Vita Florentii*, Ch. XXIV.

27. Th. à Kempis, *Vita Joh. Gronde*, Ch. I.

28. Th. à Kempis, *Vita Arn. Schoonhcviac*, § 3; *Vita Joh. Gronde*, Ch. I, § 2.

29. Th. à Kempis, *Vita Flor.*, Ch. XVI, § 4.

30. It should also be borne in mind that Thomas à Kempis was only one of the many boys who happened to be copying religious writings at Deventer. From far and near they had come to Deventer to attend school there, and, as happened with Thomas Hemerken of Kempen, to "learn to read and write the Holy Scriptures and books on moral subjects." Thus thousands of manuscripts were written at Deventer, which as a rule were taken home when the boys left the Yssel country, or, in case they entered some monastery, these manuscripts were added to the library of that monastery. It is a great pity that so few writers have investigated this phase of the influence exerted by the Brethren of the Common Life at Deventer, Zwolle, and elsewhere. The only one who appears to have mentioned the subject before the year 1924 is Dr. M. Schoengen of Zwolle, who found three manuscripts in the Episcopal Seminary at Liége which expressly mention the fact that they had been written at Deventer and Zwolle. Schoengen even claims that in the library of this institution twenty-five unpublished treatises of Groote are found (M. Shoengen, *Nederlandica in Belgische archieven*, p. 180). But after careful examination of the manuscripts in question during the summer of the year 1920, the present writer noticed that many of them were in all probability copied at Deventer, but not a single unpublished treatise written by Groote is found in any one of them. And still this subject is of such significance that results cannot fail the serious student. A few examples might illustrate the nature of this interesting problem. In the *Stadt-und Landesbibliothek* at Düsseldorf a manuscript is found, called Ms. B. 180, containing 171 folios. Some extracts from Groote's writings were written in it and other material by a certain "John Nijell at Deventer in the year 1458, when seated in the 'Nova domo clericorum,' " which was the building constructed by the Brethren of the Common Life for the purpose of accommodating poor school boys with proper board and lodging. Manuscript G. B. 8°8/3 of the *Stadt-bibliothek* at Cologne also contains a note stating that this manuscript had been written at Deventer (fol. 90b: "Explicit iste liber scriptus et completus per manus Wilhelmi Vos de Ghiecen anno Domini 1416 in profesto Valentini Daventrie"). And on fol. la of Ms. G. B. 8°76 of the same library we read the following statement: "Iste libellus pertinet fratribus s. Crucis in Colonia et vocatur Farago ea quod in eo multa ac diversa raptim undique collecta sint, et primo do servire Deo et multis aliis ut pateat in folio sequenti, ubi ponitur etiam per numerum foliorum." This table of contents is found on fol. 2a-3a, while on fol. 8b we read: "Sequuntur multa bona collecta Swollis ante annos 30a, quorum tabula in principio huius habetur." On fol. 12b we find the date 1412. Unfortunately it was not customary in those days to write such notes in the manuscripts, wherefore it is difficult to estimate how many of them were written by pupils of the Brethren of the Common Life. Only incidentally do we find indications which lead to definite conclusions. One very interesting example is the following. Manuscript G. B. 4°249 of the City Library at Cologne was written at Deventer, though we would never have known about this, if a very curious accident had not impelled the copyist to mention the fact. He had already copied the *Sermo de Nativitate Domini* in this manuscript under the title of *Tractatus magistri Gerardi dicti Groet de Daventria de quatuor generibus meditabilium*

sive contemplacionum. We are very grateful to him for that, as the *Sermo de Nativitate Domini* by Groot had been thought lost, and as it was believed that the *Tractatus de quatuor generibus meditabilium* was a separate work. Next he had copied a few extracts from Gregory (fol. 13b-15b), followed on fol. 22a by Groote's *De locatione curae animarum* and an excerpt from the *Liber apum*, called *De pluritate beneficiorum*, which he believed to be also a treatise composed by Groote (fol. 37b: "Expliciunt valde horribilia de pluritate beneficiorum visa a magistro Gerardi dicto Groet de Daventria"). The words: "visa a magistro Gerardi dicto Groet de Daventria" were scratched out by a later hand and the following note written on the margin: "Ex libro apum scripta." On fol. 38a he had begun a treatise on the ten commandments and had already come to the top of the second column of fol. 68, when his work was interrupted. A cat soiled the page on which he had been writing, wherefore the next morning he drew a picture there of the cat and added the following commentary: "Confound that wretched cat which soiled this page one night at Deventer. Care must be taken that no books are left open at night where cats are." On fol. 73b he finished the *Commentum super decem precepta,* and on fol. 73b-90a we find the *Tractatus de peccatis capitalibus sive mortalibus.*

31. According to Rosweyden he went to Mount St. Agnes in 1399 (*Vindiciae,* p. 110), and his probation lasted for six years (*Vindiciae,* p. 111), but according to the continuation of the *Chronicon Mt. St. Agnetis* by an anonymous writer, he was invested in 1406.

32. V. Becker, *L'auteur de l'Imitation,* p. 7.

33. The above selection is taken from D. V. Scully's translation of the *Sermons to the Novices Regular,* pp. XXI-XXII.

34. See: Thomas à Kempis, *Opera,* Nuremberg, 1494, fol. 84b-85a, where a biography is given by an anonymous writer. This sketch is also found in a manuscript at The Hague, and is edited in the edition of the *Imitation* by L. Peters, Leiden 1902, where on pp. XI-XV a list of the thirty-eight works is given.

35. See J. van Rooij, *Gerard Zerbolt, van Zutphen* (Nijmegen, 1936) pp. 241-250.

36. The quotations are all from: Th. à Kempis, *The Founders of the New Devotion,* ed. J. P. Arthur, pp. 59, 54, 67, 72-73, 153-160, 192-207, 238, 251, 260.

37. F. R. Cruise, *Thomas à Kempis,* pp. 159-160. Cf. E. Amort, *Ded. crit.,* p. 50.

38. A. Loth, *L'auteur de l'Im.,* pp. 531-537.

39. See: J. E. G. De Montmorency, *Th. à Kempis,* p. XIX, pp. 110-112.

40. V. Becker, *Thomas van Kempen* (1892), p. 9.

41. K. Hirsche, *Prologomena,* Vol. III, pp. 181-190.

42. O. A. Spitzen, *Nouvelle defense,* pp. 50-51. The manuscript in question contains the following note: "Notandum quod iste tractatus editus est a probo et egregrie viro magistro (master of novices) Thoma de Monte sancte Agnetis . . . descriptus ex manu autoris in Trajecto (in the bishopric of Utrecht) anno 1425." Hirsche, however, refuses to believe that this is the correct date (see his *Prologomena,* Vol. III, pp. 167, 172).

43. O. A. Spitzen, *Les Hollandismes,* p. 74.

44. K. Hirsche, *Prologomena,* Vol. III, pp. 174-181. — O. A. Spitzen, *Les Hollandismes,* p. 63.

45. O. A. Spitzen, *Th. à Kempis gehandhaafd,* pp. 58-60. On the last page of the manuscript in which Spitzen discovered this very important translation we read: "Item een boeken van gheestelijken vermaningen qui sequitur me." Hence book I was originally drawn up in Latin. This translation was made by John Scutken, the friend of Thomas à Kempis (see: O. A. Spitzen, *Les Hollandismes,* p. 61, *Nouvelle defense,* p. 42).

46. O. A. Spitzen, *Nouv. def.* p. 110; *Nalezing,* p. 35.

47. K. Hirsche, *Pologomena,* Vol. III, pp. 190-191.

48. O. A. Spitzen, *Nauv. def.,* p. 100.

49. K. Hirsche, *Prologomena,* Vol. III, p. 194. — E. Barnikol, *Studien,* p. 64.

50. O. A. Spitzen, *Les Hollandismes,* p. 62.

51. O. A. Spitzen, *Nouv. déf.,* pp. 58, 197-199.

52. L. Korth, *Die älteste deutsche Uebersetzung der "Imitatio Christi,"* pp. 89-90.

53. See: V. Becker, *Thomas van Kempen* (1892), pp. 16-19. Becker mentions copies of the years 1428, 1429, 1433, 1436, brought to Liége, Erfurt and other places.

54. J. Busch, *Chron. Wind.,* p. 58.

55. "All that the supporters of Thomas à Kempis have left," triumphantly exclaimed Wolfsgruber in his well-known work on the abbot Gersen, "is the account by Busch and the autograph of Thomas à Kempis, finished in 1441" (C. Wolfsgruber, *Gersen*, p. 74).

56. See: O. A. Spitzen, *Nouvelle défense*, p. 48. — V. Becker, *L'auteur de l'Imitation*, pp. 33-35. — J. B. Malou, *Recherches*, pp. 77-89. — V. Becker, *Derniers travaux*, pp. 49-51. — F. R. Cruise, *Thomas à Kempis*, pp. 149-157, 242-248. The best source on this question remains: E. Amort, *Ded. critica*, pp. 94-118. See also: O. A. Spitzen, *Th. à Kempis gehandhaafd*, pp. 165-177. — H. Watrigant, *La genèse des Exerc. spirit.*, p. 104.

57. See: O. A. Spitzen, *Nouv. déf.*, pp. 44-45.

58. K. Hirsche, *Prologomena*, Vol. III, pp. 11-14. — A. Loth, L'Auteur de l'Imitation, pp. 581-585. — E. Renan, *L'Auteur de l'Imitation de Jesus Christ*, pp. 320-322.

59. *De Im. Christi*, book I, ch. XXV.

60. E. Renan, *L'Auteur de l'Im*, pp. 323-334. — Wolfsgruber, *J. Gersen*, pp. 172-185 (the author is an Italian), 185-198 (written in the thirteenth century). Cf. W. Moll, *Kerkgeschiedenis*, Vol. II, part II, p. 372. Valuable is the article by Professor J. Tesser in *Ons geestelijk erf*, Vol. XXIII (1949), entitled "De eerste en de laatste faze van het auteursprobleem der Navolging in Italië (see pp. 168-203.)

61. K. Hirsche, *Prologomena*, Vol. II, pp. 2-88.

62. See pp. XVIII-XIX of the ed. of *Imitation* by J. Malaise for further proof.

63. O. A. Spitzen, *Nouv déf.*, pp. 136, 144, 162.

64. P. Hagen, *De Navolging van Christus en Thomas van Kempen*, p. 40.

65. J. F. Vregt, *Eenige ascetische tractaten*, p. 323, p. 330. They are chapters X and XIII.

66. *Ibid.*, p. 325.

67. J. B. Malou, *Recherches*, pp. 119-120 (from a letter by John Vos of Heusden, prior of Windesheim), pp. 391-402 (from the *Admonitiones of Florentius*).

68. O. A. Spitzen, *Thomas à Kempis gehandhaafd*, pp. 71-82.

69. V. Becker, *L'auteur de l'Imitation*, pp. 145-194.

70. G. Bonet-Maury, *E quibus fontibus*, pp. 15-37.

71. Found on pages 27-40 of the issue of the year 1920. See also *Zeitschrift für deutsches Alterum*, Vol. LIX, pp. 23-35. See also P. Hagen, *Untersuchungen ueber Buch II und III der "Imitatio Christi"* (Amsterdam, 1935), pp. 1-26.

72. Mss. theol. germ. 8° no. 43 and 4° no. 15. — Ms. theol. germ 8° no. 54. On fol. 42b a prayer was written (ending on fol. 47a), which is not found in the *Imitation*. It is called: "Dit is en innich gebeth alle tyd to lesende deme mynschen."

73. On fol. 1a of the manuscript in question we read: "Anneken Poises op Sunte Johannes hort dyt bock." Cf. the article mentioned in the preceding note.

74. See the notices in: *Sitzungsberichte der kön, preuss. Ak. der Wiss.*, for Jan. 1911, pp. 108-109, and in: *Neue Jahrbücher für das klassische Altertum, Geschichte und deutsche Literatur*, Vol. XXXI (1913), p. 51.

75. See J. van Rooij, *Gerard Zerbolt*, pp. 12-13.

76. J. van Rooij, *Gerard Zerbolt van Zutphen*, pp. 362-372.

77. M. Luther, *Werke: Kritische Gesamtausgabe*, Weimer ed., Vol. 56 (1938), p. 313. See also Vol. III, p. 648.

78. P. H. Watrigant, S. J., *La genèse des Exercitia Spiritualia* (Amiens, 1897), p. 29.

79. *Ibid.*, p. 30.

80. *Ibid.*, pp. 56-57, 59.

81. *Ibid.*, p. 58; p. 54.

82. *Ibid.*, pp. 28-44. — H. Böhmer, *Studien zur Gesellchraft Jesu*, Vol. I; *Loyala* (Bonn, 1914), pp. 34-45.

83. Ign. Loyola, *Exercitia Spiritualia*, ed. J. Roothaan, S. J., II. Hebdomada. De Incarnatione (p. 132): "Pro secunda hebdomada et ita deinceps, valde prodest legere subinde (aliquid) ex libris de Imitatione Christi vel Evangeliorum et vitarum Sanctorum."

84. *Ibid.*, note 9: "Notandum, primo loco poni lectionem aliquam ex libris de Imitatione Christi; haec eenim planior, facilior, neque talis, quae mentem avertere a praecipuo contemplationun: argumento posset, sed potius ad practicas conclusiones inter meditandum conceptas magis confirmandas aptissima est" (this note is by Roothaan).

85. H. Böhmer, *Studien*, Vol. I, p. 46.

86. *Ibid.*, p. 47.

87. *Ibid.*, p. 64: "Sein originellstes Werk, die exercitia spiritualia, ist im Grunde nur eine letzte Frucht der 'devotio moderna.' "

88. P. H. Watrigant, S. J. *La genèse des Exercitia Spiritualia*, p. 59. Cfr. M. Godet, *La Congregation de Montaigu* (Paris, 1912), p. 93: "Mais les veritables precurseurs des 'Exercises' se trouvent au XIVe et XVe siecle dans les Pays-Bas. Ce sont les écrivains mystiques de l'école de Windesheim, les Frères de la Vie Commune, Gérard Groote, Florent Radjevins, Jean Mombaer et surtout Gérard de Zutphen." — H. Böhmer, *Studien*, Vol. I, p. 64, note 1.

89. See Jakob Marx, "Nicolaus von Cues und seine Stiftungen zu Cues und Deventer," in *Festschrift zum Bischofs-Jubileum* (Trier, 1906), pp. 210-22.

90. C. Smits, "David van Augsburg en de invloed van zijn Profectus op de Moderne Devotie," in *Collectanea Franciscana Neerlandica I* ('s-Hertogenbosch, 1927), pp. 171-203.

91. C. Smits, *op. cit.*, pp. 192-198.

92. J. F. Meyer, *Thomae à Kempis Capita quindecim inedita* (Lübeck, 1845).

93. J. van Ginneken, *Trois textes pré-Kemistes du premier livre de l'Imitation*. Published in *Verhandelingen der Kon. Ned. Akad. van Wet. Afd. Lett.*, Vol. XLIV (Amsterdam, 1940), pp. 5-12.

94. R. R. Post, *De Moderne Devotie* (Amsterdam, 1940), pp. 151-154.

95. Edited and translated by Joseph Malaise, S. J. Published by the America Press, New York, 1937. See p. 271.

96. See J. van Rooij, *Gerard Zerbolt*, p. 41.

97. See A. Hyma, *The "De Teutonicalibus" by Gerard Zerbolt of Zutphen*, The Hague, 1923.

98. J. Huizinga, *Erasmus* (Haarlem, 1925), pp. 15-17.

99. W. Mulder, "Ter Chronologie van het leven van Geert Groote," in *Historisch Tijdschrift*, Vol. XII (1933), pp. 349-357. Mulder found in Groote's words an almost revolutionary message, but we must bear in mind that Groote wrote his letter on the Papal Schism, in which he enunciated his remarkable view, during a time in which two popes were reigning simultaneously, one in Rome and one at Avignon. People generally had little respect for the Pope. Nevertheless, Groote did not mince words, and Zerbolt also was not afraid to put his finger on certain sore spots in the hierarchy.

100. See the first printed version published by the present writer in *Archief voor de geschiedenis van het Aartsbisdom Utrecht* (1926), p. 32. The treatise fills one hundred pages, and it is a brilliant defense of the brotherhood by the greatest scholar among its members from 1384 to 1460. It is inconceivable that such a person would have bothered to take a work by Gerard Groote and change it into a composition of his own, as Professor J. van Ginneken claimed.

101. J. van Ginneken, *Trois textes pré-Kempistes du second livre de l'Imitation* (Amsterdam, 1941), p. 32.

102. One of the most devastating attacks upon the Van Ginneken thesis appeared in R. R. Post, "Hendrik van Kalkar en Geert Groote?" in *Studia Catholica*, Vol. XXI (1946), pp. 88-92. Here we discover that Groote never mentioned in his correspondence Hendrik Eger van Kalkar, who induced him to enter a Carthusian monastery and who, according to Van Ginneken, assisted Gerard Groote in the composition of *De Imitatione Christi*. Moreover, Hendrik Eger never mentioned Groote in any of his works.

Van Ginneken makes much of the fact that Groote's biography by P. Horn mentions Groote's friendship with Henry Eger, the Carthusian monk. He also indicates that in the *Conclusa et Proposita* of Groote there is a section with this title, "De Sacris Libris Studendis," while the title of Chapter V in the *Imitation* reads "De Lectione Sacrae Scripturae." The resemblance is less striking than that we mentioned above in the text, where we compared Zerbolt's phrase with that heading Chapter V in the *Imitation*. In the great treatise by Zerbolt entitled *De Reformatione Virium Animae*, we find this chapter heading (Ch. XV); "De Reformatione Intellectus per Sacram Lectionem." Zerbolt emphasizes the reading of the sacred writings, while Groote talked more about studying. In Chapter XXVII of *De Spiritualibus Ascensionibus* Zerbolt made some telling remarks about the imitation of Christ: "Et tu etiam primo hoc modo sequere Christum, esto in eius comitatu . . . Attende eius sermones et dulcissimam doctrinam et attende modum quo Christus se in omnibus habuit, quam dulciter et benigne verba illa melliflua protulit. Attende modi quo interius se habuit . . . Quod profuit inde

Pilato, Herodi, vel Pharisais, quod Christi mores vel gestus, aut praesentiam corporalem viderunt, qui eum imitari noluerunt?" In Chapter XXXII we read: "Et cogita semper quasi Christus dicat tibi: 'Haec feci ut sequaris me.' "

103. In December, 1948, an excellent article on Van Ginneken's thesis appeared in the Belgian periodical, *Ons Geestelijk Erf.* The author is B. Spaapen, S. J. He reviews two Swiss publications dealing with the original version of the *Imitation.* He concludes, on the basis of these two contributions (though he had made up his mind long before they appeared in print), that Gerard Groote certainly did not write any part of the *Imitation* in the Dutch language, although Van Ginneken stated in one of his bigger works on the subject (*Op zoek naar den oudsten teskst en den waren schrijver van het eerste boek der Navolging van Christus,* Wetteren, 1929) that Groote had written the whole of the work in Dutch. The present writer, on several occasions, has discussed this question with colleagues of Van Ginneken, and the latter presented him with a copy of the interesting volume just mentioned. But he said from the beginning that Van Ginneken's main thesis was all wrong, namely, that Groote wrote the original version of the *Imitation.* Spaapen on October 24, 1948, wrote on p. 377 of his article: "Haar *Bemerkungen* slaan enkel op de vraag naar den Oertekst der Navolging, die door P. v. Ginneken niet bevredigend is opgelost." His Eminence, Johannes Cardinal de Jong, in Vol. II of the fourth edition (p. 431) of his magisterial work, *Handboek der Kerkgeschiedenis* (1947) expresses the same opinion. Moreover, Professor J. Tesser, S. J. wrote a frank statement in his study in the city of Rome, which was published in *Ons Geestelijk Erf* for May, 1949 (p. 169): "Het staat voor ons vast dat professor van Ginneken zijn thesis historisch niet heeft bewezen." The same opinion is shared by the outstanding Roman Catholic educators in the Netherlands, including Professor R. R. Post at Nijmegen. Significant also is the rejection of Van Ginneken's thesis in the admirable study by J. Tiecke: *De Werken van Geert Groote* (Nijmegen, 1941).

Select Bibliography

Acquoy, J. G. R., Het klooster te Windesheim en zijn invloed, 3 vols., Utrecht 1875-1880.

Allen P. S., Opus Epistolarum Desiderii Erasmi Roterodami, vol. I, Oxford 1906.

Amort, E., Deductio critica qua juxta saniores criticae leges moraliter certum redditur ven. Thomam Kempensem librorum de imitatione christi authorem esse, Augsburg 1761.

Anrich, G., Martin Bucer, Strasbourg 1914.

Auger, A., Étude sur les mystiques des Pays-Bas au Moyen-Age, in: Mémoires couronnés et autres mémoires de l'académie royale de Belgique, Brussels 1891 (1902).

Barnikol, E., Luther in Magdeburg und die dortige Brüderschule, in: Theologische Arbeiten aus dem rheinischen wissenschaftlichen Predigerverein, Neue Folge, vol. XVII (Heft 17), Tübingen 1917, pp. 1-62.

.... Studien zur Geschichte der Brüder vom gemeinsamen Leben; extra issue of (Ergänzungsheft zur) : Zeitschrift für Theologie und Kunst, Tübingen 1917.

Becker, V., L'auteur de l'Imitation et les documents néerlandais, The Hague 1882.

Beer, K. C. L. M. de, Studie over de spiritualiteit van Geert Groote, Nijmegen 1938.

Bleyswyck, D. van, Beschrijvinge der stadt Delft, Delft 1667.

Block, C., Chronicle of an Augustinian monastery at Utrecht (Latin), ed. by J. G. C. Joosting, in; Bijdragen en mededeelingen van het historisch genootschap te Utrecht, The Hague 1895.

Böhmer, H., Studien zur Geschichte der Gesellschaft Jesu, vol. I, Bonn 1914.

Bömer, A., Ausgewählte Werke des münsterschen Humanisten Johannes Murmellius, Münster i. W. 1892-1895.

.... Das literarische Leben in Münster bis zur entgültigen Rezeption des Humanismus, Münster i. W. 1906.

Boerner, H., Die Annalen und Akten der Brüder des gemeinsamen Lebens im Lüchtenhofe zu Hildesheim, Fürstenwald 1905.

Bonet-Maury, G., Quaeritur e quibus nederlandicis fontibus hauserit scriptor libri cui titules est De imitatione Christi (1384-1464), Paris 1878.

Bouwmeester, W. L., Het klooster Bethlehem bij Doetinchem, Doetinchem 1903.

Brinkerink, D. A., Van den doechden der vuriger ende stichtiger susteren van Diepen Veen, Leiden 1902.

.... Biographieën van beroemde mannen uit den Deventer kring, in: Arch. voor de gesch, v. h. aarsb. Utr., vol. XXVII, pp. 400-423; vol. XXVIII, pp. 225-276, 321-343; vol. XXIX, pp. 1-37.

.... De "Vita venerabilis Ioannis Brinckerinck", in: Ned. arch. v. kerkgesch., 1901, pp. 314-354.

Brugmans, H., De kroniek van het klooster te Utrecht, in: Bijdragen en mededeelingen van het historisch genootschap te Utrecht, Amsterdam 1902.

214 The Brethren of the Common Life

Busch, J., Chronicon Windeshemense, and Liber de reformatione monasteriorum, ed. by K. Grube, in: Geschichtsquellen der Provinz Sachsen und angrenzender Gebiete, vol. XIX, Halle 1886.

Butzbach, J., Auctarium de scriptoribus ecclesiasticis, ed. by C. Kraft and W. Crecelius, in: Zeitschrift des bergischen Geschichtsvereins, vol. VII (1871), pp. 224-281.

Clarisse, A. and J., Over den geest en de denkwijze van Geert Groete, kenbaar uit zijne schriften, in: Arch. voor kerk gesch., vol. I (1829), pp. 355-398; vol. II (1830), pp. 245-395; vol. III (1831), pp. 1-90; vol. VIII (1837), pp. 1-384.

Coeverincx, G., Analecta, ed. by G. can den Elsen and W. Hoevenaars, and publ. by: Provinciaal genootschap van kunsten en wetenschappen in Noord-Brabant ('s-Hertogenbosch 1905).

Cruise, F. R., Thomas à Kempis, notes of a visit to the scenes in which his life was spent, London 1887.

Delprat, G. H. M., De broederschap van G. Groote, 2nd ed., Arnhem 1856.

Denifle, H., Cartularium universitatis Parisiensis, vol. III, Paris 1894.

Dier de Muden (Muiden), R., Scriptum de magistro Gherardo Grote, domino Florencio et multis aliis devotis fratribus, in: G. Dumbar, Analecta Daventria, vol. I, pp. 1-87.

Diest Lorgion, E. J., Bijdrage tot de geschiedenis van het fraterhuis te Groningen, in: Groningsche volksalmanak, Groningen 1851, pp. 105-118.

Dillenburger, W., Geschichte des Gymnasiums zu Emmerich, in: Jahresbericht über den Schulcursus 1845-1846 an dem königlichen Gymnasium zu Emmerich, Emmerich (1846), pp. 1-56.

............Zur Geschichte des deutschen Humanismus; Alexander Hegius und Rudolf von Langen, in: Zeitschrift für das Gymnasialwesen, vol. XXIV, Berlin 1870, pp. 481-502.

Dodt van Flensburg, J. J., De stichtings oorkonden van het Utrechtsche fraterhuis, in: Archief voor kerkelijke en wereldlijke geschiedenissen, inzonderheid van Utrecht, vol. I, Utrecht 1838, pp. 89-95.

Doebner, R., Annalen und Akten der Brüder des gemeinsamen Lebens im Luchtenhofe zu Hildesheim, in: Queelen und Darstellungen zur Geschichte Niedersachsens, Hanover 1903.

Dols, J. M. E., Bibliographie der Moderne Devotie, 2 vols., Nijmegen 1936-1937.

Doorninck, J. I. van, Bouwstoffen voor een geschiedenis van het onderwijs in Overijssel, in: Bijdragen tot de geschiedenis van Overijssel, vol. IV, Zwolle 1877, pp. 67-83, 140-157, 233-249; vol. IX (1888), pp. 97-110.

Drossaers, S. W. A., De archieven van de Delftsche statenkloosters, The Hague 1917.

Dumbar G., Analecta Daventria, vol. I, Deventer 1719.

............Het kerkelyk en wereltlyk Deventer, 2 vols., Deventer 1732-1788.

Egen, A., Der Einfluss der münsterschen Domschule auf die Ausbreitung des Humanismus, in: Festschrift zur Feier der Einweihung des Paulinischen Gymnasiums, Münster i. W. 1898, pp. 15-48.

Ekker, A. De Hieronymusschool te Utrecht (1474-1636), Utrecht 1863.

Evelt, J., Die Anfänge der Bursfelder Benedictiner-Congregation, in: Zeitschrift für vaterländische Geschichte und Alterthumskunde (Westfalens), vol. XXV, Münster i. W. 1865, pp. 121-180.

Erhard, H. A., Gedächtniss-Buch des Frater-Hauses zu Münster, in: Zeitschrift für vaterländische Geschichte und Alterthumskunde (Westfalens), vol. VI, Münster i. W. 1843, pp. 89-126.

Feith, H. O., Het klerkenhuis en het fraterhuis te Groningen, in: Bijdragen tot de geschiedenis en oudheidskunde inzonderheid van de provincie Groningen, vol. VI, Groningen 1869, pp. 1-24.

Feugen, G., Onuitgegeven brieven van-en aan Geert Groote, in: Ons Geestelijk Erf, vol. XV (1941), pp. 5-51.

Fredericq, P., Corpus documentorum inquisitionis haereticae pravitatis neerlandicae, vol. II, Ghent and the Hague 1896.

Gallee, J. H., Middeleeuwsche kloosterregels: I. De regel der Windesheimsche vrouwenkloosters; II. Het boek der statuten van het klooster Bethlehem bij Hoorn, in: Ned. arch. v. Kerkgesch., vol. V (1895), pp. 250-322, 345-420.

Gantesweiler, P. T. A., Chronik der Stadt Wesel, Wesel 1881.

Geesink, G. H. J. W. J., Gerard Zerbolt van Zutfen, Amsterdam 1879.

Gelder, H. E. van, De Latijnsche school te Alkmaar, vol. I, Alkmaar 1905.

Gerretsen, J. H., Florentius Radewijns, Nijmegen 1891.

Ginneken, J. van, Op zoek naar den oudsten tekst en den waren schrijver van het eerste boek der Navolging van Christus, Wetteren 1929.

............Trois textes pré-Kempistes du premier livre de l' Imitation, Amsterdam 1940.

............Trois textes pré-Kempistes du second livre de l' Imitation, Amsterdam 1941.

............Geert Groote's levensbeeld, Amsterdam 1942.

Godet, M., La congrégation de Montaigu (1490-1580), Paris 1912.

Groote, G., Epistolae, ed. J. G. R. Acquoy: Gerardi Magni epistolae XIV, Amsterdam 1857.

............*Epistolae*, ed. W. Mulder.

............Conclusa et proposita non vota, in: Thomas à Kempis, Opera omnia, Antwerp 1615, pp. 915-921, and in. Archief voor kerkgesch., vol. III (1831), pp. 371-383.

............Defense and explanation of his Sermo contra focaristas, ed. J. Clarisse, in: Archief voor kerkgesch, vol. VIII (1837), pp. 108-117.

............Dicta quaedam, in: Th. à Kempis, Vita Gerardi Magni, ch. XVIII.

............Dit sijn de vijf poente, die meester Geert de Groote in den volke 't Utrecht predicte, ed. W. Moll, in: Studien en bijdragen op 't gebied der theologie, vol. I, pp. 409-411.

............Een goede leer, ed. W. Moll; see under Moll.

............De locatione ecclesiarum, ed. J. Clarisse, in: Arch. voor kerkgesch., vol. VIII (1837), pp. 119-152.

............De matrimonio, ed. J. Clarisse, in: Arch. voor kerkgesch., Vol. VIII, pp. 159-249.

............Protestatio de veridica Evangelia praedicatione, in: Th. à Kempis, Opera, Antwerp 1615, pp. 914-915; also in: G. Bonet-Maury, Groote, pp. 95-96, and in: Arch. voor kerkgesch., vol. I (1829), pp. 359-360.

............Sermo contra focaristas, ed. A. and J. Clarisse, in: Arch. voor kerkgesch., vol. I, pp. 364-379; vol. II, pp. 307-395; vol. VIII, pp. 5-107.

............Sermo de paupertate, n W. Moll, Geert Groote's sermoen voor Palmzondag over de vrijwillige armoede, in: Studien en bijdragen op 't gebied der theologie, vol. II, pp. 425-469 (the sermon itself: pp. 432-469).

216   *The Brethren of the Common Life*

............Sermo de nativitate Domini: see under A. Hyma.
............De simonia ad beguttas, in: R. Langenberg, Quellen und For-
schungen zur Geschichte der deutschen Mystik, Bonn 1902, pp. 3-33.
............Tractatus de quatuor generibus meditabilium sive contem-
placionum. See A. Hyma.
............Zedelijke toespraak, ed. J. Van Vloten, in: Nieuw arch, voor
kerkgesch., vol. II (1854), pp. 295-307.
............Zedelijke toespraak, in: G. Monet-Maury, Gérard Groote, pp.
96-98.
Gysbertszoon, H. van Arnhem, Kronyk van het fraterhuis te Gouda, in:
Bijdragen en mededeelingen van het historisch genootschap te Utrecht,
vol. XX, Amsterdam 1898.
Hegius, A., Dialogi, Deventer 1503.
Heussen, H. F. van, and Ryn, H. van, Qudheden en gestichten van Deventer, Leiden 1725.
Hirsche, K., Prologomena zu einer neuen Ausgabe der Imitatio Christi,
3 vols., Berlin 1873-1894.
Hofman, J. H., De boekerij van St. Michiel te Zwolle, in: Arch. v. d.
gesch. v. h. aartsh. Utr., vol. IV (1877), pp. 387-389.
............De broeders van 't Gemeene Leven en de Windesheimsche
kloostervereeniging, in: Arch. v. d. gesch. v. h. aartsb. Utr., vol. II
(1875), pp. 217-275: vol. V (1878), pp. 80-152.
Hoogeweg, H., Verzeichnis der Stifter and Klöster Niedersachsens vor
der Reformation, Halle and Leipsic 1908.
Horn, P., Vita Gerardi Magni, ed. by W. J. Kühler, in: Ned. arch. voor
k,erkgesch., n. s. (1909), pp. 325-370.
Hullu, I. de, Bescheiden betreffende de Hervorming in Overijssel, vol. I
(1522-1546), Deventer 1899.
Hulshof, A., Verslag van een onderzoek te Rostock naar handschriften,
drukwerken en bescheiden belangrijk voor de geschiedenis van Nederland, The Hague 1909.
Hyma, A., The Christian Renaissance: A history of the "Devotio Moderna," Grand Rapids, Mich., 1924; New York 1925.
............The Imitation of Christ (ed.), New York 1927.
............The Youth of Erasmus, Ann Arbor, Mich., 1930.
............Is Gerard Zerbolt of Zutphen the author of the "Super modo
vivendi"? in: Ned. Ar. voor kerkgeschiedenis, n. s., vol. XVI (1920),
pp. 107-128.
............The "De libris Teutonicalibus" by Gerard Zerbolt of Zutphen,
in: Ned. Ar. voor Kerkg., n. s., Vol. XVII (1922), pp. 42-70.
............Het "Scriptum pro quodam inordinate gradus ecclesiasticos et
praedicationis affectante" door Gerard Zerbolt van Zutphen, in: Ned.
Ar. voor Kerkg., n. s., Vol. XX (1927), pp. 179-232.
............Het "Tractatus de quatuor generibus meditationum" of "Sermo de nativitate Domini", door Geert Groote, in: Ar. v. de gesch.
v. h. Aartsbisdom Utrecht, vol. LI (1925), pp. 1-31.
............Het traktaat "Super modo vivendi devotorum hominum simul
commorantium," in: Ar. v. de gesch. v. h. Aartsb. Utr., vol. LII
(1926), pp. 1-100.
............Drie-en-twintig brieven van Geert Groote, in: Ar. v. de gesch.
v. h. Aartsb. Utr., vol. LIII (1928), pp. 1-53; vol. LIV (1929), pp.
1-49. Of these 23 letters only one had been published previously.
Jostes, F., Johannes Veghe, ein deutscher prediger des 15ten jahrhunderts,
Halle 1883.

Kempis, Th. à, Opera, Nuremberg 1494. Contains biographical notices called by Rosweyden: Vita Thomae à Kempis Canonici Regularis auctore incerto paene coaevo (the Stadtbibliothek at Cologne has a copy, which was consulted by the author).

............Opera. ed. J. Badius Ascensius, Paris 1523. Contains: Vita beati Thomae Malleoli.

............Opera omnia, ed. R. P. Henrici Sommalii, S. J., Antwerp 1615.

............Chronicon Montis S. Agnetis, una cum vindiciis Kempensibus Heriberti Rosweydi pro libro De imitatione Christi, Antwerp 1621. On p. 137 this chronicle is continued by another writer.

............Opera omnia, ed. J. Pohl, 7 vols., Freiburg 1902-1921.

............Works, vol. 1: Prayers and meditations on the life of Christ, ed. W. Duthoit, London 1908: vol. II: The founders of the New Devotion, ed. J. P. Arthur, London 1905; vol. III: The chronicle of the Canons Regular of Mount St. Agnes, ed. J. P. Arthur, London 1906; vol. IV: Sermons to the Novices Regular, ed. V. Scully, London 1907; vol. V: The incarnation, life, and passion of our Lord, ed. V. Scully, London 1907.

Kentenich, G., Noch einmal "Die Handschriften der Imitatio Christi und die Autorschaft des Thomas," in: Zeitschrift für Kirchengeschichte, vol. XXIV, Gotha 1903, pp. 594-604.

............Zum Imitatio Christi-Street, in: Zeitschrift für Kirchengeschichte, vol. XXVI, Gotha 1905, pp. 467-470.

Kettlewell, S., The authorship of the De Imitatione Christi, London 1877.

Keussen, H., Die Matrikel der Universität Köln (1389-1559), vol. I (1389-1466), Bonn 1892.

............Der Dominikaner Matthäus Grabow und die Brüder des gemeinsamen Lebens, in: Mittheilungen aus dem Stadtarchiv Köln, vol. XIII, Cologne 1887, pp. 29-47.

Korth, L., Die älteste deutsche Uebersetzung der "Imitatio Christi", in: Mittheilungen aus dem Stadtarchiv Köln, vol. XIII, Cologne 1887, pp. 88-92.

Kronenberg, M. E., De bibliotheek van het Heer-Florenshuis te Deventer, in: Ned. archief voor kergeschiedenis, nieuwe serie, vol. IX (1912), pp. 150-164, 252-300, 313-322.

Kückelhahn, L., Sturm, Strassburgs erster Schulrektor, Leipzig 1872.

Kühler, W. J., Johannes Brinckerinck en zijn klooster te Diepenveen, Rotterdam 1908.

............Levensbeschijvingen van devote zusters te Deventer, in: Archief voor de gesch. v. h. aartsb. Utrecht, 1910, pp. 1-68.

Landeen, W., The Devotio Moderna in Germany in the fifteenth century: A study of the Brethren of the Common Life. Doctoral dissertation, University of Michigan 1939.

............De vita Gerardi Magni. See under: Horn, P.

Lesker, B., Die Rostocker Fraterherren, Frankfurt 1887.

Lindeboom, J., Het Bijbelsch humanisme in Nederland, Leiden 1913.

Lindeborn, J., Historia sive notitia episcopatus Daventriensis, Cologne 1670.

Lisch, G. C. F., Geschichte der Buchdruckerkunst in Mecklenburg, bis zum Jahre 1540, in: Jahrbücher des Vereins für mecklenb. Gesch. und Alterthumskunde, vol. IV (1839), part I (pp. 1-62): Buchdruckerei der Brüder vom gemeinsamen Leben zu St. Michael in Rostock; vol. VI, pp. 209-281: Urkunden-Sammlung: Urkunden der Brüder vom gemeinsamen Leben zu Rostock.

Löffler, K., Heinrich von Ahaus und die Brüder vom gemeinsamen Leben in Deutschland, in: Hist. Jahrbuch der Görres-Gesellschaft, Vol. XXX, München 1909, pp. 762-79.

..........Neues über Heinrich von Ahaus, in: Zeitsch. für Gesch. und Altertumskunde Westfalens, vol. LXXIV (1916), pp. 229-240.

..........Das Fraterhaus Weidenbach in Köln, in: Annalen des historischen Vereins für den Niederrhein, vol. CII, Cologne 1918, pp. 99-128.

..........Das Gedächtnisbuch des Kölner Fraterhauses Weidenbach, in: Ann. des hist. Ver. f. d. Niederrhein, vol. CIII (1919), pp. 1-47.

Loth, A., L'Auteur de l'Imitation. Nouvel examen de la question d'aprés un manuscrit de 1406, in: Revue des questions historiques, 1873, pp. 527-616.

Malou, J. B., Recherches historiques et critiques sur le véritable auteur du livre de l'Imitation de Jésus-Christ, Paris and Tournai 1858.

Man, D. de, Hier beginnen sommige stichtege punten van onsen oelden zusteren, The Hague 1919.

Marx, J., Festschrift zum Bischofs-Jubiläum 1906, Trier 1907; pp. 129-243: Nikolaus von Cues and seine Stiftungen zu Cues and Deventer.

Massaeus, Chr., Chronicorum multiplicis historiae libri XX, Antwerp 1540.

Meyer, O., Die Brüder des gemeinsamen Lebens in Würtemberg, Tübingen 1913.

Miller, E. W., and Scudder, J. W., Wessel Gansfort, New York 1917.

Moll, W., Geert Groote de ketterhamer, in: Studien en Bijdragen, ed. Moll and De Hoop Scheffer, vol. I (1870), pp. 343-346.

..........Geert Groote's dietsche vertalingen beschreven en toegelicht, in: Verhandelingen der koninklijk akademie van wetenschappen, afdeeling letterkunde, vol. XIII, Amsterdam 1880.

..........Johannes Brugman en het Godsdienstig leven onzer vaderen in de vijftiende eeuw, 2 vols., Amsterdam 1854.

Mooren, J., Nachrichten über Thomas à Kempis, Crefeld 1855.

Müller, H., Les origines de la Compagnie de Jésus; Ignace et Lainez, Paris 1898.

Muller, S., Openbare verzamelingen der gemeente Utrecht. Catalogussen van de bij het Stads-archief bewaarde archieven. Eerste afdeeling: De aan de stad Utrecht behoorende archieven, Utrecht 1913.

..........De Moderne Devotie te Utrecht, in: Ned. archief voor kerkgeschiedenis, nieuwe serie, vol. XII (1915), pp. 16-34.

Mulder, W., Gerardi Magni epistolae, Antwerp 1933.

Nordhoff, J. B., Denkwürdigkeiten aus dem Münsterschen Humanismus, Münster 1874.

Parmet, A., Rudolf von Langen. Leben und gesammelte gedichte des ersten münsterschen humanisten. Münster 1869.

Paulsen, F., Geschichte des gelehrten Unterrichts auf den deutschen Schulen and Universitäten vom Ausgang des Mittelalters, vol. I, Leipzig 1896.

Post, R. R., De Moderne Devotie, Amsterdam 1940.

Pomerius, H., De origine monasterii Viridisvallis una cum vitis b. Joannis Rusbrochii primi prioris huius monasterii et aliquot coaeterneorum ejus, in: Analecta Bollandia, vol. IV, Paris, Brussels, and Geneva 1885, pp. 263-322.

Preger, W, Beiträge zur Geschichte der religiösen Bewegung in den Niederlanden in der 2. Hälfte des 14. Jahrhunderts, in: Abhandlungen ker kön. bayer. Akademie der Wissenschaften, III Cl., vol. XXI, Munich 1894, pp. 1-64.

Puyol, P. E., L'Auteur du livre de Imitatione Christi, 2 vols., Paris 1899-1900.

Radewijns, F., Omnes inquit artes. See: Unpubl. sources, under Deventer.
...........Tractatulus de spiritualibus exercitiis, in: Vregt, J. F., Eenige ascetische tractaten, pp. 383-427.

Reichling, D., Ortwin Gratius; sein Leben and Werken; eine Ehrenrettung, Heiligenstadt 1884.
...........Johannes Murmellius; sein Leben und seine Werke, Freiburg i. Br. 1880.
...........Die Reform der Domschule zu Münster im Jahre 1500, Berlin 1900.

Renan, E., L'Auteur de l'Imitation de Jésus-Christ, in: Études d' histoire religieuse, Paris 1880, pp. 317-336.

Renaudet, A., Érasme, sa vie et son oeuvre jusqu'en 1517 d'après sa correspondance, Revue historique, vol. CXI, pp. 225-262; vol. CXII, pp. 241-274.
...........Jean Standonk, un Réformateur Catholique avant la Réforme, in: Bulletin de la société de l'histoire du Protestantisme francais, Paris 1908, pp. 5-81.
...........Préréforme et Humanisme à Paris (1494-1517), Paris 1916.

Richter, J. H., Geschichte des Augustinerklosters Frenswegen in der Grafschaft Bentheim, Hildesheim 1913.

Rhijn, M. van, Wessel Gensfort, The Hague 1917.

Roelfsema, E. H., De Fraters en het Fraterhuis te Groningen, in: Gron. volksalmanak, 1920, pp. 28-39.

Roersch, O., L'humanisme belge à l'époque de la renaissance, Brussels 1910.

Rogge, H. C., Gerardus Listrius, in: Ned arch. voor kerkgesch., vol. VII (1897), pp. 207-220.

Rooij, J. van, Gerard Zerbolt van Zutphen, Nijmegen 1936.

Rootselaar, W. F. N., Amersfoort, geschiedkundige bijzonderheden, Amersfoort 1897.
...........Amersfoort (777-1580), 2 vols., Amersfoort 1878.

Rosweyden H., Vindiciae Kempenses, Antwerp 1583.
...........Vita Thomae à Kempis ex variis auctoribus concinnata, in his Vindiciae.

Schevichaven, H. D. J. van, Oud-Nijmegens kerken, kloosters, gasthuizen, stichtingen en openbare gebouwen, Nijmegen 1909.

Schoengen, M., Die Schule von Zwolle von ihren Anfängen bis zu dem Auftreten des Humanismus, Freiburg i. Br. 1898.
...........Nederlandica in Belgische archieven, in: Nederlandsch archievenblad, vol. XVII, pp. 177ff.
...........Jacobus Traiecti alias de Voecht narratio de inchoatione domus clericorum in Zwollis, Amsterdam 1908.

Schmitz-Kallenberg, L., Monasticon Westfaliae, Münster 1909.

Schwarz, W. E., Studien zur Geschichte des Klosters Marienthal, in: Zeitschrift für Geschichte und Altertumskunde Westfalens, vol. LXXII, Münster 1914, pp. 48-151.

Slee, J. C. van, Het necrologium en cartularium van het convent der reguliere kanunikessen te Diepenveen, in: Arch. voor de gesch. v. h. aartsb. Utrecht vol. XXXIII (1908), pp. 318-485.

Sohm, W., Die Schule Johann Sturms und die Kirche Strassburgs in ihrem gegenseitigen Verhältnis (1503-1581), München, Berlin 1912.
Spitzen, O. A., Thomas à Kempis als schrijver der Navolging van Christus gehandhaafd, Utrecht 1880.
............Nalezing op mijn Thomas à Kempis als schrijver der Navolging van Christus gehandhaafd, Utrecht 1881.
............Les Hollandismes de l'Imitation de Jésus-Christ et trois anciennes versions du livre. Réponse à M. le Chevalier B. Veratti, Utrecht 1884.
Spoelhof, W., Concepts of religious nonconformity and religious toleration as developed by the Brethren of the Common Life in the Netherlands, 1374-1489. Doctoral dissertation, University of Michigan 1946.
Sturm, Joh., Consilium curatoribus scholarum Argentorati propositum VI. die Kal. Martii 1538, in: G. Bonet-Maury, De opera scholastica fratrum vitae communis in Neerlandia, p. 90.
Tieck, J. G. J., De werken van Geert Groote, Utrecht 1941.
Tolensis, F., Vita Thomae Malleoli à Kempis, in: Th. à Kempis, Opera, ed. H. Sommalius, Antwerp 1615, pp. 27-31.
Ullman, C., Reformers before the Reformation, vol. II, Edinburgh 1855.
Veil, H., Zum Gedächtnis Johannes Sturms. Eine Studie über J. Sturms Unterrichtsziele und Schuleinrichtungen mit besonderer Berücksichtigung seiner Beziehungen zu dem niederländischen Humanismus, in: Festschrift zur Feier des 350 jährigen Bestehens des Protestantischen Gymnasiums zu Strassburg, Strasbourg 1888, pp. 1-[132].
Velden, H. E. J. M. van der, Rodolphus Agricola (Roelof Huusman), Leiden 1909.
Vregt, J. F., Eenige ascetische tractaten, afkomstig van de Deventersche broederschap van het gemeene leven, in verband gebracht met het boek van Thomas à Kempis, de Navolging van Christus, in: Archief voor de geschiedenis van het aartsbisdom Utrecht, vol. X, Utrecht 1882, pp. 321-498.
Waterton, E., Thomas à Kempis and the Imitation of Christ, London 1883.
Watrigant, P. H., La genèse des Exercitia spiritualia, Amiens 1897.
Wiese, J., Der Pädagoge Alexander Hegius und seine Schüler, Berlin 1892.
Wolters, A., Reformationsgeschichte der Stadt Wesel, Bonn 1868.
Wüstenhoff, U. J. M., "Florentii parvum et simplex exercitium," naar een Berlijnsch handschrift medegedeeld, in: Nederlandsch Archief voor kergeschiedenis, vol. V (1895), pp. 89-105.
Zerbolt, G., Opuscula duo ad vitam corrigendam recteque instituendam quibusvis accomodo. — I. — De reformatione interiori seu virium animae. — II. De spiritualibus ascensionibus, Cologne 1539.
............Super modo vivendi devotorum hominum simul commorancium. See: A. Hyma.
............De libris teutonicalibus, or An liceat libros divinos transferre in vulgare. See: A. Hyma.

Index